FARMHOUSE WEEKNIGHTS

FARMHOUSE WEEKNIGHTS

QUICK AND WHOLESOME RECIPES FOR DINNER

MELISSA BAHEN
CREATOR OF **LULU THE BAKER**

Gibbs Smith

First Edition
29 28 27 26 25   5 4 3 2 1

Text © 2025 Melissa Bahen
Photographs © 2025 Melissa Bahen

All rights reserved. No part of this book may be reproduced by any means whatsoever without written permission from the publisher, except brief portions quoted for purpose of review. No part of this book may be used or reproduced in any manner for the purpose of training artificial intelligence technologies or systems.

Published by
Gibbs Smith
570 N. Sportsplex Dr.
Kaysville, Utah 84037

1.800.835.4993 orders
www.gibbs-smith.com

Designed by Sheryl Dickert
Production design by Renee Bond
Printed and bound in China

Library of Congress Control Number: 2024951488
ISBN: 978-1-4236-6833-6
Ebook ISBN: 978-1-4236-6834-3

This product is made of FSC® -certified and other controlled material.

MIX
Paper | Supporting responsible forestry
FSC® C208677
www.fsc.org

To my big, beautiful family: Speedy, Addie, Ellie, James, George, Mom, Dad, Chaz, Jasmine, Penelope, Henry, Holly, Emily, Thomas, Max, Owen, Alice, Lucy, Anna, and Zach.

"Put your hands up and ask the eternal question:

What's for dinner?"

CONTENTS

Introduction 9

Breakfast for Dinner 15
Breakfast Sandwiches 16
Cheesy Eggs-in-a-Basket 19
Cheesy Egg & Hashbrown Breakfast Bake 23
Coffee Shop Bacon & Cheese Egg Bites 24
San Antonio Breakfast Tacos 27
French Toast Waffles 28

Soups 31
Anne's Lentil Soup 32
White Bean & Ham Soup 35
Black Bean Soup 36
Dr. B.'s Southwest Three-Bean Soup 39
Garden Minestrone 41
Creamy Tomato Cheese Soup 44
Roasted Cauliflower & White Cheddar Soup 47
Lulu the Baker's Famous Cheesy Chowder 48
Homestyle Chicken Noodle Soup 51
Mom's Chicken Tortilla Soup 52
Taco Soup 54
Nana's Quick & Hearty Soup 57
Pasta Fagioli 58

Salads 61
Annie & Brooke's Kale Salad 62
Blue Valley Spinach Salad with Feta & Avocado 65
Loaded, Lemony Caesar Salad with Homemade Dressing 66
Classic Cobb Salad with Lemon-Shallot Vinaigrette 69
Emily's South Lane Chopped Salad with Cilantro-Lime Vinaigrette 71
Harvest Salad with Creamy Herb-Dijon Vinaigrette 74
Italian Pasta Salad 77
Toasted Ramen Noodle Salad 78
Mediterranean Quinoa Salad 81
Taco Salad 82

Sandwiches 85
Green Goddess Veggie Sandwiches 86
Slow Cooker Barbecue Chicken Sandwiches 89
Caprese Grilled Cheese Sandwiches 93
Chicken Pesto Paninis 94
Chicken Salad Sandwiches 97
Turkey-Bacon-Avocado Clubs 98
Turkey & Cranberry Plymouth Rock Sandwiches 101

Meatball Subs 102
Philly Cheesesteaks 105
Slow Cooker Sausage & Pepper Sandwiches 106

Pastas 109
Cheese Tortellini with Pesto & Veggies 110
Lemon Garlic Spaghetti 113
Chicken Tetrazzini 114
One-Pan Weeknight Lasagna 116
Sausage & Pesto Pasta 119
Shrimp Scampi 120
Cajun Alfredo Pasta with Kielbasa 123
Mac & Cheese with Toasted, Buttered Breadcrumbs 124
Stella Blues' Pasta 127
Weeknight Beef Stroganoff 128

Slow Cooker Entrées 131
Easy Pot Roast 132
Carnitas 135
Smothered Pork Chops 136
Sweet Shredded Pork 139
Taco Chicken 140
Teriyaki Chicken 143
Mom's Garlic Butter Chicken 144

Skillets, Sheet Pans & Bakes 147
Bean & Cheese Tostadas 148
Cornbread-Topped Tex-Mex Bake 150
Sheet Pan Honey-Lime Chicken Fajitas 153
Tropical Fried Rice 155
Emily's Cheesy Chicken & Stuffing Bake 158
Mini Meatloaves 161
Crispy Chicken Parmesan 162
Easy Flatbread Pizzas 165

After-Dinner Treats 169
Oatmeal Toffee Cookies 170
Snickerdoodles 173
Speedy's Chocolate No-Bake Cookies 174
Chocolate Chip Cookies 177
Triple Chocolate Cookies 178
Easy Peanut Butter Cup Brownies 181
Aunt Myrl's German Cookies 182
Peanut Butter Pretzel Magic Cookie Bars 185
Peanut Butter Scotcheroos 186
S'mores Bars 189
Brown Butter Crispy Cereal Treats 190
Donut Shortcake 193
Double Chocolate Cake 194

Acknowledgments 197

Vegetarian Recipes 198

30-Minute (or Less!) Recipes 199

Index 201

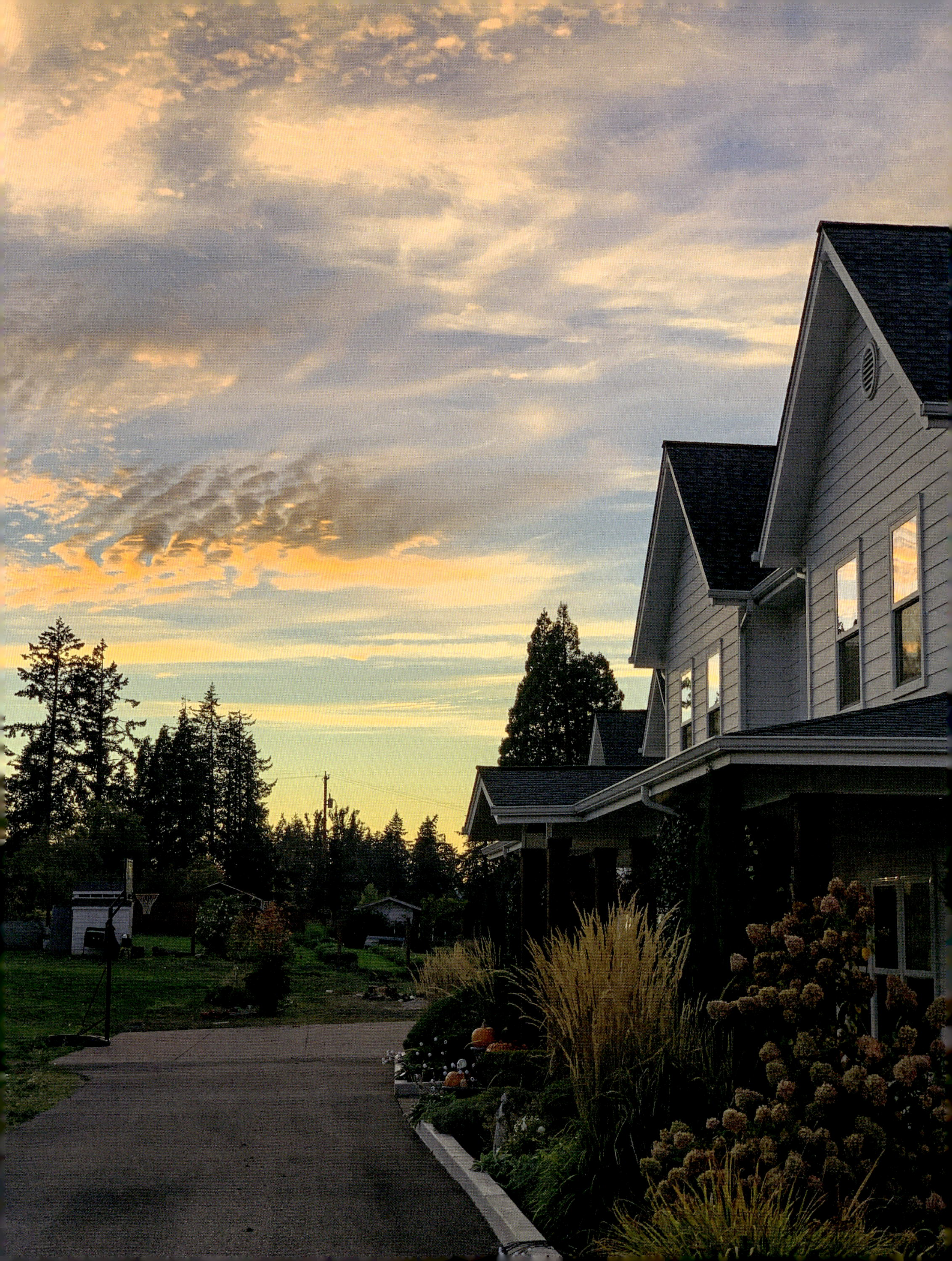

INTRODUCTION

I USED TO WONDER when my kids were really little (and when we had fewer of them!) if we would always have time to sit down together for a regular family dinner every night. We had mostly been successful at it up to that point, and I just assumed that would always be the case. At the time it didn't seem that hard. But wow, how things have changed! For the past several years—or really all of the years in recent memory, if I'm being honest—we have been so busy. Weeknights are filled with getting home late from work, school and community meetings, homework, projects, kids' sports and activities, lessons, and more. Everyone in our household is busy, and sometimes it feels like weeks go by without a proper weeknight dinner.

And I've realized that life is that way for all of us sometimes, regardless of where we work, what we do, or how big our household is. Some seasons of life are just hectic. But in the midst of all this busyness—and maybe even because of it—I still find value in sitting down for a home-cooked meal at the end of a long day whenever possible. It gives all of us a chance to relax, to flex our creative muscles, to focus on something other than the stresses of the day. We can get off our feet for a few minutes and share the highs and lows of our day with the people we live with, and hear about theirs in return. Cooking and eating give us moments of peace and togetherness when those are sometimes hard to find.

Farmhouse Weeknights, by necessity and design, is a different book than *Farmhouse Weekends*. *Farmhouse Weekends* was full of recipes designed specifically for long, lazy, luxurious weekends when time feels unlimited. That's just not going to fly on a busy weeknight at my house! The recipes I've created for *Farmhouse Weeknights* have the same list of wholesome ingredients, with plenty of fresh produce and most things made from scratch, but they were all designed to be ready quickly and with minimal prep.

My overarching goal when coming up with the idea for this book, and something I kept in mind while I was writing it, was to make it as useful as possible—to think of every conceivable way it could help you get dinner on the table on busy nights. With that in mind, we built lots of great features into the book:

- Every recipe lists the amount of prep time, cooking time, and total time from start to finish. I tried to be really realistic when writing these, but everybody goes at their own pace. You might be faster or slower, but these times will give you a good ballpark.

- Every chapter comes with serving suggestions to make the recipes in that chapter part of a complete meal (except for the desserts).

- Every recipe has a list of useful shortcuts that can save you time if you want to use them.

- The vegetarian recipes are identified with this icon:

- The recipes that can be made in 30 minutes or even less time are identified with this icon:

- In addition to the regular ingredient index, there are special indexes at the back of the book that list just the vegetarian recipes and just the recipes ready in 30 minutes or less.

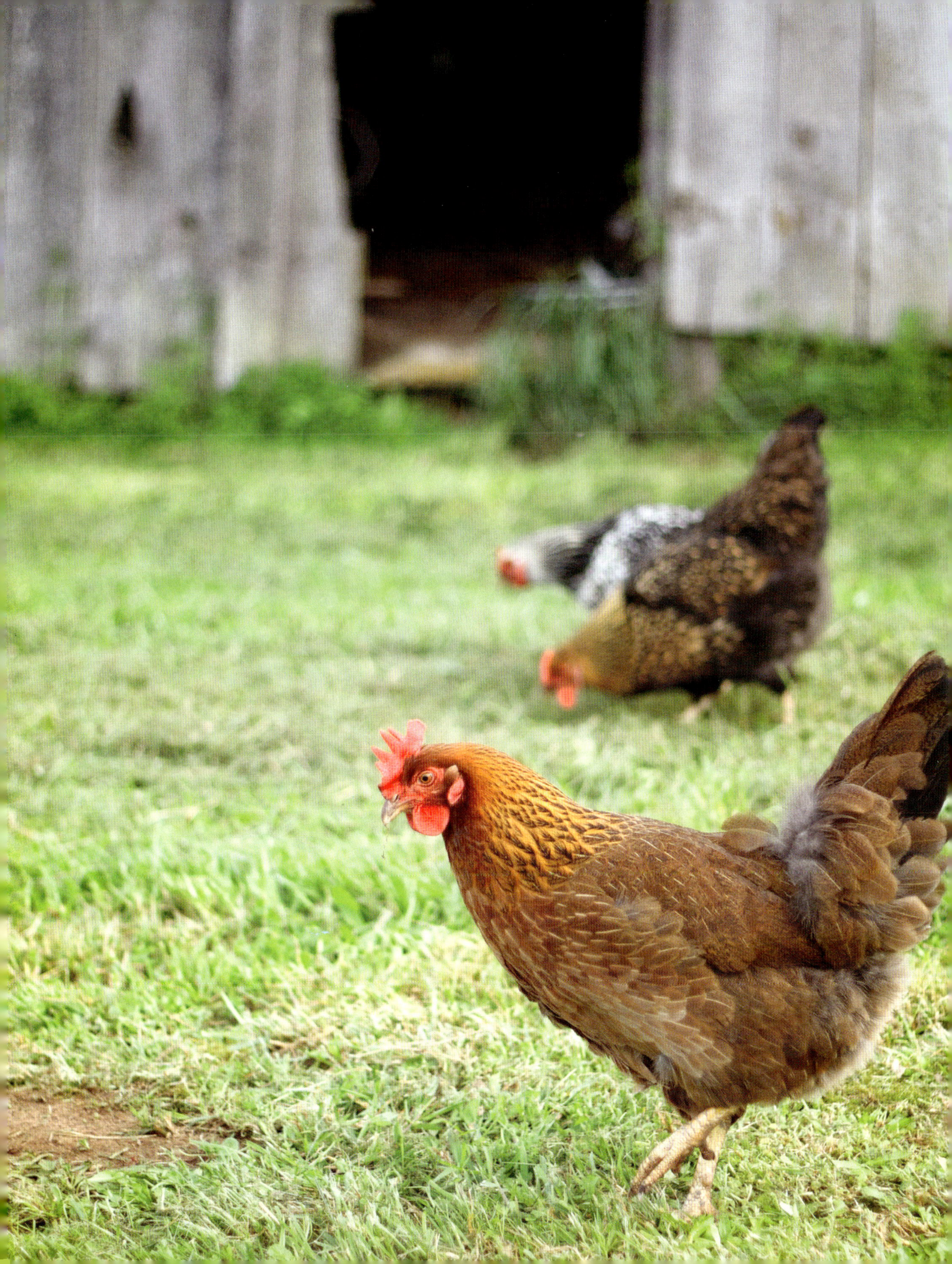

KITCHEN SHORTCUTS

One of my pet peeves is kitchen shaming, and we'll have none of that here. Shortcuts are not only time-savers but also lifesavers, so consider this your official permission to use them all. On weeknights, if I'm making one thing from scratch, I'm almost never making two or three things from scratch. Here are some of the kitchen shortcuts I use regularly.

Meats
- Shredded or chopped rotisserie chicken
- Pre-cooked, ready-to-heat bacon
- Pre-cooked, ready-to-heat meatballs
- Pre-cooked, ready-to-heat sausage patties

Produce
- Salad kits
- Precut fruit from the produce section (especially the pineapple and watermelon options)
- Store-bought veggie trays
- Steam-in-the-bag fresh or frozen veggies
- Frozen minced garlic cubes (the freshest option) or minced garlic in a jar or squeeze tube
- Frozen grated ginger cubes (again, freshest) or grated ginger in a jar or squeeze tube
- Pre-chopped veggies from the grocery store (just make sure they look fresh)

Breads
- Packaged dinner rolls, especially Hawaiian rolls
- Grocery store French bread loaves
- Garlic bread
- Garlic knots
- Boxed muffin mixes and cornbread mix

Miscellaneous
- Pre-cooked quinoa
- Store-bought fresh pesto (refrigerated, not the kind in a shelf-stable jar)
- Bottled dressings and marinades
- Pre-shredded and pre-sliced cheeses (not in every case but, honestly, in most cases)

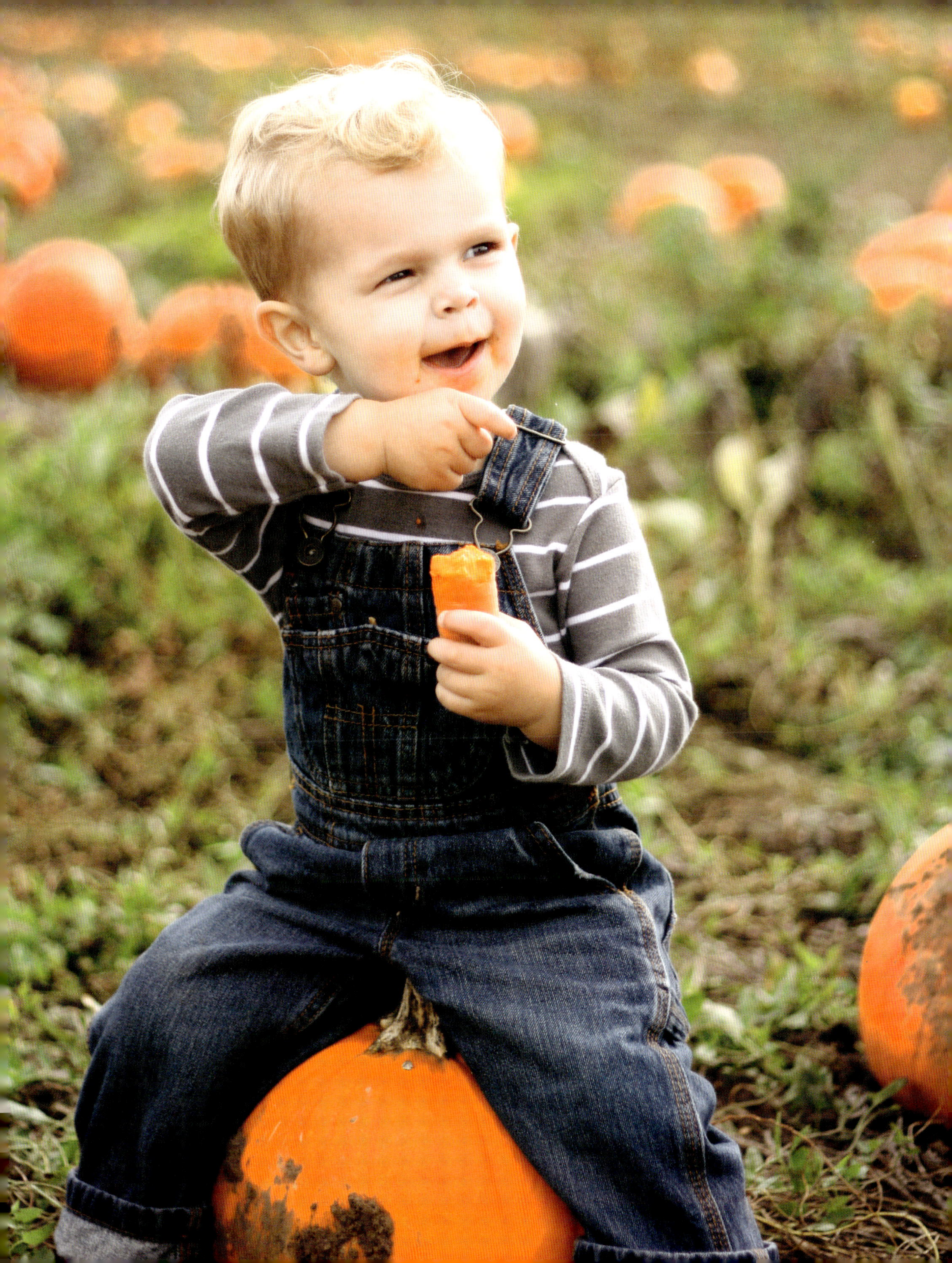

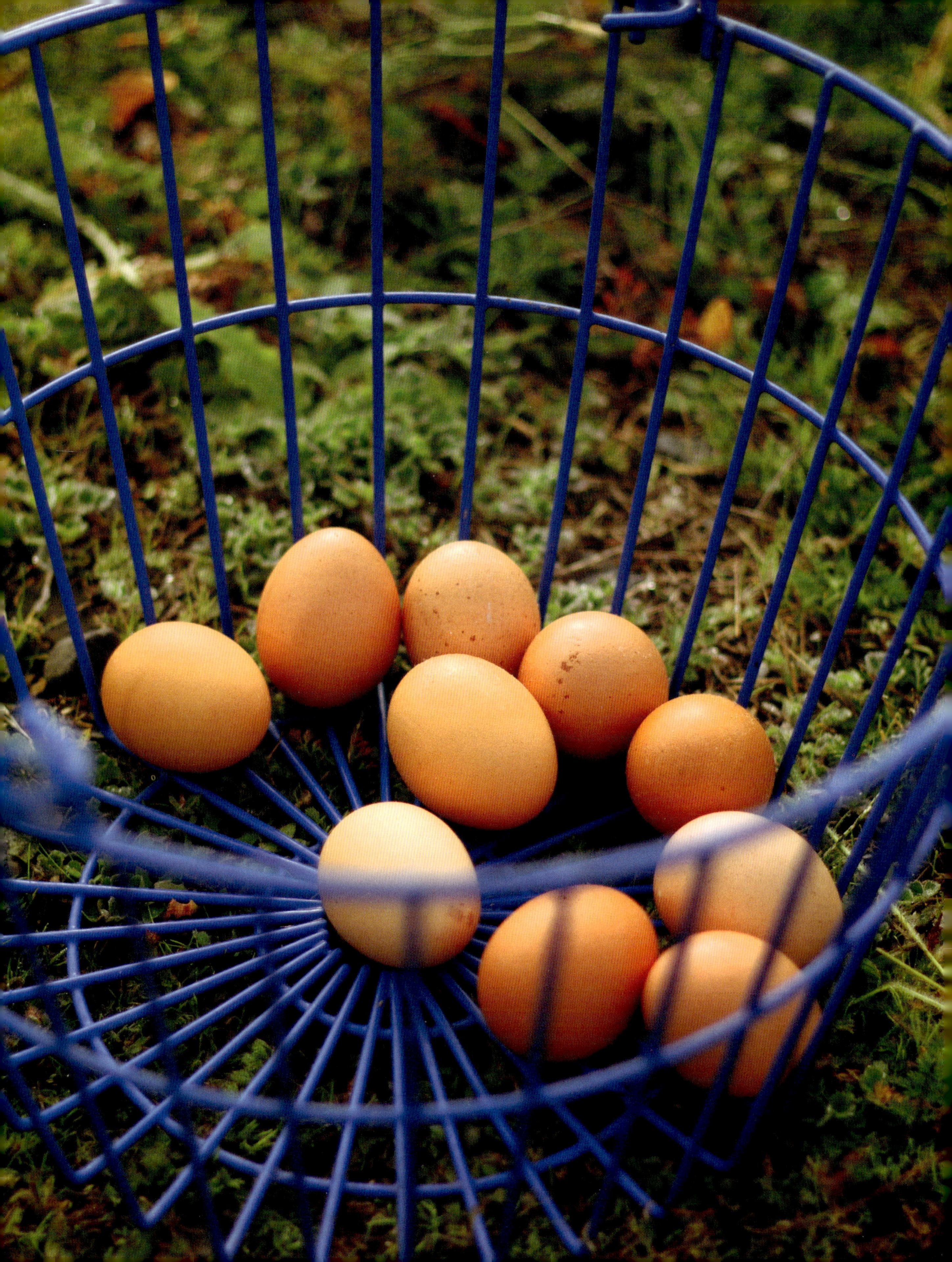

BREAKFAST FOR DINNER

SERVING BREAKFAST FOR DINNER has to be hands down one of the easiest ways to get a dinner that everyone loves on the table in a short amount of time. We turn to our breakfast faves often when we have a busy weeknight. We usually opt for a savory breakfast to serve at dinnertime, but I don't think anyone has ever suggested a sweet option, like the French Toast Waffles on page 28, and been turned down.

Round these dinners out by serving them with:

FRESH FRUIT

YOGURT

JUICE

TOAST, ENGLISH MUFFINS, OR MUFFINS

BACON, BREAKFAST SAUSAGE, OR HAM

Breakfast Sandwiches 🥓

We are huge fans of breakfast sandwiches in this house! We enjoy them in the morning (usually on the weekends) for breakfast, and love to have them for dinner on busy nights. I'm giving you three different options because they're all a little different and we honestly love them all equally. The croissant sandwiches are fancy, the English muffin sandwiches are classic, and the bagel sandwiches are decadent and packed with flavor. Feel free to mix it up and find your favorite combos! All of the amounts listed are per person, so you can make the exact amount you want for your household.

Prep: 10 minutes | Cook: 10 minutes | Total: 20 minutes | Makes 1 sandwich; scale up for your household

#1: THE CROISSANT-WICH

2 slices bacon or 2 slices deli ham

1 or 2 eggs

Kosher salt

Freshly ground black pepper

1 ounce medium cheddar cheese, either shredded or sliced

1 large croissant, halved like a hamburger bun

#2: THE ENGLISH MUFFIN-WICH

2 slices bacon or 2 slices deli ham or 1 or 2 breakfast sausage patties, cooked

1 to 2 eggs

Kosher salt

Freshly ground black pepper

1 ounce medium cheddar cheese, either shredded or sliced

1 English muffin, lightly toasted and buttered

#3: THE DOUBLE CHEESE BAGEL-WICH

Onion & chive cream cheese (or garden veggie or plain)

2 slices bacon

1 or 2 eggs

Kosher salt

Freshly ground black pepper

1 ounce medium cheddar cheese, either shredded or sliced

1 everything bagel (or whatever savory bagel flavor you want!), lightly toasted

1. Preheat the oven to 350°F. Tear off 1 square of aluminum foil for each sandwich.

2. Cook or heat the bacon and sausage (ham doesn't need its own cooking time) as needed on a griddle, in a large skillet, or in the microwave until cooked to your liking, then lay on a paper towel–lined plate and blot off any excess grease with another paper towel.

continued

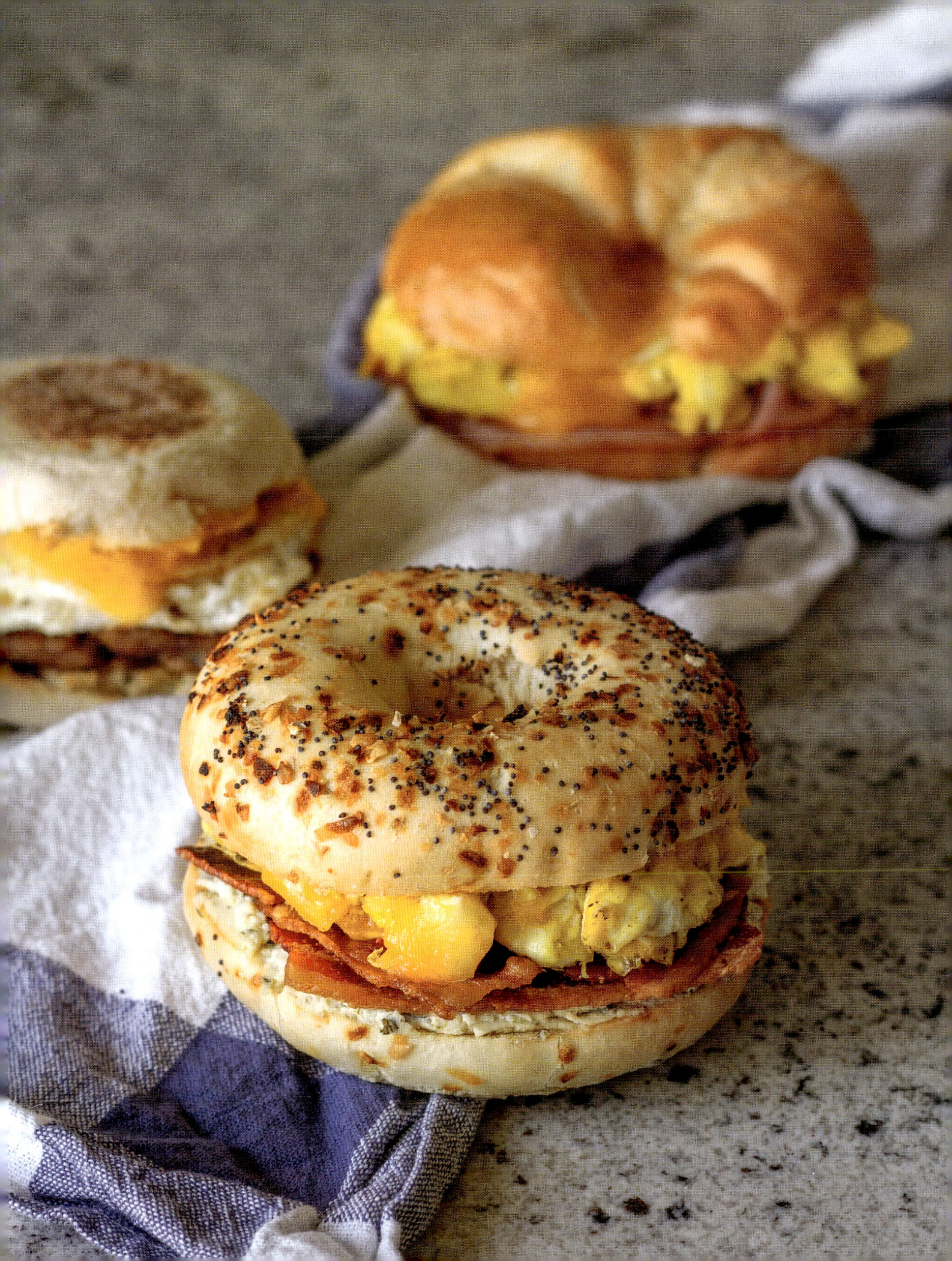

3. Make the scrambled or fried eggs. Spray a nonstick skillet with nonstick cooking spray and put it on the stove over medium-low heat. For scrambled eggs, crack the eggs into a separate bowl and scramble with a fork. Pour the eggs into the nonstick skillet, season with salt and pepper, and cook, gently stirring frequently, until the eggs are cooked through. For fried eggs, crack them straight into the pan, season with salt and pepper, and fry until the white is cooked through and the yolk is cooked to your liking, flipping as necessary.

4. Divide the eggs, meat, cheese, and any other ingredients among your bread of choice. Wrap each sandwich up in foil and place in the oven for 5 minutes, until the cheese is melted and the sandwiches are hot.

SHORTCUTS & NOTES

- Pre-cooked bacon (We like the black package from Costco.)

- Pre-cooked frozen sausage patties

- Pre-sliced or pre-shredded cheese

Cheesy Eggs-in-a-Basket

This dish goes by several names: Eggs-in-a-Basket, Boy Scout Eggs, and Egg in a Hole, just to name a few. I remember my mom making them when I was little, and they always seemed really special. I can't remember when I started making this particular cheesy-sourdough version, but it became an instant family favorite. It's ridiculously easy to make and has only a handful of humble ingredients, but the end result still manages to feel special.

Prep: 5 minutes | Cook: 12 minutes | Total: 17 minutes | Serves 4

4 large slices sourdough bread

2 tablespoons butter, softened

4 eggs

Kosher salt

Freshly ground black pepper

1 cup shredded cheddar cheese

1. Preheat a large griddle over medium-low heat.

2. Use a 3- to 3½-inch round cookie cutter to cut a hole in the center of each piece of sourdough bread. Depending on how thick and big your slices of bread are, you can make the holes a little smaller or a little larger, but that'll be a trial-and-error thing you'll just have to figure out on your own! With the bread we use, a 3-inch cutter works perfectly.

3. Butter 1 side of each piece of bread, cutouts included.

4. Put all of the bread butter-side down on the griddle. Place a tiny amount of butter on the griddle in each hole, then crack an egg in each hole. Sprinkle the eggs with kosher salt and black pepper.

5. Sprinkle the shredded cheese as evenly as you can on each piece of sourdough (try to avoid the egg!) and circle cutout. If you have anything large enough to cover the griddle loosely, like a large, rimmed baking sheet, you can set that gently over everything to help the cheese melt, but this is optional. Cook for 5 to 6 minutes, until the cheese has started to melt and the bottom of all the bread is golden.

continued

6. Use a large, flat spatula to gently flip over each piece of bread. Try not to make a mess, but also keep in mind that these will be delicious no matter how they look. Allow each piece of bread to cook until the egg is cooked through completely and the cheese on the bottom is golden, crispy, and no longer gooey, 5 to 6 more minutes.

7. Carefully flip the eggs-in-a-basket back over, making sure to keep the crispy cheese on each piece intact, and serve immediately, with circle cutouts on the side.

SHORTCUTS & NOTES

- Pre-shredded cheese

- If you want runny egg yolks, don't add the egg to the hole in the sourdough until after you've flipped it over the first time. Once the bread is cheese-side down, add your egg. You can monitor the doneness of the egg by gently jiggling it with your spatula, and you'll probably need to flip the whole thing several times instead of just twice. You can also cover the griddle as you did in step 5 to help the egg whites cook through faster. You don't want runny egg whites! My husband loves to dip his cheesy circle cutout into his runny yolk.

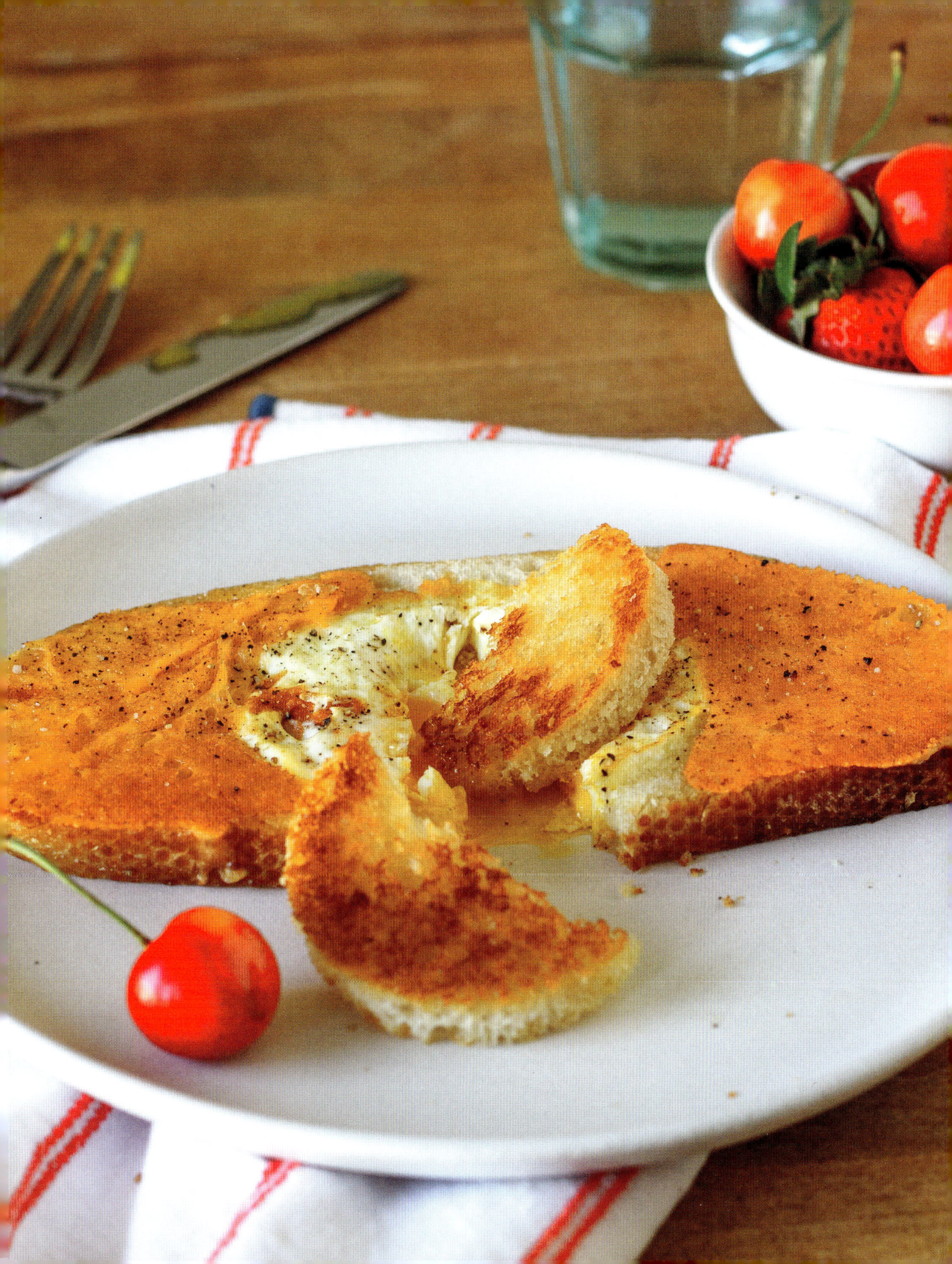

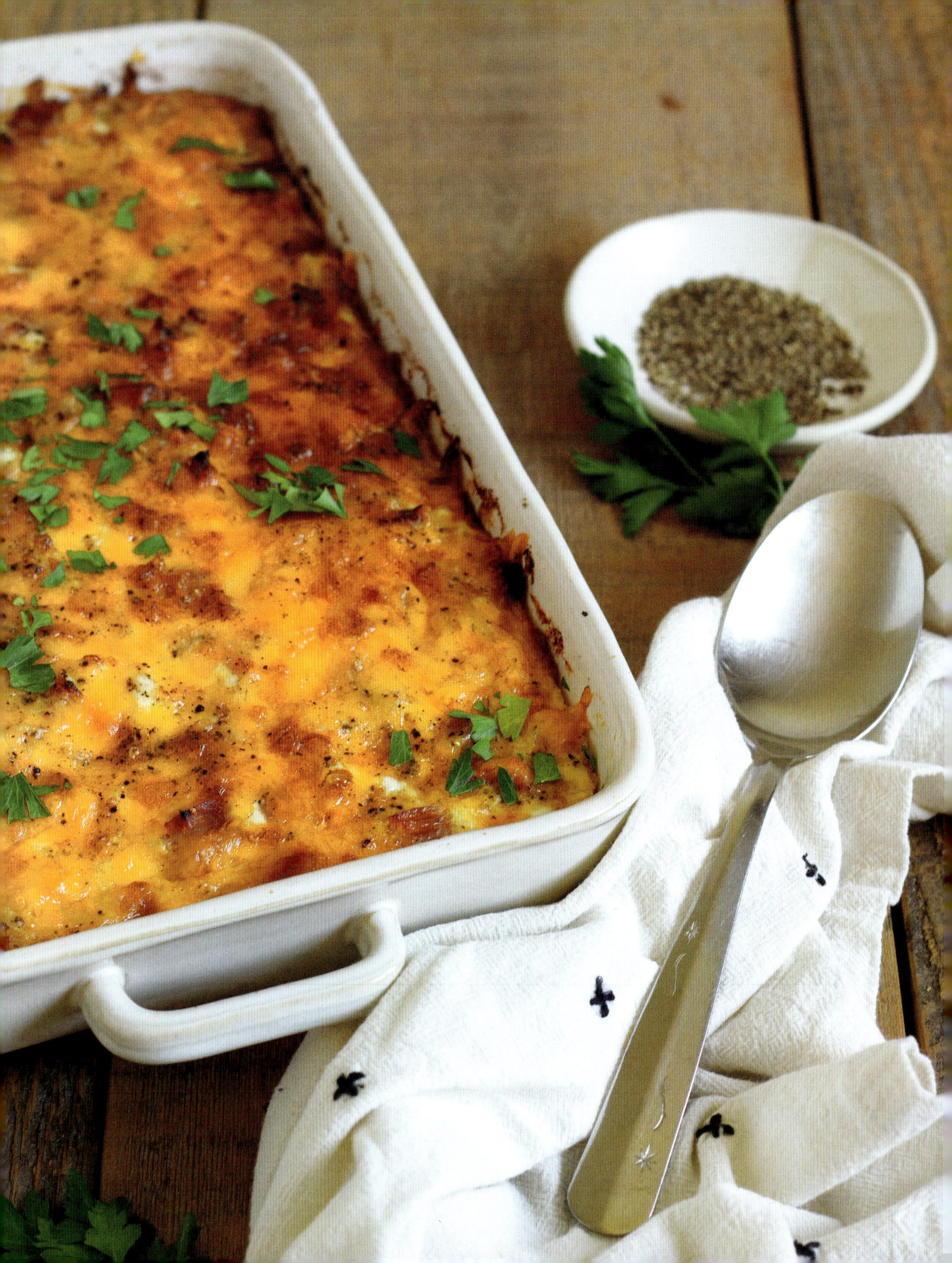

Cheesy Egg & Hashbrown Breakfast Bake

Casseroles might not win any awards for glamor, but they're easy and delicious, which is worth a lot on a busy night. My family has been making a cheesy ham-and-egg breakfast casserole for as long as I can remember, and this tasty version is even heartier thanks to the addition of buttery hashbrowns. The Southwestern variation is equally delicious and is perfect for meatless meals.

Prep: 10 minutes | Cook: 45 minutes | Total: 55 minutes | Serves 12

20 ounces frozen hashbrowns, thawed

¼ cup butter, melted

1 teaspoon seasoned salt

Freshly ground black pepper

12 ounces ham, diced

2 cups shredded cheddar cheese, divided

8 eggs

1 cup milk

½ teaspoon garlic salt

⅛ teaspoon mustard powder

⅛ teaspoon onion powder

1 tablespoon minced fresh parsley, for garnishing

1. Preheat the oven to 350°F and spray a 9 x 13-inch baking dish with nonstick cooking spray.

2. Put the thawed hashbrowns in the baking dish, drizzle with the butter, seasoned salt, and a pinch of black pepper, and toss to coat. Add the ham and 1 cup of cheese and toss again.

3. In a medium bowl or a large liquid measuring cup (at least 4 cups), combine the eggs, milk, garlic salt, mustard powder, and onion powder. Whisk until well combined. Pour evenly over the top of the hashbrown mixture.

4. Sprinkle the remaining 1 cup of cheese evenly over the top and bake for 45 minutes, until the eggs are puffed and a knife inserted in the center of the casserole comes out wet but clear.

5. Sprinkle the parsley on top and serve.

SHORTCUTS & NOTES

- Pre-shredded cheese

- Pre-diced ham

- For a Southwestern (and meatless!) variation, replace the diced ham with 1 (15-ounce) can of black beans, drained and rinsed; 1 (15.25-ounce) can of corn, drained; and 1 (4-ounce) can of diced green chiles, drained. Replace the parsley garnish with minced fresh cilantro, and serve with salsa on the side.

Coffee Shop Bacon & Cheese Egg Bites

One of my favorite recipes from *Farmhouse Weekends* is the White Cheddar & Zucchini Egg Bites. And one of my favorite quick breakfasts to grab when I'm out running errands is a coffee shop egg bite with bacon and Gruyère. So of course, I had to tinker with my recipe until I had a perfect copycat version of the coffee shop fave. These mini crustless quiches are savory and satisfying, and now you don't have to leave the house to enjoy them.

Prep: 15 minutes | Cook: 20 minutes | Total: 35 minutes | Serves 6 (2 egg bites each)

8 slices bacon, cooked and crumbled (about 1.6 ounces)

8 eggs

½ cup whole-milk cottage cheese

½ cup (about 2 ounces) shredded Gruyère cheese

½ cup (about 2 ounces) shredded Monterey jack cheese

½ teaspoon salt

Freshly ground black pepper

10 shakes hot sauce

1. Preheat the oven to 325°F. Set a 9 x 13-inch baking dish on the bottom rack of the oven. Bring about 2 cups water to a boil. I use a tea kettle for that, but a small saucepan is great, too.

2. While the oven preheats, spray a 12-cup muffin tin with nonstick cooking spray. Divide the cooked, crumbled bacon evenly among the muffin cups.

3. In a blender, combine the eggs, all three cheeses, salt, pepper, and hot sauce. Blend on high until smooth, about 30 seconds.

4. Pour the egg mixture into the muffin cups. I usually fill mine halfway to start, then add a little more to each cup until the mixture is gone.

5. Place the muffin tin in the oven. Pour the boiling water into the 9 x 13-inch pan below it. This will create a steamy environment in your oven, which will give the egg bites a creamier texture. Close the door and bake the egg bites for 20 minutes. They should be lightly golden on top and have pulled away from the sides of the pan when they are finished. Cool for a few minutes before serving.

SHORTCUTS & NOTES

- Pre-cooked bacon (We like the black package from Costco.)

- Pre-shredded cheeses

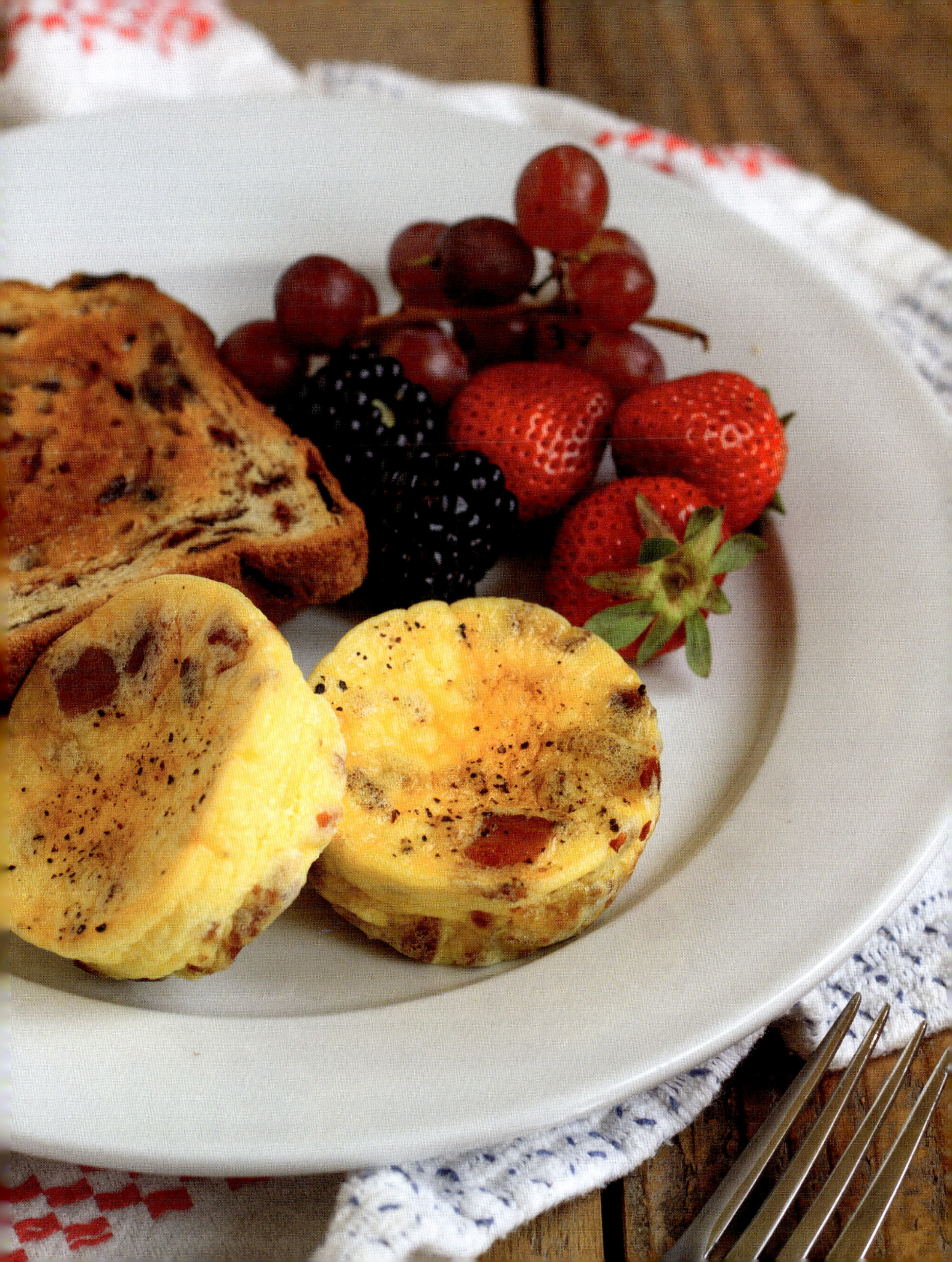

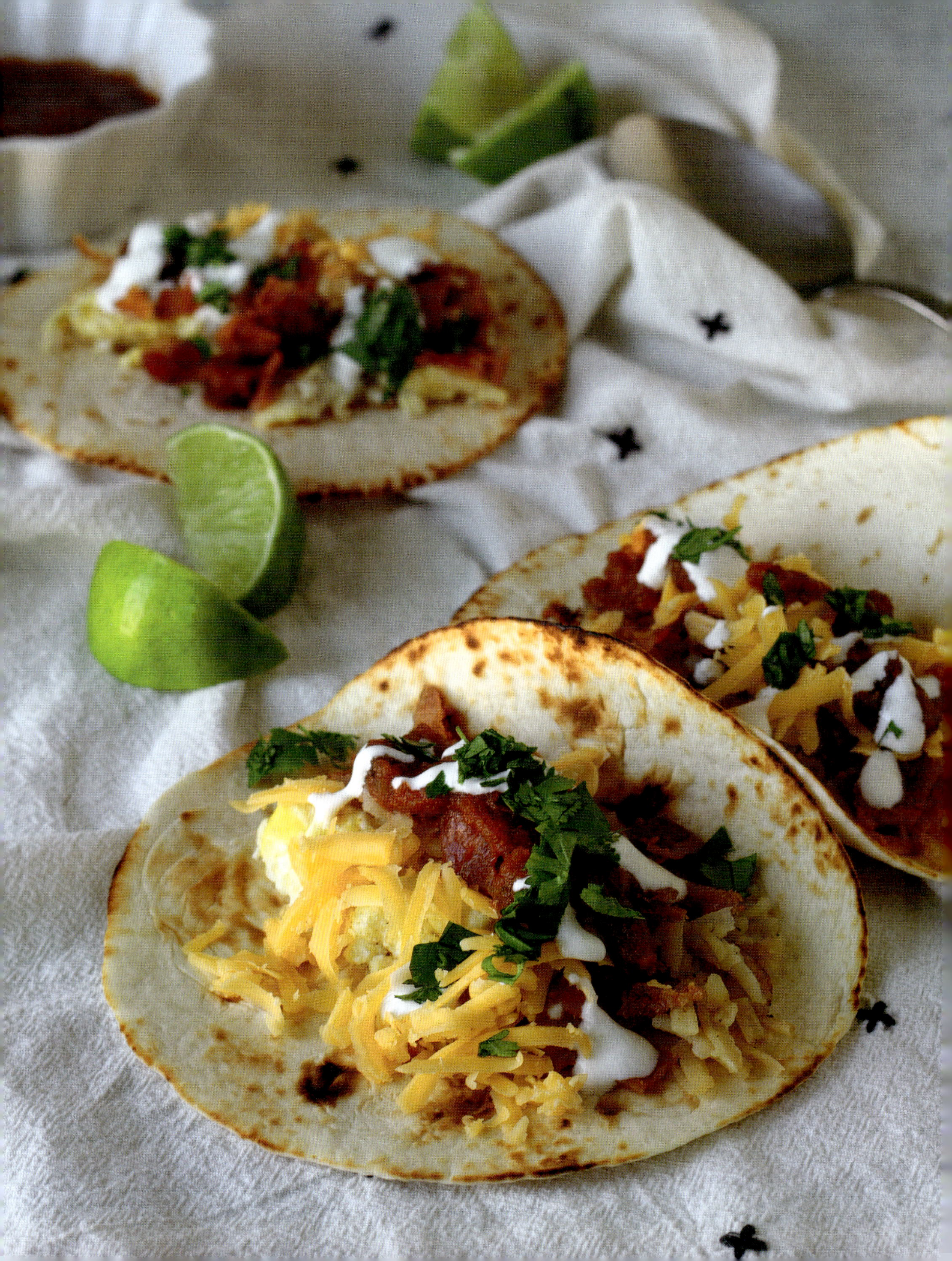

San Antonio Breakfast Tacos

We lived in San Antonio for a few years when I was just starting elementary school, and I was too young to remember much... except for the food. I remember a lot of good food in San Antonio, and these breakfast tacos are probably the one that has made the largest and most lasting impact on my life. Everyone in my extended family loves them. We have them often at our house for both breakfast and dinner, and when we get together for family reunions with my parents and siblings, they are always on the menu.

Prep: 10 minutes | Cook: 20 minutes | Total: 30 minutes | Serves 8 (2 tacos each)

16 fajita-size flour tortillas

8 eggs

Kosher salt

Freshly ground black pepper

2 cups shredded cheddar cheese

1 pound bacon, cooked and crumbled

4 cups hashbrowns, cooked

Sour cream, cilantro-lime crema (page 149), salsa, pico de gallo, hot sauce, diced onions (green, red, pickled, white, or yellow), diced avocado or guacamole (page 154), for topping

1. Preheat the oven to 200°F. Stack up the flour tortillas and wrap them in aluminum foil, then put them in the oven to warm.

2. Spray a nonstick skillet with nonstick cooking spray and put it on the stove over medium-low heat. Crack the eggs into a bowl and scramble with a fork. Pour the eggs into the prepared skillet, season with salt and pepper, and cook, gently stirring frequently, until the eggs are cooked through. Turn the heat off, sprinkle the cheese evenly over the eggs, and cover with a lid or some aluminum foil until the cheese is melted.

3. Get all of your components out, set up your taco bar, and let eaters build their own breakfast tacos.

SHORTCUTS & NOTES

- Pre-cooked bacon (We like the black package from Costco.)

- Pre-chopped ham (if using ham)

- Pre-shredded cheese

- Store-bought salsa or pico de gallo

- You can really customize these to your liking. You can upgrade the tortillas to burrito size, in which case these go from breakfast *tacos* to breakfast *burritos*. You can use any kind of cheese you like. One of my sisters uses frozen diced red potatoes instead of the hashbrowns, and we sometimes like using Tater Tots. And we usually use bacon in our breakfast tacos, but I love them just as much with breakfast sausage or diced ham instead. You could even do a meat-lovers' breakfast taco and use all three kinds of meat.

French Toast Waffles

French toast is one of my family's favorite easy meals. When we don't feel like making anything or when we're just too busy to focus on dinner, French toast is a delicious option we all not only agree on but also get excited for. The waffle-iron treatment in this recipe takes regular French toast up a notch. And then the whipped cream and fresh strawberries take it up another notch each, so this French toast is at least three notches above average!

Prep: 10 minutes | Cook: 20 minutes | Total: 30 minutes | Serves 5 or 6 (2 or 3 pieces each)

6 eggs

2 cups half-and-half

2 tablespoons granulated sugar

2 teaspoons vanilla extract

½ teaspoon ground cinnamon or pumpkin pie spice

½ teaspoon salt

16 pieces thick-sliced sandwich bread, like Texas toast

Butter, maple syrup, whipped cream, and sliced fresh strawberries, for serving

1. Plug in a waffle iron and let it preheat.

2. In a medium bowl, whisk together the eggs, half-and-half, sugar, vanilla, cinnamon, and salt.

3. Pour the egg mixture into a shallow baking dish or pie pan. Submerge a piece of bread in the egg mixture, making sure it's fully soaked, then put it in the waffle maker. Repeat until the waffle maker has as many slices of bread as it can hold. Ours holds 4. Close the waffle maker and let it cook until the French toast is golden. For our waffle maker, this takes about 5 minutes, but your waffle maker might be different.

4. When a round of French toast is golden, remove each piece from the waffle maker (I use a fork to gently lift them out), and serve immediately with butter, maple syrup, whipped cream, and sliced strawberries.

5. Repeat with the remaining ingredients until all the French toast is made and your group is happy and full.

SHORTCUTS & NOTES

- If you don't have a waffle iron (or if you just don't want to use it), you can make regular French toast on a big griddle on your stovetop. Put the griddle over medium-low heat and cook the French toast for 3 to 5 minutes per side, until deep golden brown. One of the benefits of cooking French toast on a griddle is that you can butter the griddle first to make the French toast extra crispy on the edges and extra buttery and delicious.

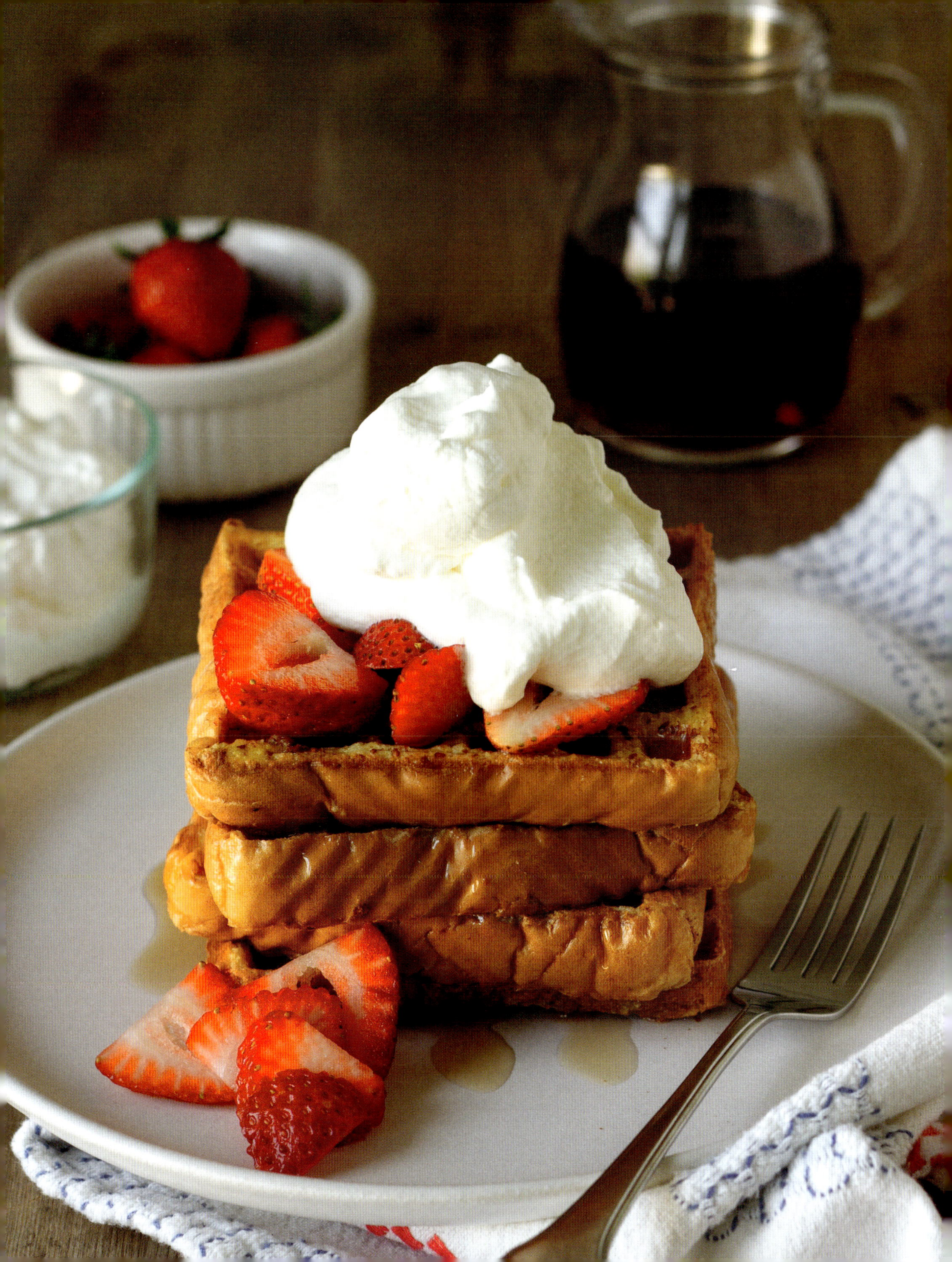

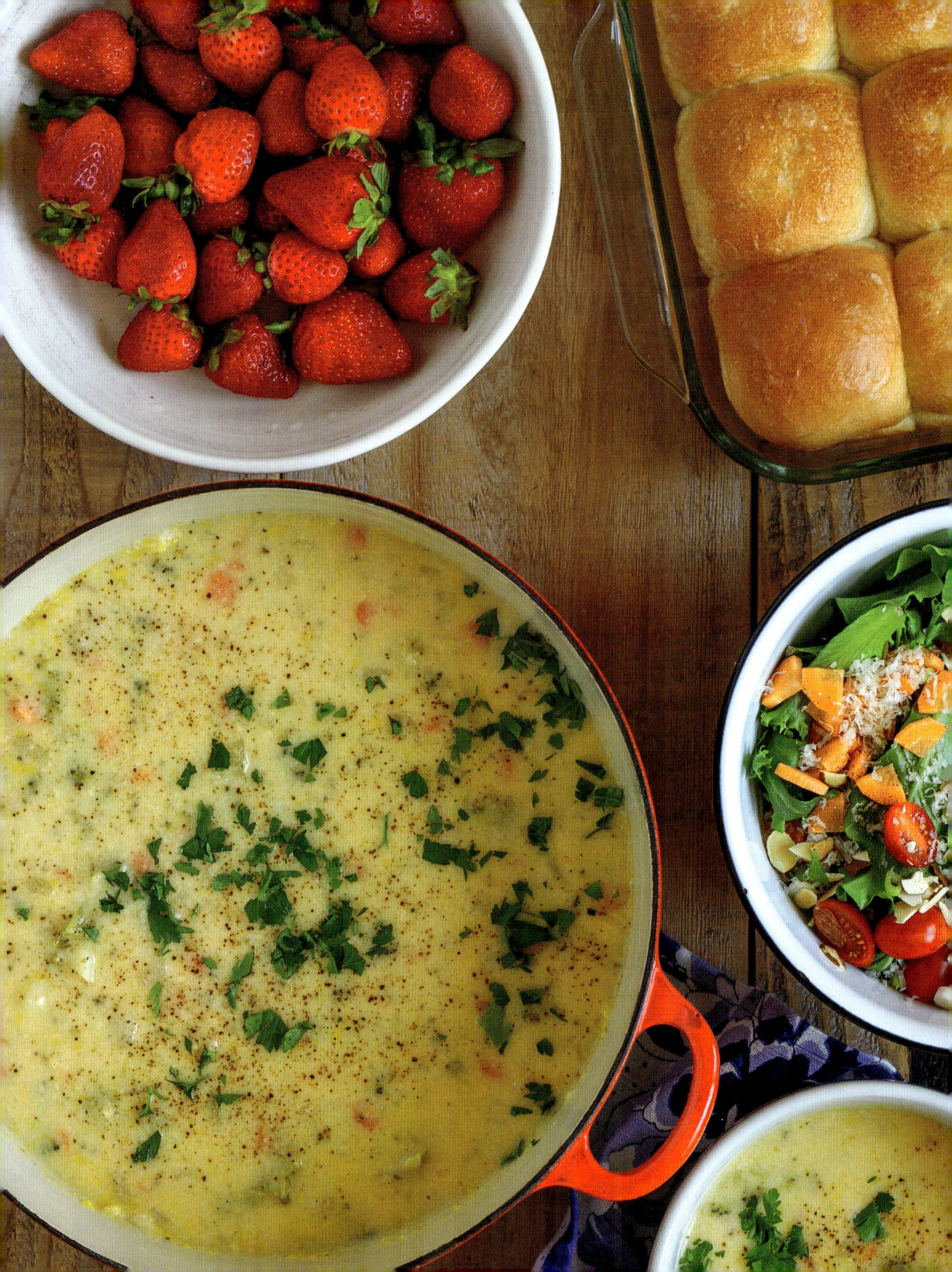

SOUPS

SOUP IS SUCH A GREAT dinner option. Soups are usually either quick to make or require very little work, tend to be hearty and comforting, and often reheat just as well if not better the next evening. We sometimes think of soup as a fall/winter/spring dinner, but all but the very heartiest of soups work just as well in the summer.

Round these dinners out by serving them with:

A GREEN SALAD (PAGES 61–83)

FRENCH BREAD FROM THE GROCERY STORE BAKERY, CORNBREAD, MUFFINS, DINNER ROLLS, HAWAIIAN ROLLS, OR GARLIC BREAD

SANDWICHES (PARTICULARLY GRILLED CHEESE)

FRESH FRUIT

Anne's Lentil Soup

My friend Anne shared this recipe many years ago on social media, and I could tell immediately that it was going to become just as much a favorite in my family as it was in hers. It is chock-full of veggies and lentils, so it's really filling without being heavy. It is warm, cozy, and comforting in the cold months but light enough for summer dinners, too. And it is 100 percent plant-based, so it's a great option for Meatless Mondays all year long.

Prep: 10 minutes | Cook: 50 minutes | Total: 1 hour | Serves 8 to 10

Extra-virgin olive oil or your favorite neutral cooking oil

1 medium onion, small diced

2 medium carrots, peeled and small diced

2 celery stalks, small diced

1 teaspoon minced garlic, or 1 clove garlic, minced

1 pound brown lentils

8 cups water

1 (16-ounce) can diced tomatoes

1 tablespoon dried cilantro

2½ teaspoons salt

½ teaspoon dried oregano

Freshly ground black pepper

2 tablespoons red wine vinegar

Dried cilantro, for garnish, optional

1. Drizzle about 1 tablespoon of oil in the bottom of a large, heavy-bottom Dutch oven or pot. Over medium heat, sauté the onion, carrots, and celery for about 10 minutes. Add the garlic and cook for 1 additional minute.

2. While the vegetables are sautéing, rinse and pick through the lentils to remove any small stones or dirt. Add the drained lentils, water, diced tomatoes with their liquid, cilantro, salt, oregano, and pepper to the pot. Bring the mixture to a boil, cover, reduce the heat, and simmer for 30 to 35 minutes, until the lentils are tender. Remove from the heat, stir in the vinegar, and add more salt, pepper, and vinegar to taste. Garnish with cilantro if using.

SHORTCUTS & NOTES

- 2½ to 3 cups pre-chopped mix of onion, carrots, and celery

- Pre-minced garlic (frozen cubes, or a jar or squeeze tube)

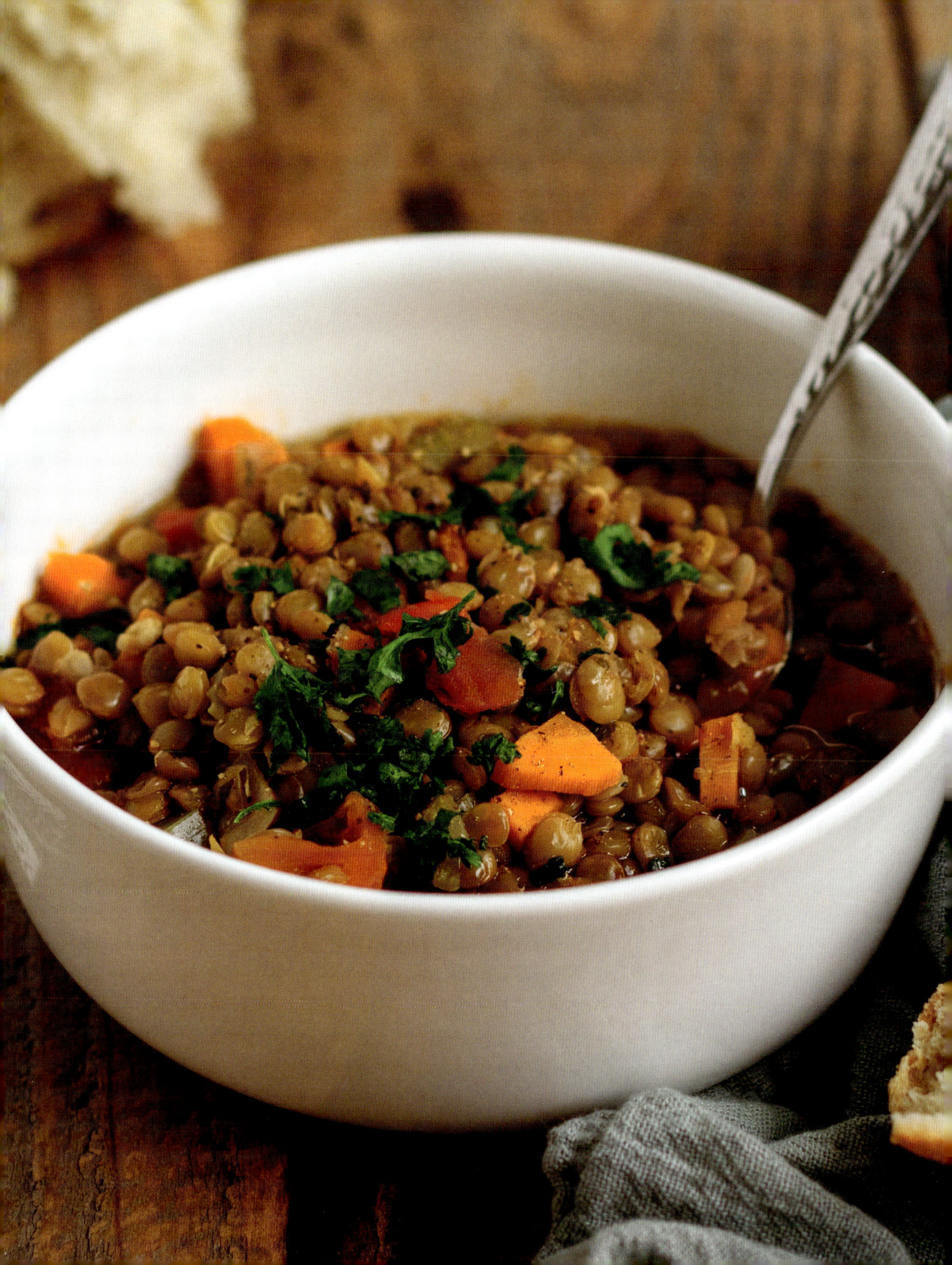

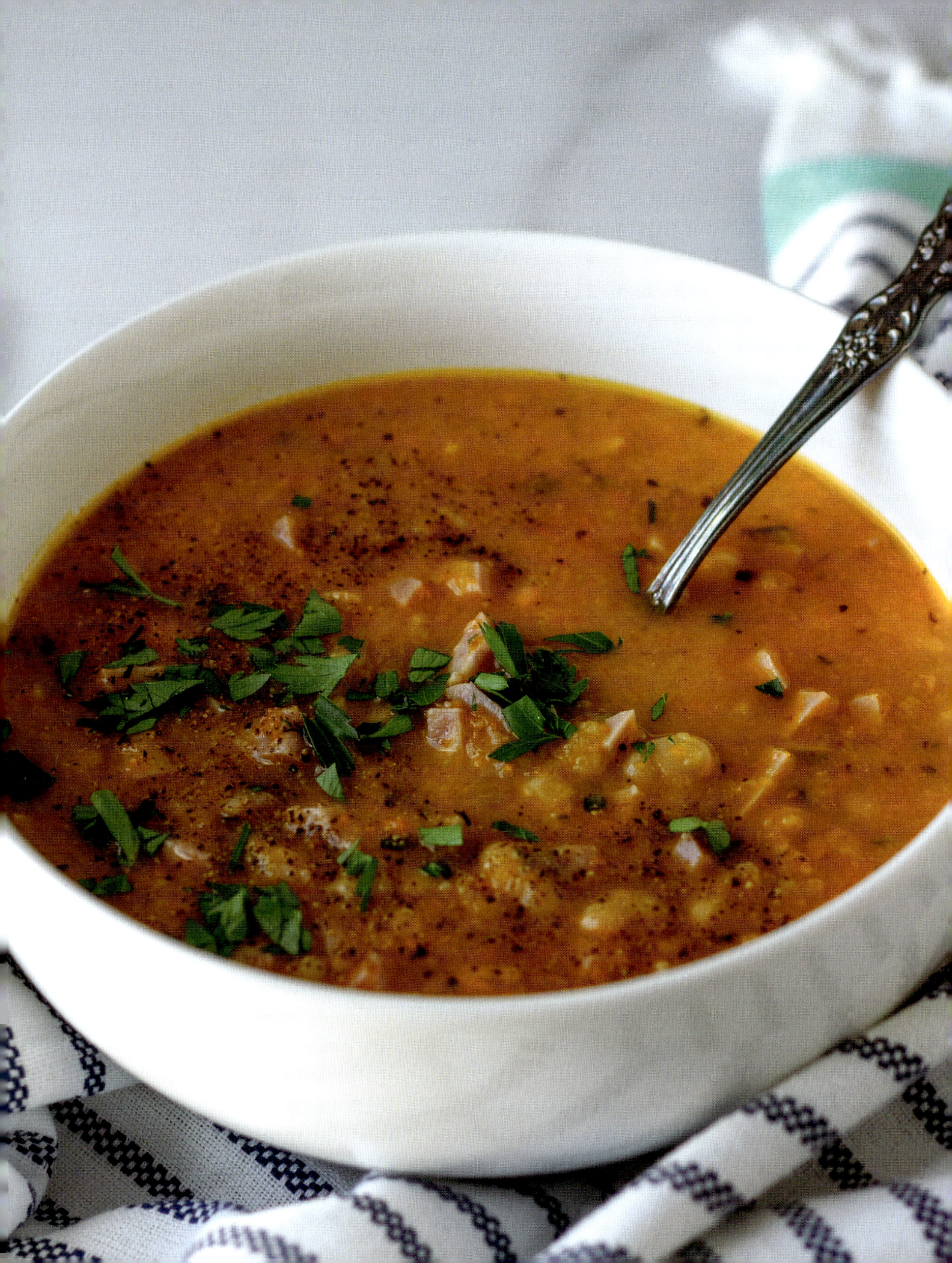

White Bean & Ham Soup

This yummy soup reminds me of a cross between bean-and-bacon and split pea with ham. It has lovely layers of smoky and tangy flavors and a pretty amber color. It is perfect for evenings where you want something quick and cozy for dinner, and the leftovers reheat wonderfully for lunch the next day.

Prep: 5 minutes | Cook: 40 minutes | Total: 45 minutes | Serves 8 to 10

¼ cup butter

2 cups diced onion

2 cups diced carrots

1 cup diced celery

1 pound ham, diced (about 3 cups) plus a few big chunks or 1 big slice for sautéing

4 teaspoons minced garlic, or 4 garlic cloves, minced

4½ cups low-sodium chicken broth

4 (15.5-ounce) cans white beans, drained and rinsed, divided

2 bay leaves

1 teaspoon smoked paprika

1 teaspoon Italian seasoning

Freshly ground black pepper

4 teaspoons apple cider vinegar

1 tablespoon minced fresh parsley

Kosher salt

1. In a large, heavy-bottom soup pot or Dutch oven over medium heat, melt the butter. Add the diced onion, carrots, and celery, plus the big chunks or slice of ham (not the 3 cups diced). Sauté the vegetables and ham for about 8 minutes, until tender and golden. Add the garlic and sauté for 1 to 2 minutes more. Add the broth and 2 cans of beans.

2. Remove from the heat and use a pair of tongs to remove the ham from the pot. Set it aside. Use an immersion blender to make the vegetable and bean mixture into a thick purée. Some chunks are fine; it shouldn't be perfectly smooth.

3. Return to the heat, put the big ham back in the pot (STILL NOT THE DICED HAM), and add the remaining 2 cans of beans, the bay leaves, the smoked paprika, the Italian seasoning, and pepper. Bring to a simmer, cover, and cook for 20 minutes, stirring frequently to make sure nothing is sticking to the bottom of the pot.

4. Remove and discard the big piece of ham and the bay leaves. Add the 3 cups of diced ham, the vinegar, and fresh parsley. Continue cooking for 2 to 3 more minutes, until everything is heated through. Salt and pepper to taste and serve.

SHORTCUTS & NOTES

- 5 cups pre-chopped mix of onion, carrots, and celery

- Pre-diced ham and a slice of deli ham for sautéing

- Pre-minced garlic (frozen cubes, or a jar or squeeze tube)

Black Bean Soup

I first started enjoying black bean soup in college. In those days, my black bean soup recipe involved a little paper cup filled with dried beans and spices, with microwave instructions on the back. My black bean soup and I have come a long way from those days! This from-scratch version might take a little longer than 60 seconds in the microwave, but it tastes amazing, with a bright, lightly spiced flavor and creamy texture. I'm generally all about toppings, but I think this soup is fantastic as is. If you must add toppings, I'd go with crumbled cotija, chopped cilantro, and a little sour cream.

Prep: 10 minutes | Cook: 35 minutes | Total: 45 minutes | Serves 6 to 8

1 large onion, diced

4 celery stalks, diced

½ red bell pepper, diced

2 tablespoons extra-virgin olive oil or your favorite neutral cooking oil

4 teaspoons minced garlic, or 4 garlic cloves, minced

2 (14.5-ounce) cans chicken or vegetable broth

3 (15-ounce) cans black beans, undrained

1 teaspoon ground cumin

1 teaspoon salt, plus more as needed

¼ teaspoon ground coriander

Freshly ground black pepper

¼ cup fresh lemon juice (from 1 to 2 lemons)

1. In a large, heavy-bottom Dutch oven or saucepan, sauté the onion, celery, and bell pepper in the olive oil over medium heat until tender, about 10 minutes. Add the garlic and cook for 1 to 2 minutes more. Add the broth and 1 can of black beans. Bring to a simmer, then remove from the heat.

2. Blend the soup either with an immersion blender or in a countertop blender until smooth. If you are using a countertop blender, leave the lid slightly askew and cover it with a kitchen towel while blending. This will allow steam to escape but also protect both your hand and the kitchen from splatters and steam. After blending, pour the soup pack into the saucepan.

3. Return the soup to medium heat, add the remaining 2 cans of black beans, plus the cumin, salt, coriander, black pepper, and lemon juice. Simmer, covered, for 20 minutes. Add salt and black pepper to taste, and serve.

SHORTCUTS & NOTES

- Pre-chopped onions, celery, or bell peppers
- Pre-minced garlic (frozen cubes, or a jar or squeeze tube)

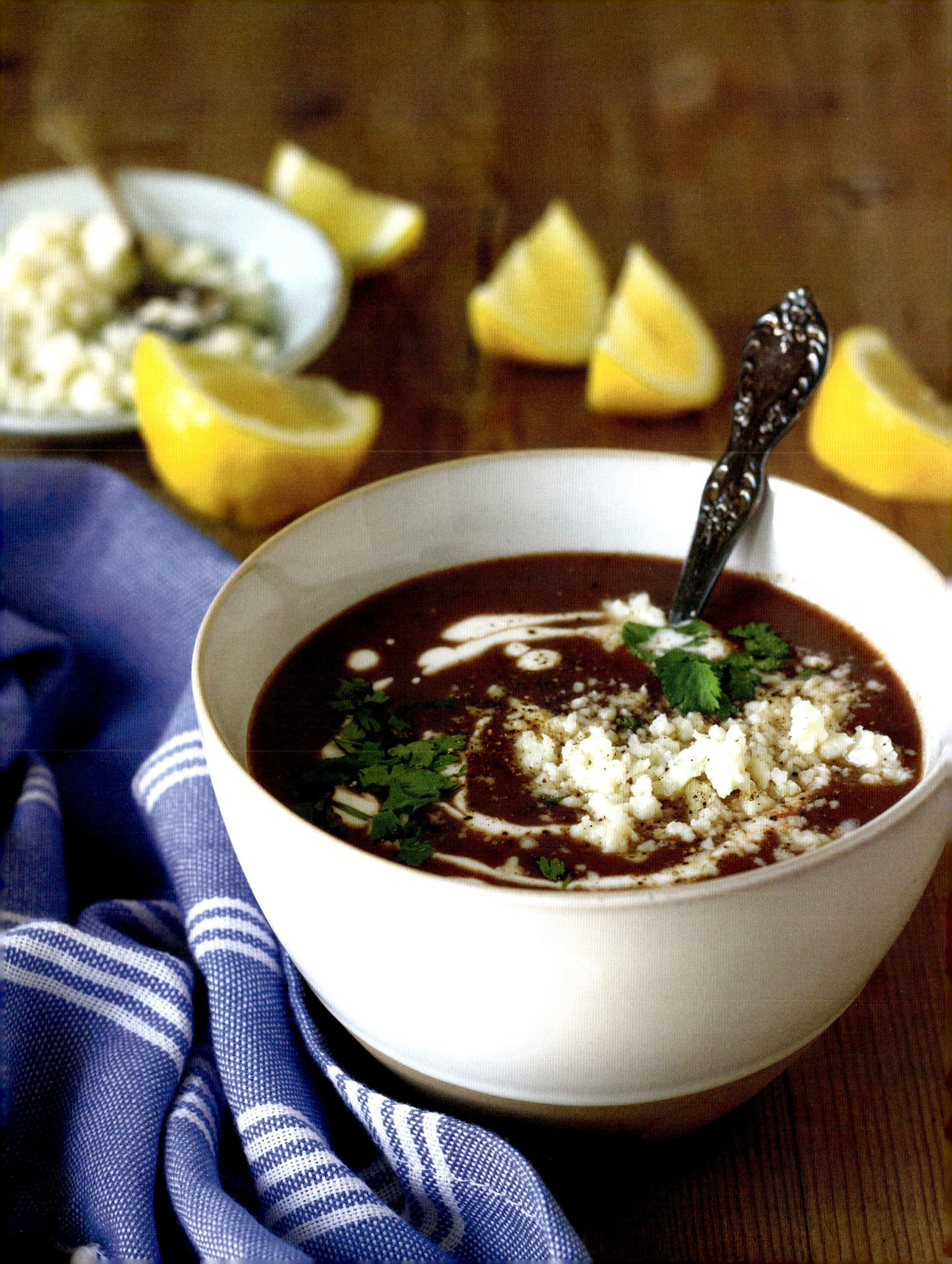

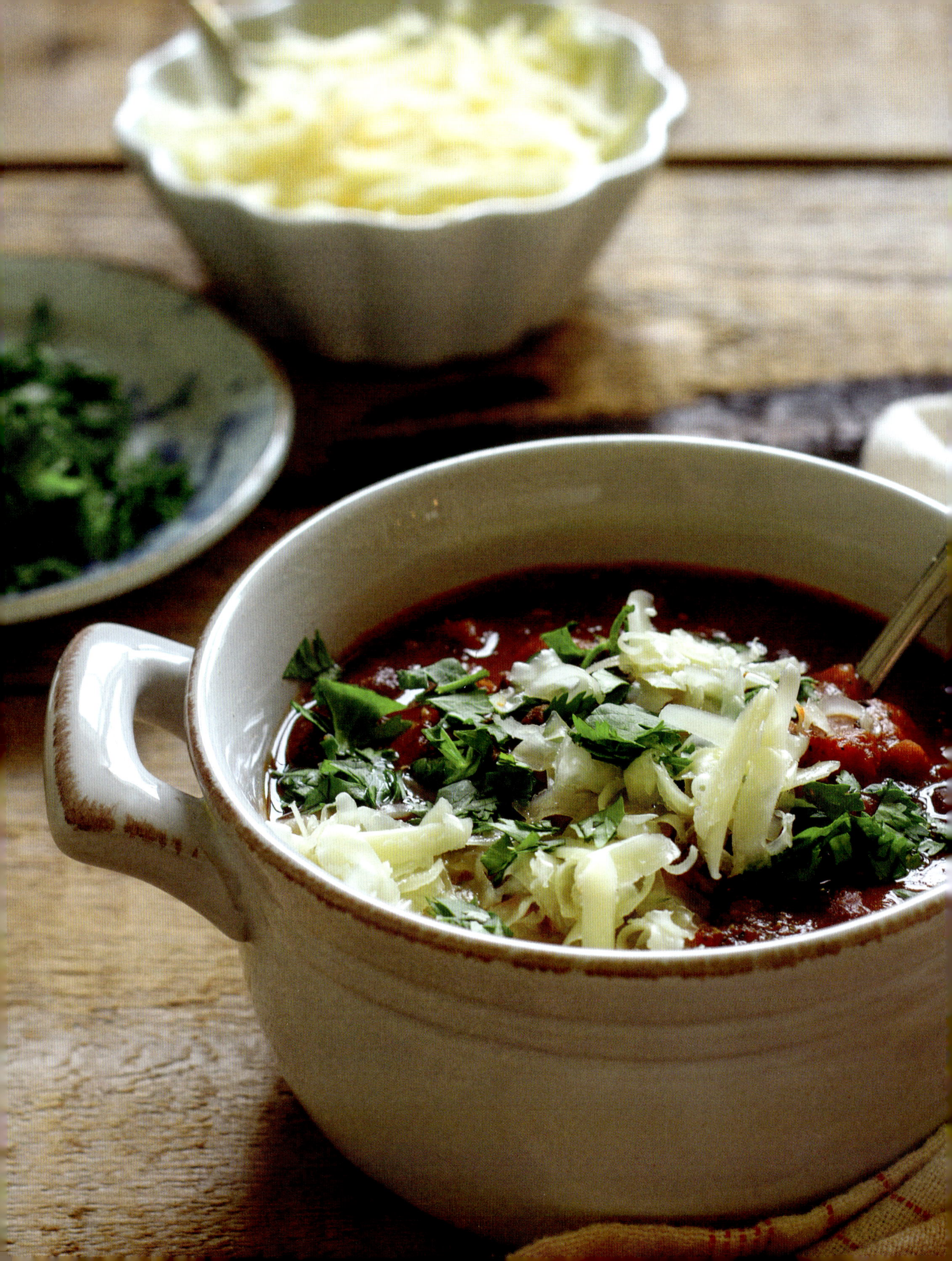

Dr. B.'s Southwest Three-Bean Soup

In my second year of college, I decided to take Intro to Marine Biology because I'd always loved the ocean. My friend happened to be the teaching assistant for the class and said to me one day, "Hey, you know that ten-week field study we do every year in Monterey Bay? Someone just dropped out and I told the professor you'd go in their place." And—completely uncharacteristically—I said yes. I spent ten weeks studying marine biology up close on the central coast of California, sleeping on the floor of an unfurnished apartment with four other students, exploring rocky tide pools and mudflats at low tide, and just having the time of my 20-year-old life. The professor, Dr. Lee Braithwaite, became one of my favorite people in the whole world. He made this soup for us one day after a field trip. I think he even cooked it on a hot plate in the lab! It's flavorful and satisfying—the perfect end to a long work day—and every time I make it, I think of Dr. B. and that magical summer I spent at the ocean.

Prep: 10 minutes | Cook: 30 minutes | Total: 40 minutes | Serves 6

Extra-virgin olive oil or your favorite neutral cooking oil

6 ounces Canadian bacon, diced

1 cup diced onion

½ cup red bell pepper, small diced

2 garlic cloves, minced, or 2 teaspoons minced garlic

1 teaspoon ground cumin

1 teaspoon chili powder

¼ teaspoon smoked paprika

1 (15-ounce) can petite diced tomatoes, undrained

1 (15-ounce) can black beans, drained and rinsed

1 (15-ounce) can red kidney beans, drained and rinsed

1 (15-ounce) can pinto beans, drained and rinsed

1 cup tomato-based red salsa of choice (Dr. B. used Pace chunky salsa)

1 (8-ounce) can tomato sauce

1 (14.5-ounce) can beef broth

1 cup water

1½ teaspoons fresh thyme

2 tablespoons red wine vinegar

Salt

Freshly ground black pepper

Shredded cheddar or Monterey jack cheese and chopped fresh cilantro, for topping

continued

1. In a large, heavy-bottom Dutch oven or pot over medium heat, drizzle about 1 tablespoon of olive oil. Add the Canadian bacon, onion, bell pepper, garlic, cumin, chili powder, and smoked paprika. Sauté for 10 minutes, until the onion and pepper are tender.

2. Add the tomatoes, beans, salsa, tomato sauce, broth, water, and thyme. Bring to a simmer, cover, and cook for 20 minutes. Add the vinegar, salt, and black pepper to taste. Serve with cheese and cilantro on top.

SHORTCUTS & NOTES

- Pre-chopped onions and bell peppers
- Pre-minced garlic (frozen cubes, or a jar or squeeze tube)
- Pre-shredded cheese (for topping)

Garden Minestrone

If I ask my husband what kind of soup he would like to see on the dinner menu for the week, nine times out of ten, the answer is minestrone. I've probably tweaked this recipe a hundred times over the years until it's my idea of perfect: absolutely packed with fresh vegetables and flavor, flavor, flavor!

Prep: 10 minutes | Cook: 30 minutes | Total: 40 minutes | Serves 8

- 8 ounces small dried pasta (orzo, ditalini, or small shells or elbows)
- ⅓ cup extra-virgin olive oil or your favorite neutral cooking oil
- 1 cup diced onion
- 1 cup chopped leek, white and light green parts (about 1 medium leek)
- 2 cups diced carrots
- 1 cup diced celery
- 2 cups diced zucchini
- 2 cups diced yellow squash
- 1 tablespoon minced garlic, or 3 garlic cloves, minced
- ¼ cup minced fresh parsley, plus more for garnishing
- 1 teaspoon fresh thyme
- 1 (28-ounce) can diced tomatoes
- 4 cups vegetable broth or chicken broth
- 1 (15.5-ounce) can kidney beans, drained and rinsed
- 1 (15.5-ounce) can white beans, drained and rinsed
- 1 tablespoon tomato paste
- ¼ cup pesto
- Juice of ½ lemon
- Salt
- Freshly ground black pepper
- Freshly shredded Parmesan cheese, for topping

continued

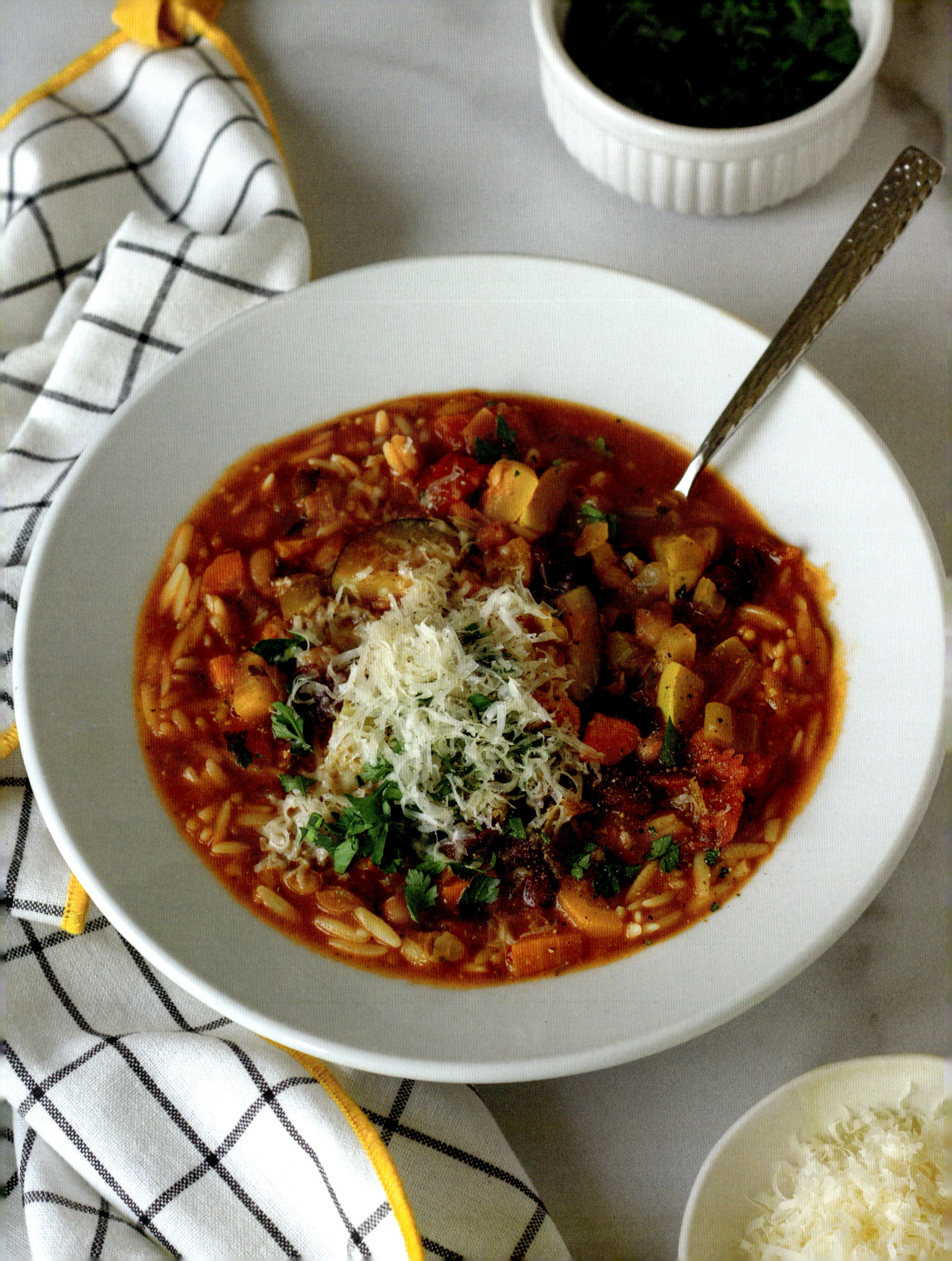

1. Put a large pot of salted water over high heat and bring to a boil. Cook the pasta according to the package instructions. Pour into a colander, rinse, and set aside.

2. While waiting for the pasta water to boil and for the pasta to cook, start the soup. In a large, heavy-bottom pot, heat the olive oil over medium heat. Add the onion, leek, carrots, and celery and sauté until tender, about 10 minutes. Add the zucchini, squash, garlic, parsley, and thyme and cook until fragrant, 3 minutes. Add the diced tomatoes (with liquid), broth, beans, and tomato paste. Bring to a boil, cover, reduce the heat, and simmer for 15 minutes.

3. Add the pesto and lemon juice to the soup, then salt and pepper to taste.

4. Serve the soup over cooked pasta, and top with Parmesan cheese and parsley.

SHORTCUTS & NOTES

- 4 cups pre-chopped mix of onion, carrots, and celery

- Pre-sliced zucchini and yellow squash (It's already sliced, but if you go this route, chop them a little smaller.)

- Pre-minced garlic (frozen cubes, or a jar or squeeze tube)

- Store-bought pesto (We like the one from Costco.)

- I think most store-bought, pre-shredded Parmesan cheese is very different from freshly shredded Parmesan. Parmesan is one case where I almost always just grate it myself.

- For a delicious variation with even more veggies, leave out the cooked pasta and add about 1 pound coarsely chopped green cabbage when you add the zucchini.

Creamy Tomato Cheese Soup

Creamy tomato soup (served with grilled cheese sandwiches, of course!) is a comfort food classic, and it's not hard to see why. It's easy to make, even on busy nights, and leaves you feeling warm, happy, and satisfied. It's been one of my favorite meals since I was a kid, and it pops up on our dinner menu regularly. This recipe uses cheddar in place of the usual Parmesan cheese, and I think you'll love it.

Prep: 5 minutes | Cook: 35 minutes | Total: 40 minutes | Serves 4 or 5

2 tablespoons butter

1 cup chopped onion

2 teaspoons minced garlic, or 2 garlic cloves, minced

1 (28-ounce) can San Marzano tomatoes

1 (14.5-ounce) can vegetable broth or chicken broth

1 teaspoon kosher salt

Freshly ground black pepper

½ cup heavy cream

4 ounces medium cheddar cheese, plus more for garnishing

1 tablespoon pesto

Fresh basil, for garnishing, optional

1. In a medium soup pot or heavy-bottom Dutch oven, melt the butter over medium heat. Add the onion and sauté until translucent, about 5 minutes. Add the garlic and sauté for 1 to 2 minutes. Add the tomatoes with their juices, broth, salt, and pepper, bring to a simmer, and cook, uncovered, for 20 minutes.

2. Remove from the heat. Blend the soup either with an immersion blender or in a countertop blender until smooth. If you are using a countertop blender, leave the lid slightly askew and cover it with a kitchen towel while blending. This will allow steam to escape but also protect both your hand and the kitchen from splatters and steam. After blending, pour the soup back into the saucepan.

3. Return the soup to medium heat, add the cream, cheddar, and pesto and cook, stirring, just until hot. Serve immediately, garnished with more cheese and basil if using.

SHORTCUTS & NOTES

- Pre-chopped onion

- Pre-minced garlic (frozen cubes, or a jar or squeeze tube)

- You know I love pre-shredded cheese, but in this case, if you have time, shredding the cheddar yourself will help it melt into the soup better. But it'll taste delicious either way!

- Store-bought pesto (We like the one from Costco.)

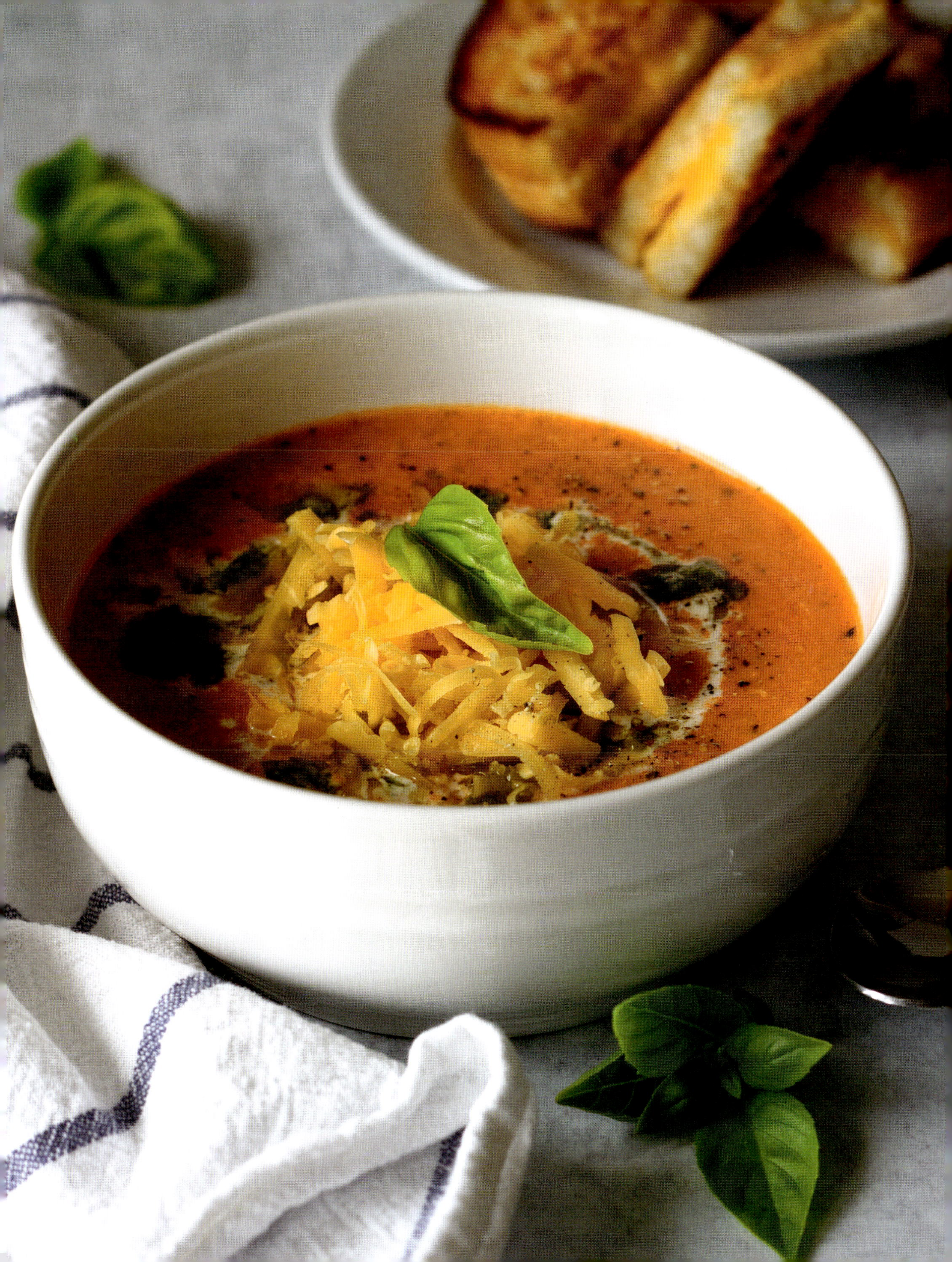

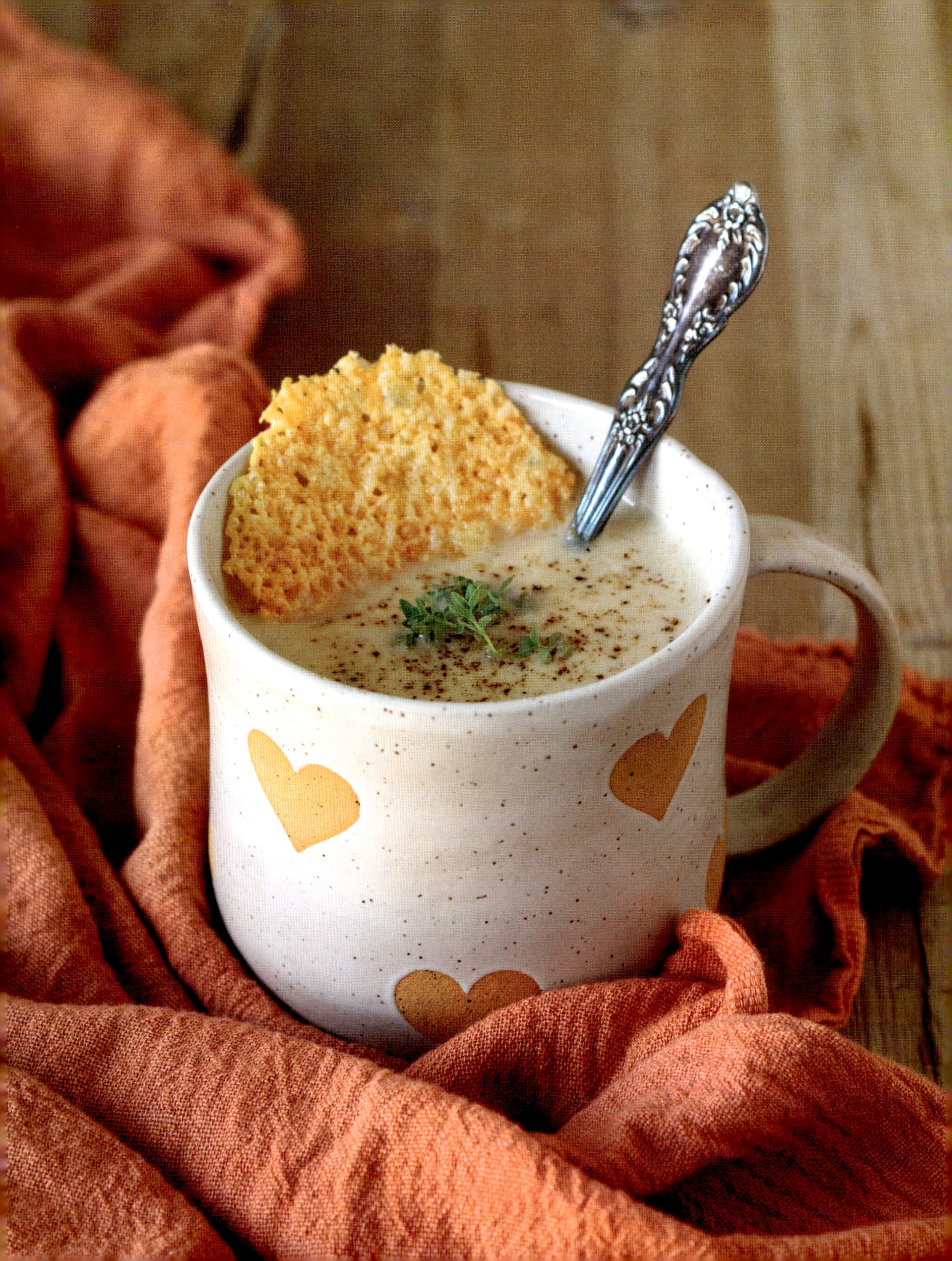

Roasted Cauliflower & White Cheddar Soup

I started making this cozy soup several years ago, and it became an instant favorite. We have it often, especially when the days are short and chilly. Roasting the cauliflower before adding it to the soup gives it a rich, deep flavor, which goes beautifully with the nutty cheddar and fresh, herby thyme.

Prep: 10 minutes | Cook: 40 minutes | Total: 50 minutes | Serves 6 to 8

2 pounds cauliflower, chopped

Extra-virgin olive oil or your favorite neutral cooking oil

1½ teaspoons kosher salt, plus more as needed

Freshly ground black pepper

1 large onion, diced

4 teaspoons minced garlic, or 4 garlic cloves, minced

1 tablespoon fresh thyme, plus more for garnishing, optional

6 cups vegetable broth or chicken broth

3 cups shredded sharp white cheddar cheese

1½ cups half-and-half

1. Preheat the oven to 400°F. Place the cauliflower in a single layer on a rimmed baking sheet. Drizzle generously with olive oil (about 3 tablespoons), season with kosher salt and pepper, and roast for 20 minutes, until the cauliflower is golden brown.

2. When the cauliflower has been in the oven for about 10 minutes, put the onion in a large, heavy-bottom Dutch oven or saucepan. Drizzle with about 1 tablespoon of olive oil and sauté over medium heat for 10 minutes. Add the garlic and thyme and sauté for 1 to 2 more minutes.

3. When the cauliflower is done roasting, add it and the broth to the saucepan. Bring to a boil, cover, reduce the heat, and simmer for 15 minutes.

4. Remove from the heat and blend either with an immersion blender or in a countertop blender until smooth. If you are using a countertop blender, leave the lid slightly askew and cover it with a kitchen towel while blending. This will allow steam to escape but also protect both your hand and the kitchen from splatters and steam. After blending, pour the soup back into the saucepan.

5. Return the soup to medium heat, add the cheese and half-and-half, and cook until heated through. Add salt and pepper to taste, then serve with some thyme if using.

SHORTCUTS & NOTES

- Pre-prepped cauliflower florets

- Pre-chopped onion

- Pre-minced garlic (frozen cubes, or a jar or squeeze tube)

- This is a case where shredding the cheese yourself will result in a smoother soup, but I have definitely used pre-shredded white cheddar before and lived to tell the tale.

- The crispy cheese garnish pictured in the photo is just an optional crunchy bite that looks pretty.

Lulu the Baker's Famous Cheesy Chowder

My family has loved cheesy chowder for nearly 20 years, and it has been the most popular recipe on my blog, *Lulu the Baker*, for more than a decade. And with good reason! It is creamy, cheesy, savory, and satisfying. Served with a fresh salad and a loaf of crusty bread, some warm sourdough, or a batch of fluffy dinner rolls, it makes a deliciously cozy supper.

Prep: 10 minutes | Cook: 35 minutes | Total: 45 minutes | Serves 8 to 10

¼ cup butter

1 cup diced onion

2 cups diced carrots

1 cup diced celery

2 tablespoons minced garlic, or 6 garlic cloves, minced

8 cups vegetable broth or chicken broth

2 pounds russet potatoes, peeled and diced

2 tablespoons all-purpose flour

1 cup water

1⅓ cups milk

1 (10.8-ounce) bag frozen broccoli florets, coarsely chopped

4 cups shredded medium cheddar cheese

Kosher salt

Freshly ground black pepper

Minced fresh parsley, for garnishing, optional

1. In a large, heavy-bottom Dutch oven or saucepan, melt the butter over medium heat. Add the onion, carrots, and celery and sauté over medium heat until tender, about 10 minutes. Add the garlic and cook for 1 to 2 additional minutes.

2. Add the broth and potatoes, turn the heat up to high, and bring to a boil. Reduce the heat just enough that the soup stays at a simmer and cook until the potatoes are tender, about 10 minutes.

3. In a small bowl, whisk the flour with the water until smooth. Add it to the large saucepan and simmer 1 to 2 minutes. Add the milk and broccoli and cook until the broccoli is tender and the soup is heated through, about 5 minutes.

4. Remove the soup from the heat. Stir in the cheese and allow to melt, add salt and pepper to taste, and serve with a sprinkling of parsley if using.

SHORTCUTS & NOTES

- 4 cups pre-chopped mix of onion, carrots, and celery

- Pre-minced garlic (frozen cubes, or a jar or squeeze tube)

- This is a case where shredding the cheese yourself might result in a smoother soup. That being said, I use pre-shredded cheddar all the time when I make this and it turns out great.

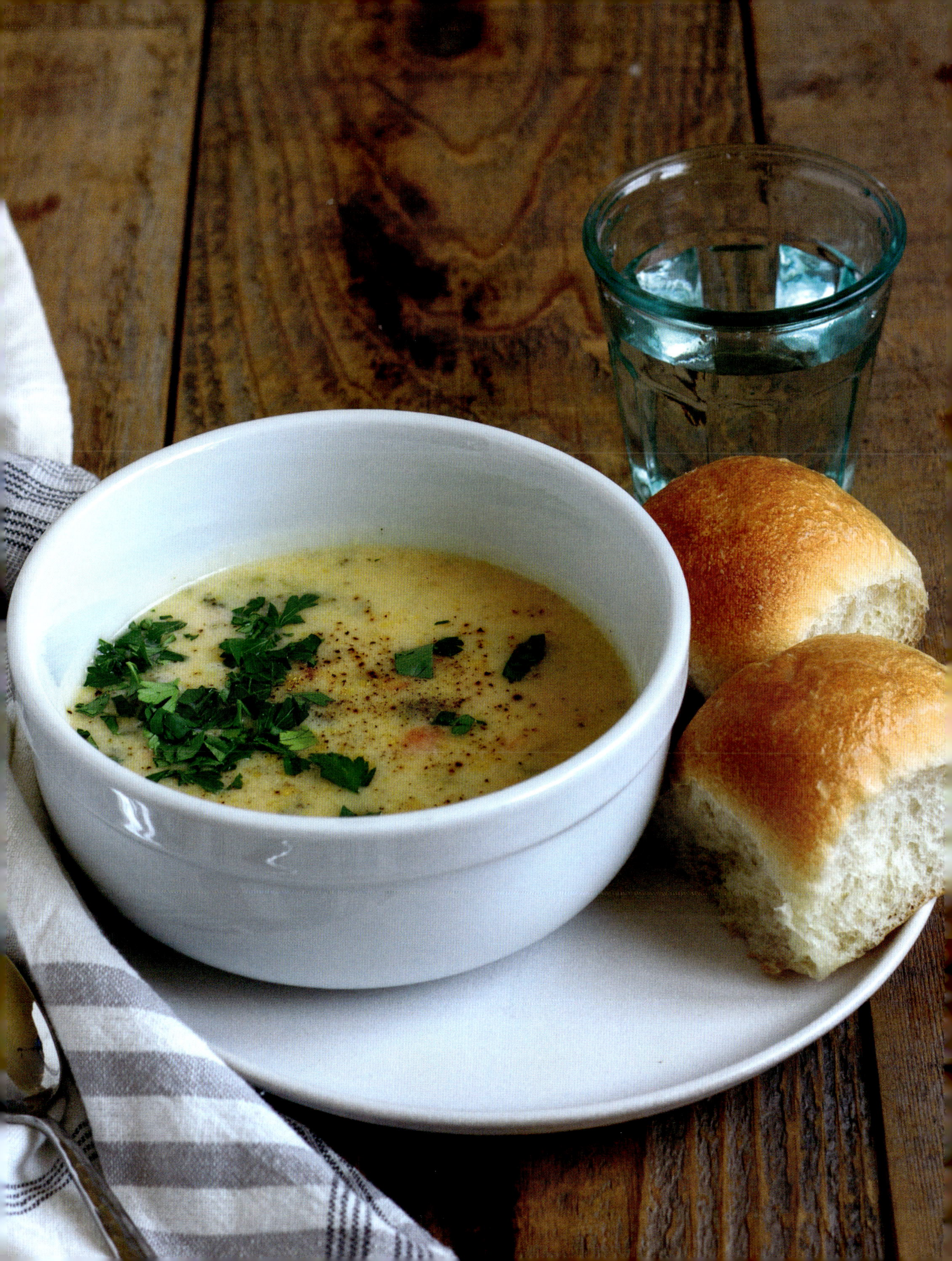

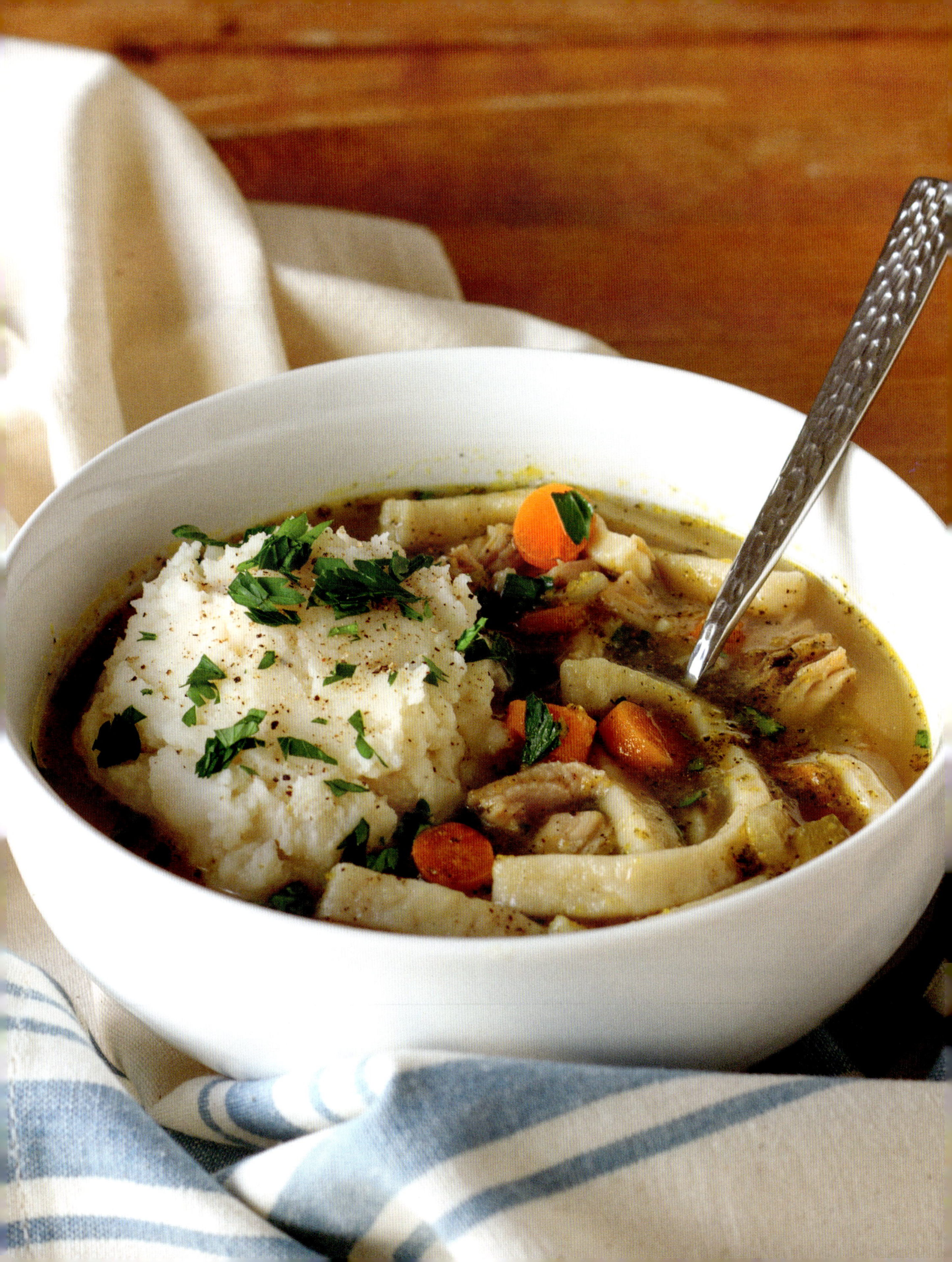

Homestyle Chicken Noodle Soup

Please don't think I'm a monster when I tell you this: I don't really love chicken noodle soup. I know! It's like the most classic of classic comfort foods. I've just never really thought chicken noodle soup was that great. But when my friend Annie made this recipe for me more than a decade ago, I fell in love with it. The broth is herby and salty and delicious, but I think the real star of the show is the noodles. Annie makes hers from scratch, but to save time, I buy them at the grocery store. There's one tiny catch: You cannot just use regular old pasta or egg noodles. Look for homestyle egg noodles in the freezer case or kluski in the dried pasta section. They are fat little noodles that are creamy, light beige, and totally opaque, not at all like a regular egg noodle. They are really top-notch and well worth the extra couple of minutes it takes to hunt them down.

Prep: 15 minutes | Cook: 40 minutes | Total: 55 minutes | Serves 8

2 tablespoons butter

1 cup diced onion

1 cup diced celery

2 cups sliced carrots

1 tablespoon minced garlic, or 3 garlic cloves, minced

12 cups chicken broth

1 teaspoon dried sage

1 teaspoon salt

½ teaspoon freshly ground black pepper

1 (12-ounce) package homestyle egg noodles or dried kluski

2 cups (about 12 ounces) chopped cooked chicken breast

Minced fresh parsley, for garnishing, optional

1. In a large, heavy-bottom Dutch oven or pot over medium heat, melt the butter. Add the onion, celery, and carrots and sauté for 10 minutes. Add the garlic and cook for 1 additional minute. Add the broth, sage, salt, and pepper and bring to a boil.

2. When the soup is at a full boil, add the noodles and cook according to the package directions, which should be 20 minutes or less depending on what brand of noodles you're using.

3. Add the chicken and continue cooking just until the chicken is heated through, about 5 minutes. Serve immediately, garnished with some parsley if using.

SHORTCUTS & NOTES

- 4 cups pre-chopped mix of onion, carrots, and celery

- Pre-minced garlic (frozen cubes, or a jar or squeeze tube)

- Rotisserie chicken

- This soup is extra delicious served over mashed potatoes, which is how I first had it and how I like to serve it. When we make mashed potatoes for any reason, we always portion out and freeze any leftovers to use in cases just like this, where we might want them on a busy night. You can also use your favorite premade mashed potatoes from the store.

Mom's Chicken Tortilla Soup

I love my mom's chicken tortilla soup! I have a photocopy of her original recipe, which she wrote on fancy parchment paper with a fancy calligraphy pen when I was a kid. The broth is savory and smoky, with lots of herbs and spices and a rich tomato flavor.

Prep: 10 minutes | Cook: 40 minutes | Total: 50 minutes | Serves 8 to 10

1 tablespoon extra-virgin olive oil or your favorite neutral cooking oil

2 cups diced onions

2 (4-ounce) cans chopped green chiles

4 teaspoons minced garlic, or 4 cloves garlic, minced

2 teaspoons ground cumin

2 teaspoons chili powder

1 teaspoon ground coriander

1 teaspoon dried oregano

½ teaspoon smoked paprika

Freshly ground black pepper

6 cups water

1 (14.5-ounce) can low-sodium chicken broth

2 (12-ounce) cans tomato juice

1 (15-ounce) can tomato sauce

2 medium tomatoes, diced

1 tablespoon Worcestershire sauce

2 teaspoons salt, plus more as needed

2 pounds shredded cooked chicken

Tortilla chips, minced green onions, diced avocado, sour cream, shredded Monterey jack cheese, hot sauce, chopped cilantro, and lime wedges, for topping

1. Heat the oil in a large Dutch oven or heavy-bottom saucepan over medium heat. Sauté the onions, chiles, garlic, cumin, chili powder, coriander, oregano, smoked paprika, and pepper until the onions are tender, 10 minutes.

2. Add the water, broth, tomato juice, tomato sauce, diced tomatoes, Worcestershire sauce, and salt. Turn the heat up to high and bring to a boil. Reduce the heat so that the soup is still simmering, then cover and simmer for 30 minutes, stirring occasionally.

3. Just before serving, stir in the chicken and add salt and pepper to taste.

4. Serve in bowls, topped with crushed tortilla chips, green onions, avocado, sour cream, shredded Monterey jack cheese, hot sauce, and chopped cilantro. Serve with lime wedges on the side.

SHORTCUTS & NOTES

- Pre-chopped onions
- Pre-minced garlic (frozen cubes, or a jar or squeeze tube)
- Rotisserie chicken
- A Tex-Mex restaurant I loved in college made their tortilla soup the following way, and it really is great: Load up your bowl with chicken and any toppings you want (along with rice and beans if that's your preference), then ladle the broth over the top of everything. Their broth was different from this one, but the method works just as well here.

Taco Soup

I don't want to pigeonhole this soup by saying it's a tasty alternative to chili … but it is a very, very tasty alternative to chili! It has a lot of the same basic ingredients as a standard beef-and-bean chili, but with a more Tex-Mex flavor profile. I've tried lots of different taco soup recipes over the years, but this one remains my favorite.

Prep: 5 minutes | Cook: 25 minutes | Total: 30 minutes | Serves 8

1 pound ground beef

½ cup diced onion

**1 teaspoon minced garlic, or
1 garlic clove, minced**

1 (15.25-ounce) can corn, drained

1 (15.5-ounce) can pinto beans, undrained

1 (15.5-ounce) can kidney beans, undrained

1 (14.5-ounce) can diced tomatoes, undrained

1 (1-ounce) packet taco seasoning (see page 140 for a homemade version)

1 (1-ounce) packet ranch seasoning

2 cups low-sodium beef broth

Salt

Freshly ground black pepper

Sour cream, diced avocado, shredded cheese, crushed tortilla chips, sliced olives, and lime wedges, for topping

1. In a large, heavy-bottom Dutch oven or pot over medium heat, cook the ground beef, crumbling it with a large spoon or spatula. Add the onion and cook until the ground beef is brown and cooked through, 7 to 8 minutes. Drain any extra grease.

2. Add the garlic, corn, beans with their juices, tomatoes with their juices, seasonings, and broth. Simmer, covered, for 15 to 20 minutes. Add salt and pepper to taste, then serve with toppings of choice.

SHORTCUTS & NOTES

- Pre-chopped onion
- Pre-minced garlic (frozen cubes, or a jar or squeeze tube)
- Pre-shredded cheese (for topping)

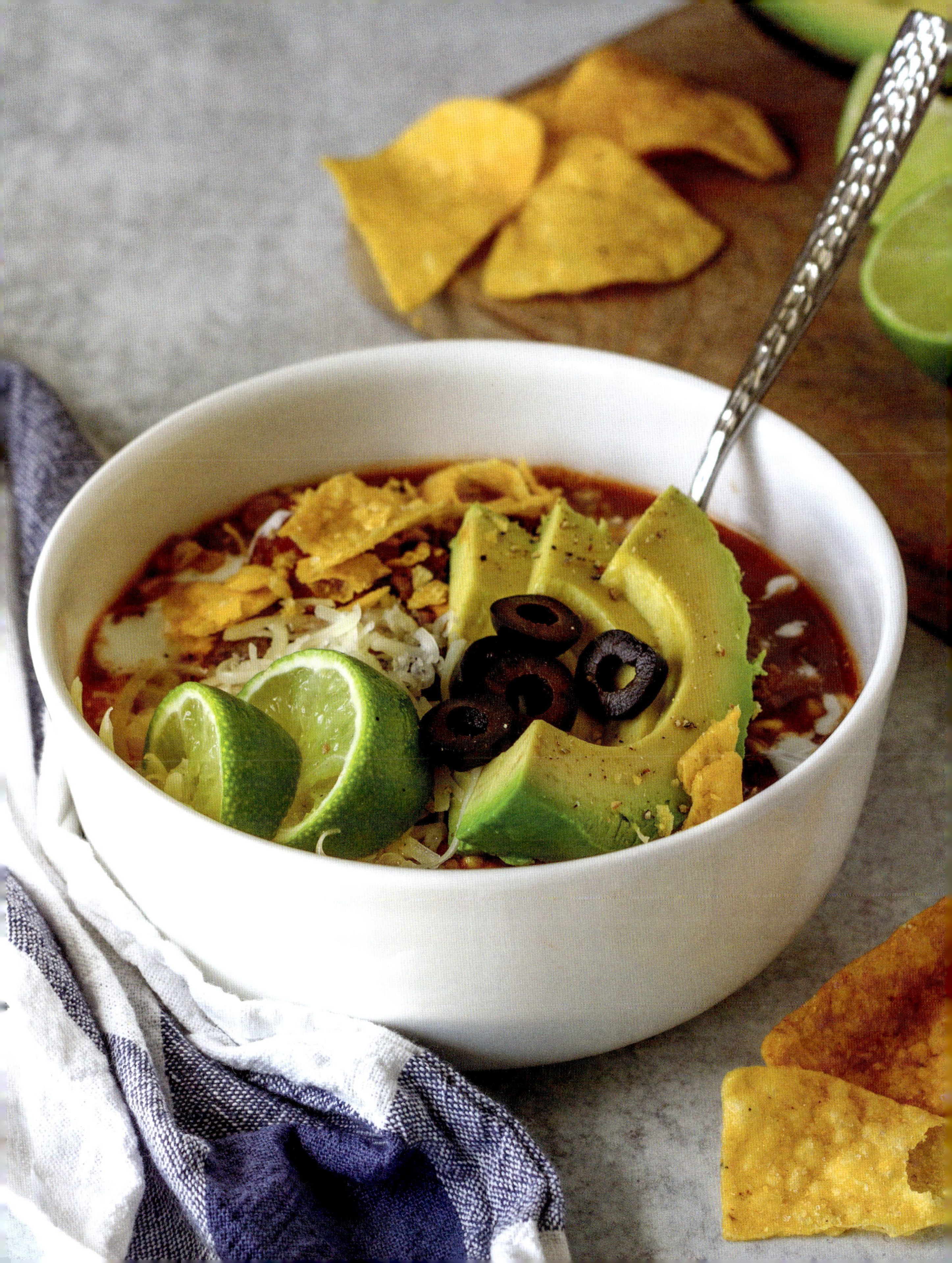

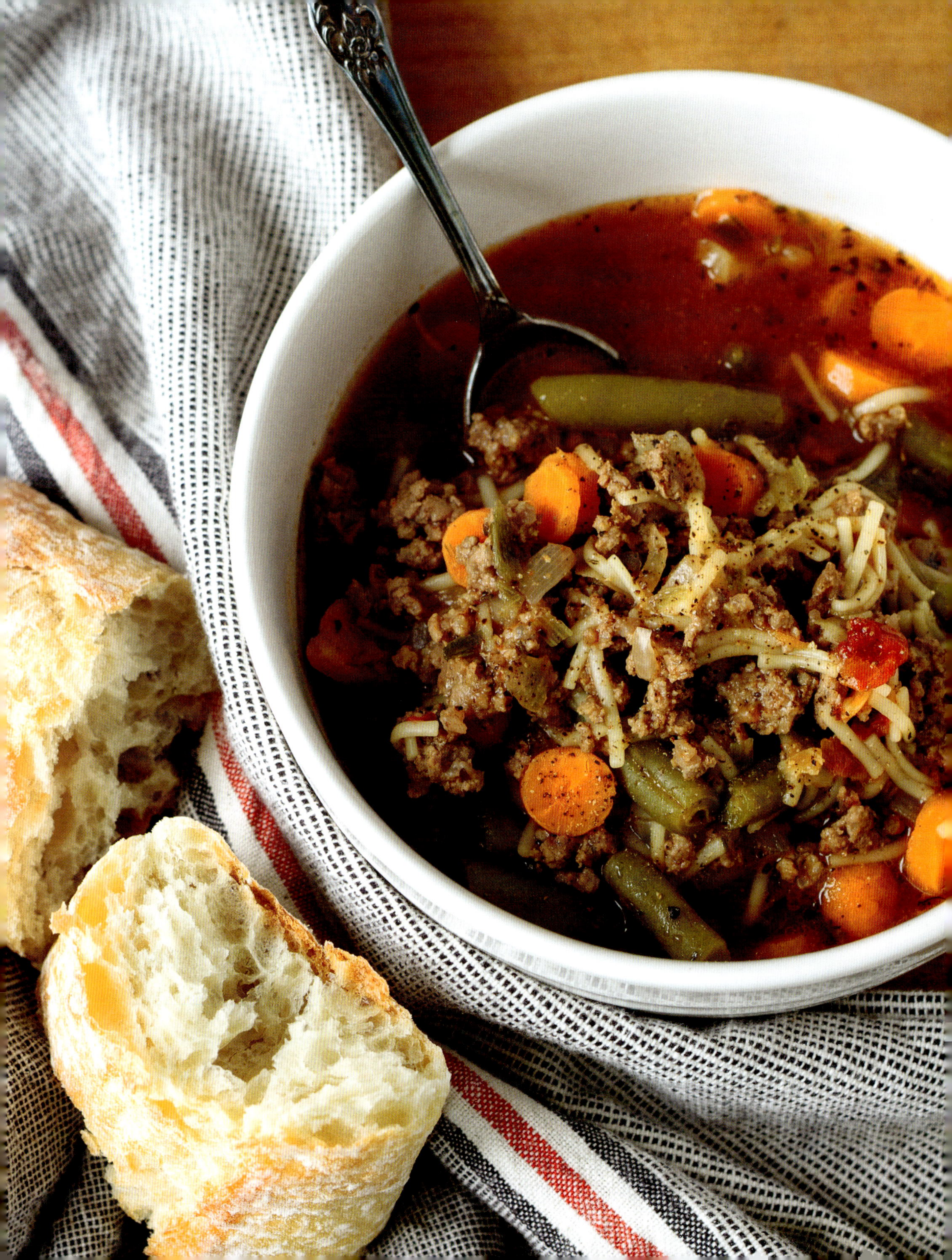

Nana's Quick & Hearty Soup

I love this recipe for lots of reasons. (1) The recipe comes from my grandma, Nana. She got the recipe from a friend when her family was young, then passed it down to my mom who passed it down to me when I was a newlywed. (2) The ingredient list is full of pantry staples, which means you can keep the ingredients on hand for busy nights that pop up unexpectedly. (3) It's ready in 30 minutes or less. And most importantly, (4) it is hearty, old-fashioned, comforting, and oh-so-tasty.

Prep: 10 minutes | Cook: 20 minutes | Total: 30 minutes | Serves 4

- 1 (1.4-ounce) package Knorr Vegetable Recipe Mix
- 8 cups water
- 1 (2.2-ounce) pouch Lipton Noodle Soup Mix (it comes in a box with 2 pouches; you only need 1 pouch)
- 1 pound ground beef
- 1 cup diced onion
- Kosher salt
- Freshly ground black pepper
- 1 (14.5-ounce) can carrots, drained
- 1 (14.5-ounce) can green beans, drained
- 1 (8-ounce) can tomato sauce
- ½ teaspoon dried oregano
- ½ teaspoon dried basil

1. In a large saucepan or soup pot, combine the Knorr Vegetable Recipe Mix with the water. Bring to a boil over high heat, then reduce the heat and simmer the soup, uncovered, for 5 minutes. Add the Lipton Noodle Soup Mix to the pot and continue simmering for 5 minutes.

2. While the soup mixes simmer, brown the ground beef and onion in a skillet over medium heat, about 10 minutes, lightly seasoning with kosher salt and pepper. Drain off any excess grease.

3. Add the ground beef, carrots, green beans, tomato sauce, oregano, and basil to the soup. Cook at a simmer until heated through, about 5 minutes. Add salt and pepper to taste, then serve.

Pasta Fagioli

I really debated where to put this stick-to-your-ribs Italian stew. It makes sense in the soup chapter, but it also verges on just being a very saucy pasta. Regardless of what chapter you find the recipe in, pasta fagioli is hearty and heavenly, full of veggies and beef, tangy tomatoes and tender beans, and lots and lots of pasta.

Prep: 10 minutes | Cook: 35 minutes | Total: 45 minutes | Serves 6 to 8

1 pound ground beef or ground turkey

Kosher salt

Freshly ground black pepper

1 large onion

1 large carrot

2 celery stalks

1 tablespoon extra-virgin olive oil or your favorite neutral cooking oil

1 teaspoon minced garlic, or 1 garlic clove, minced

3 cups low-sodium beef broth

1½ cups water

1 (28-ounce) can crushed tomatoes

1 (15.5-ounce) can white beans, drained and rinsed

1 teaspoon dried basil

1 teaspoon dried oregano

6 ounces dried ditalini or other small pasta

Grated or shredded Parmesan cheese, for serving

Minced fresh parsley, for garnishing, optional

1. In a large, heavy-bottom Dutch oven or soup pot, brown the beef over medium heat until cooked through, 7 to 8 minutes. Season with salt and pepper.

2. While the ground beef is cooking, dice your vegetables. You should have about 1½ cups of onion, and ½ cup each of carrot and celery.

3. Drain any excess grease from the cooked ground beef, then add the olive oil to the pot and sauté the onion, carrot, celery, and garlic for 5 minutes, until fragrant.

4. Add the beef broth, water, tomatoes with their juices, beans, basil, and oregano. Turn the heat up to high and bring the soup to a boil.

5. Add the dried pasta, reduce the heat but keep the soup at a simmer, and cook until the pasta is al dente, about 9 minutes. Stir frequently to keep the pasta from sticking to the bottom of the pot. Add salt and pepper to taste, and serve topped with Parmesan cheese and parsley if using.

SHORTCUTS & NOTES

- 2½ to 3 cups pre-chopped mix of onion, carrots, and celery

- Pre-minced garlic (frozen cubes, or a jar or squeeze tube)

- I think most store-bought, pre-shredded Parmesan cheese is very different from freshly grated Parmesan. Parmesan is one case where I almost always just grate it myself.

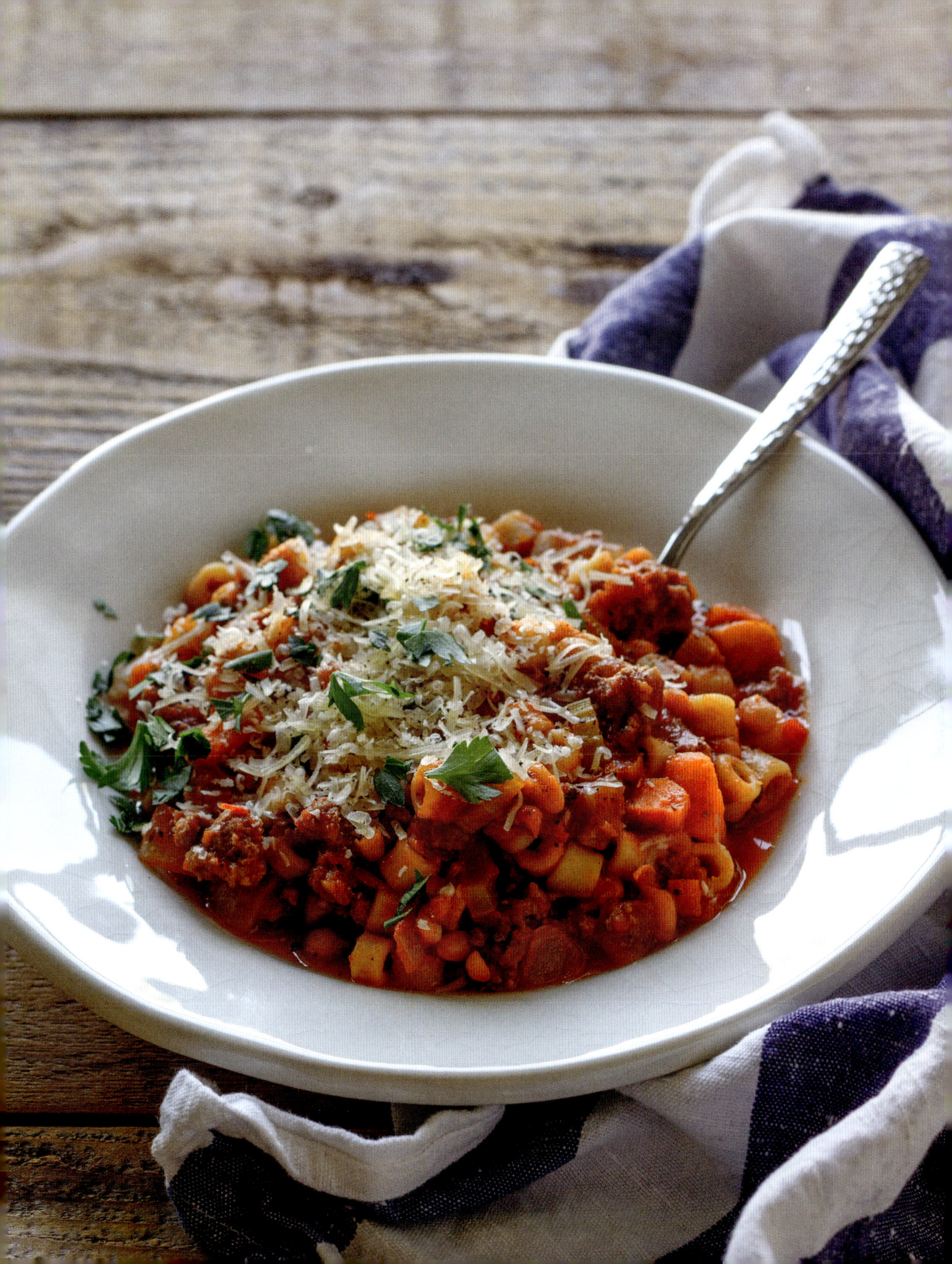

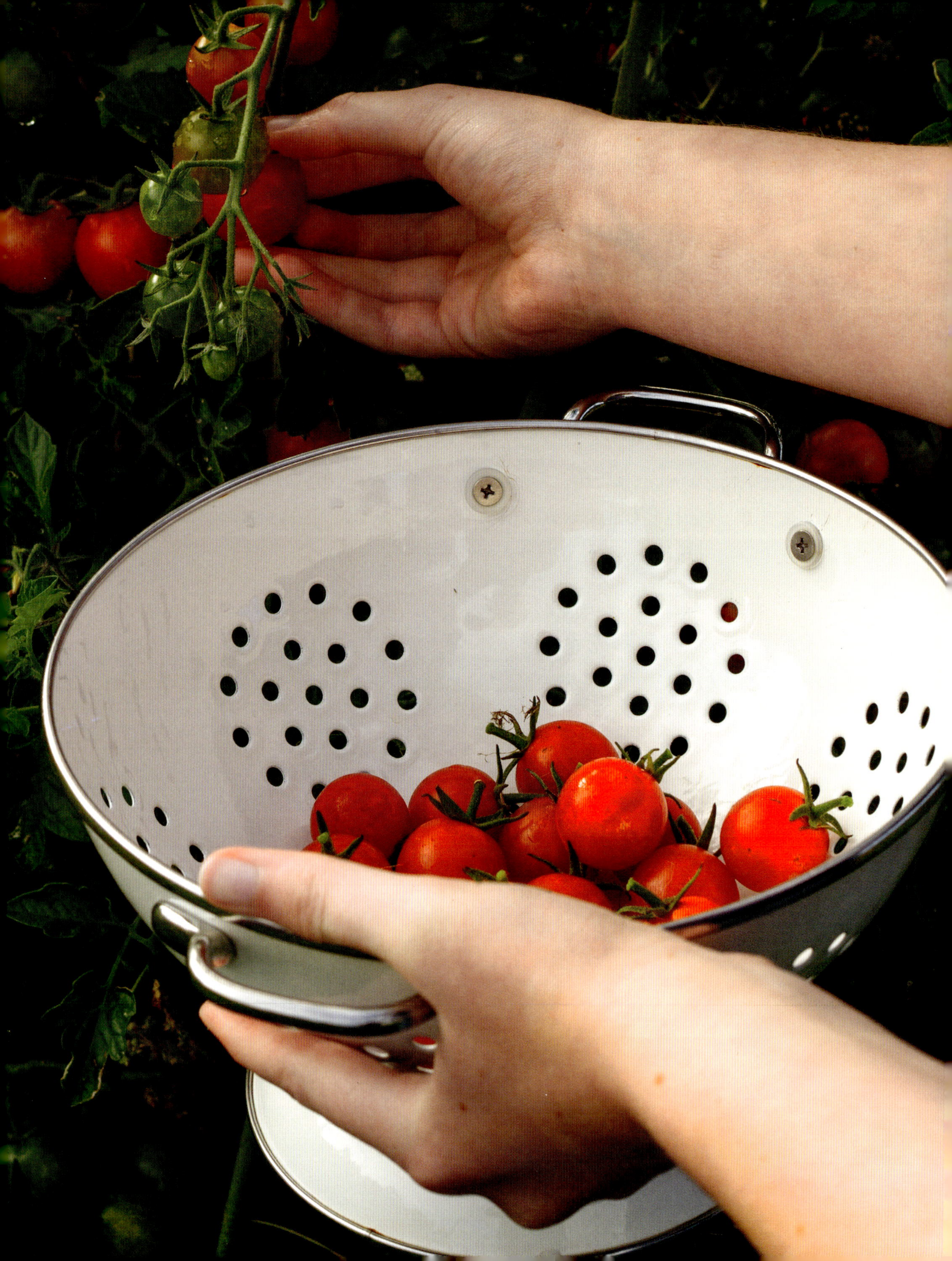

SALADS

A BIG SALAD FOR DINNER has so many good things going for it. A salad is easy for household members to customize to their liking. You can make it as hearty or as light as you want based on your dinner needs for the day. And salads are full of layers of color, texture, and flavor.

Round these dinners out by serving them with:

FRENCH BREAD FROM THE GROCERY STORE BAKERY,
CORNBREAD, MUFFINS, DINNER ROLLS,
HAWAIIAN ROLLS, OR GARLIC BREAD

FRESH FRUIT

Annie & Brooke's Kale Salad

I first had this fancy-but-easy salad at my friend Brooke's annual Christmas bingo party several years ago, but she got the recipe from our friend Annie, so I'm attributing it to both, with love. It's a very pretty salad with lovely contrasts in flavors and textures, and best of all, it's super easy to make thanks to a whole bunch of shortcuts. The delicious dressing is made up of two store-bought dressings, most of the veggies are pre-chopped and come in a bag of broccoli slaw, and you can certainly candy your own pecans, but I always use a bag of already sweet ones from the produce section of the grocery store. The only real work required to make it is to chop the kale and give it a little massage to make it tender.

Prep: 10 minutes | Cook: 0 minutes | Total: 10 minutes | Serves 6 to 8

---

1 bunch lacinato kale, ribs removed, chopped

4 tablespoons Briannas blush wine vinaigrette, or brand of choice

4 tablespoons Briannas poppyseed dressing, or brand of choice

1 (12-ounce) package broccoli slaw

½ cup crumbled Gorgonzola cheese

½ cup sweetened dried cranberries

½ cup candied or honey-roasted pecans

1. Put the kale in a large serving bowl, pour the blush wine vinaigrette over, and gently massage the kale for 1 to 2 minutes. This helps make it tender.

2. Add the poppyseed dressing, broccoli slaw, Gorgonzola, dried cranberries, and pecans and toss to combine.

SHORTCUTS & NOTES

- Lacinato kale is also called Tuscan kale and dinosaur kale. Sometimes I can only find it in the organic produce section at my grocery store. I see it often at farmers markets and summer produce stands, and it's easy to grow in a backyard garden. It comes in bunches of long, skinny leaves with a dark green, almost blueish color and a really cool, pebbly texture. If you can't find lacinato kale, I would use packaged baby kale and skip the massage step. Don't use curly kale; it can be quite bitter.

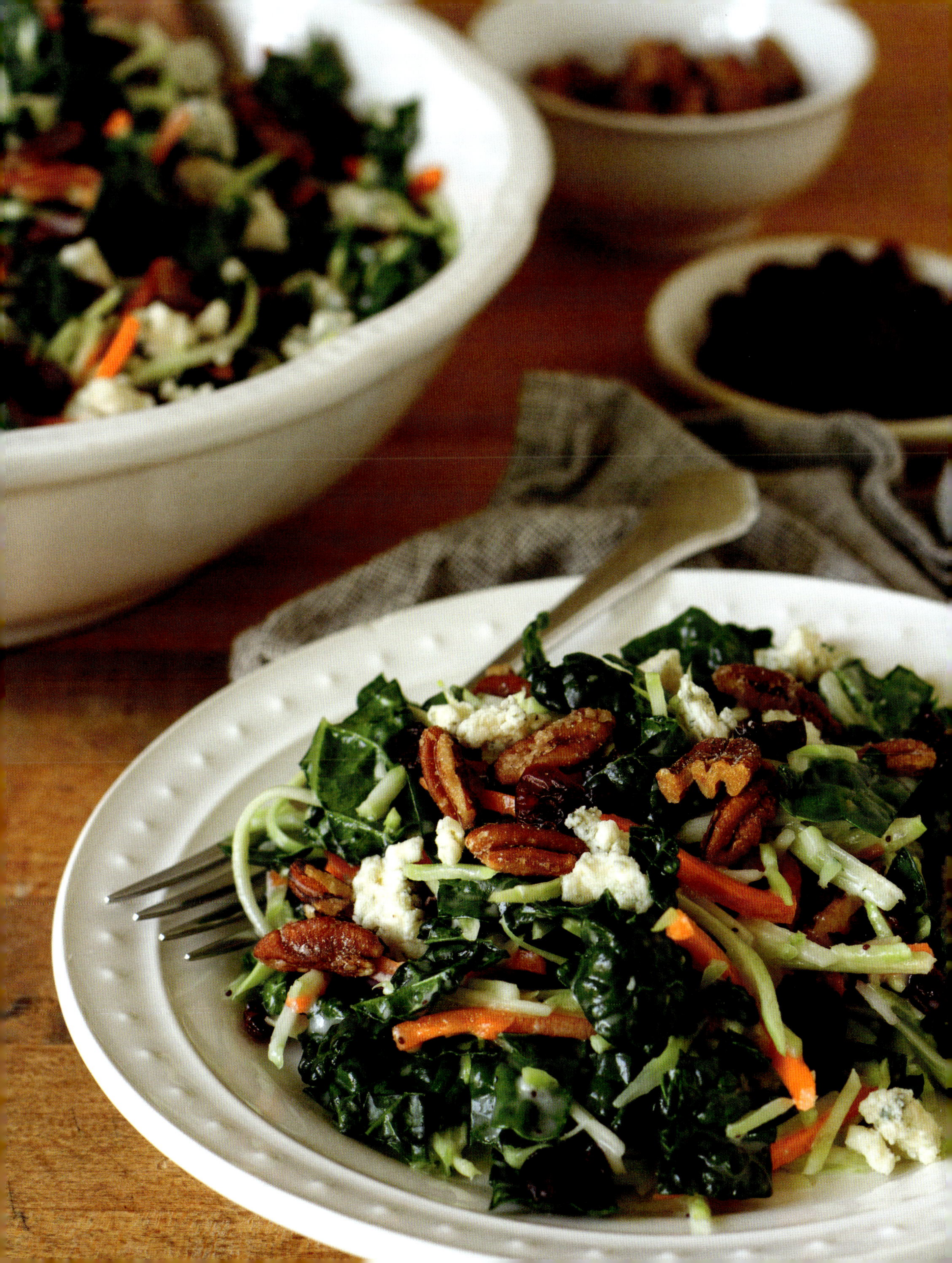

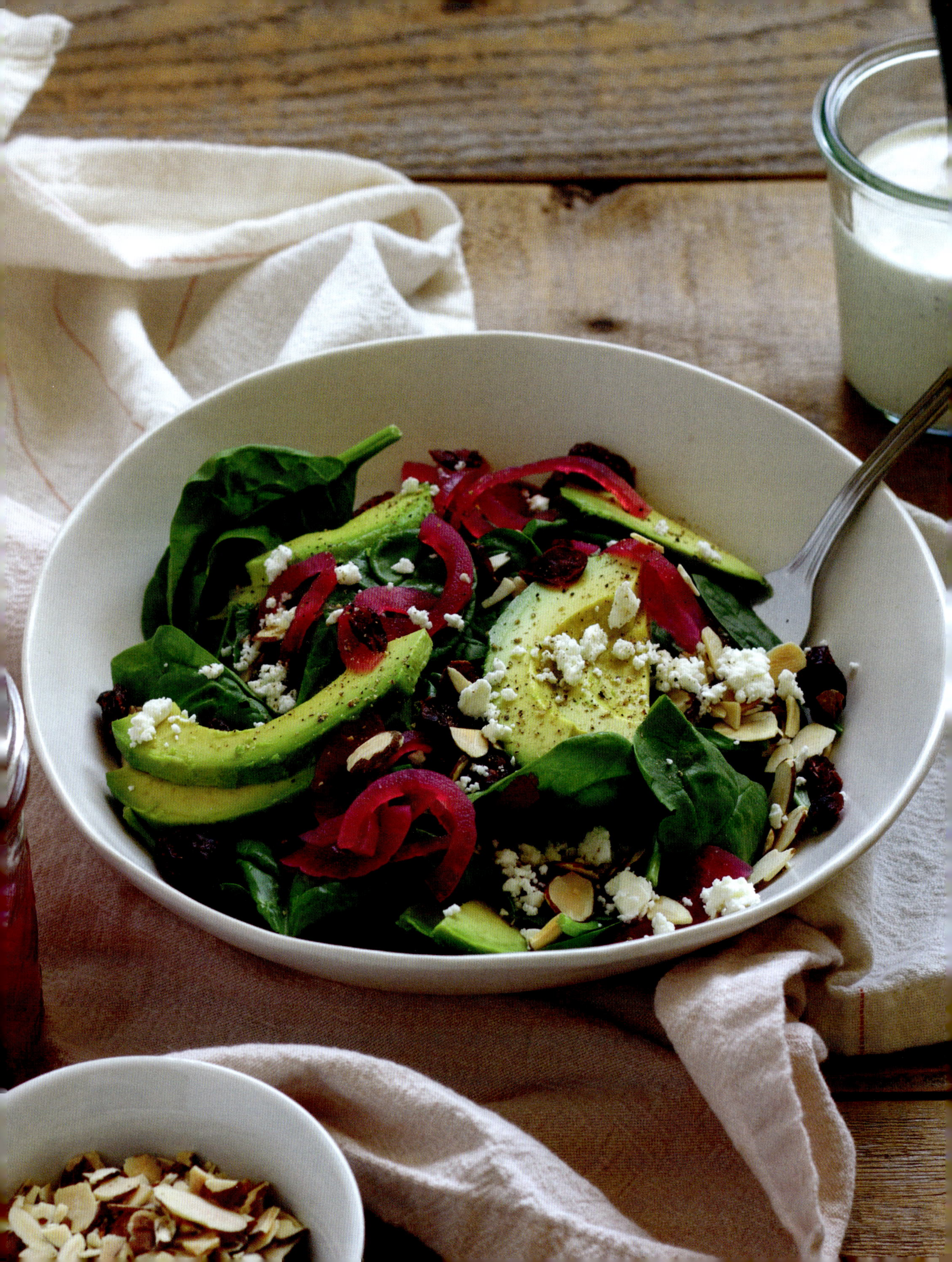

Blue Valley Spinach Salad with Feta & Avocado

There's a great little coffee shop across the street from my husband's office that serves pretty delicious food, too. They have yummy breakfasts and tasty paninis, but my go-to order is their spinach salad. It's got the perfect blend of sweet and salty flavors, some crunchy ingredients and some creamy ingredients, and my favorite dressing, ranch.

Prep: 10 minutes | Cook: 0 minutes | Total: 10 minutes | Serves 6

1 (10-ounce) package baby spinach

¾ cup sweetened, dried cranberries

¾ cup roasted sliced almonds

¾ cup crumbled feta cheese

Pickled red onion (see bonus recipe)

2 medium or 3 small avocados, peeled, pitted, and sliced

Ranch dressing, of choice

1. Divide the spinach among six plates.

2. Divide the dried cranberries, almonds, feta, pickled red onion, and sliced avocados equally among the six plates as the topping.

3. Drizzle with your favorite ranch dressing, then serve.

SHORTCUTS & NOTES

- Use roasted sliced almonds from the produce section, usually near the croutons.

- Our favorite ranch dressing is homemade Hidden Valley Ranch using the packet that says "Restaurant-Style Dressing" and "Buttermilk Recipe" on the front. It is the very best.

- You can easily make this a heartier salad by adding some protein, like grilled chicken or salmon.

Bonus Recipe! Pickled red onions are so easy and taste good on all kinds of salads and entrées. In a small saucepan, combine 1 medium red onion, thinly sliced, ½ cup water, ¼ cup white vinegar, ¼ cup apple cider vinegar, 1 teaspoon sugar, and a big pinch of kosher salt. Simmer on the stove until the mixture is pink and the onions are tender-crisp, about 8 minutes. Allow to cool before using, and store extras in the refrigerator in a container with a lid.

Loaded, Lemony Caesar Salad with Homemade Dressing

I love a good, classic Caesar salad, but I also feel completely comfortable adding a bunch of not-classic ingredients. This loaded Caesar is amazing, if I do say so myself. The bacon, the avocado, the tomatoes and slivered almonds—they're all completely delicious additions to a savory Caesar. And whatever you do, don't skip the squeeze of fresh lemon! It is the best part.

Prep: 20 minutes | Cook: 0 minutes | Total: 20 minutes | Serves 6 to 8

FOR THE DRESSING

½ cup mayonnaise

½ cup or 1 ounce freshly shredded Parmesan cheese

2 tablespoons fresh lemon juice

1 tablespoon water

1 teaspoon minced garlic, or 1 garlic clove, minced

1 teaspoon Dijon mustard

1 teaspoon Worcestershire sauce

Freshly ground black pepper

FOR THE SALAD

3 romaine lettuce hearts, chopped or torn into bite-size pieces

12 to 16 ounces diced cooked chicken breast (see page 70)

6 to 8 slices bacon, cooked and crumbled

2 avocados, diced

Grape tomatoes

Roasted sliced almonds

Croutons

Freshly shredded Parmesan cheese

Lemon wedges

1. To make the dressing, combine all dressing ingredients in a blender or food processor and process until smooth. Pour the dressing into an airtight container with a lid, and refrigerate until needed.

2. To make the salad, layer all ingredients as desired on individual plates or one large serving dish. Top with the Caesar dressing and a squeeze of lemon wedge per person, toss, and enjoy.

SHORTCUTS & NOTES

- Pre-minced garlic (frozen cubes, or a jar or squeeze tube)

- Your favorite already-cooked chicken (Rotisserie chicken works, and Costco has some grilled chicken bites that we love.)

- Pre-cooked bacon (We like the black package from Costco.)

- Roasted sliced almonds from the produce section, usually near the croutons

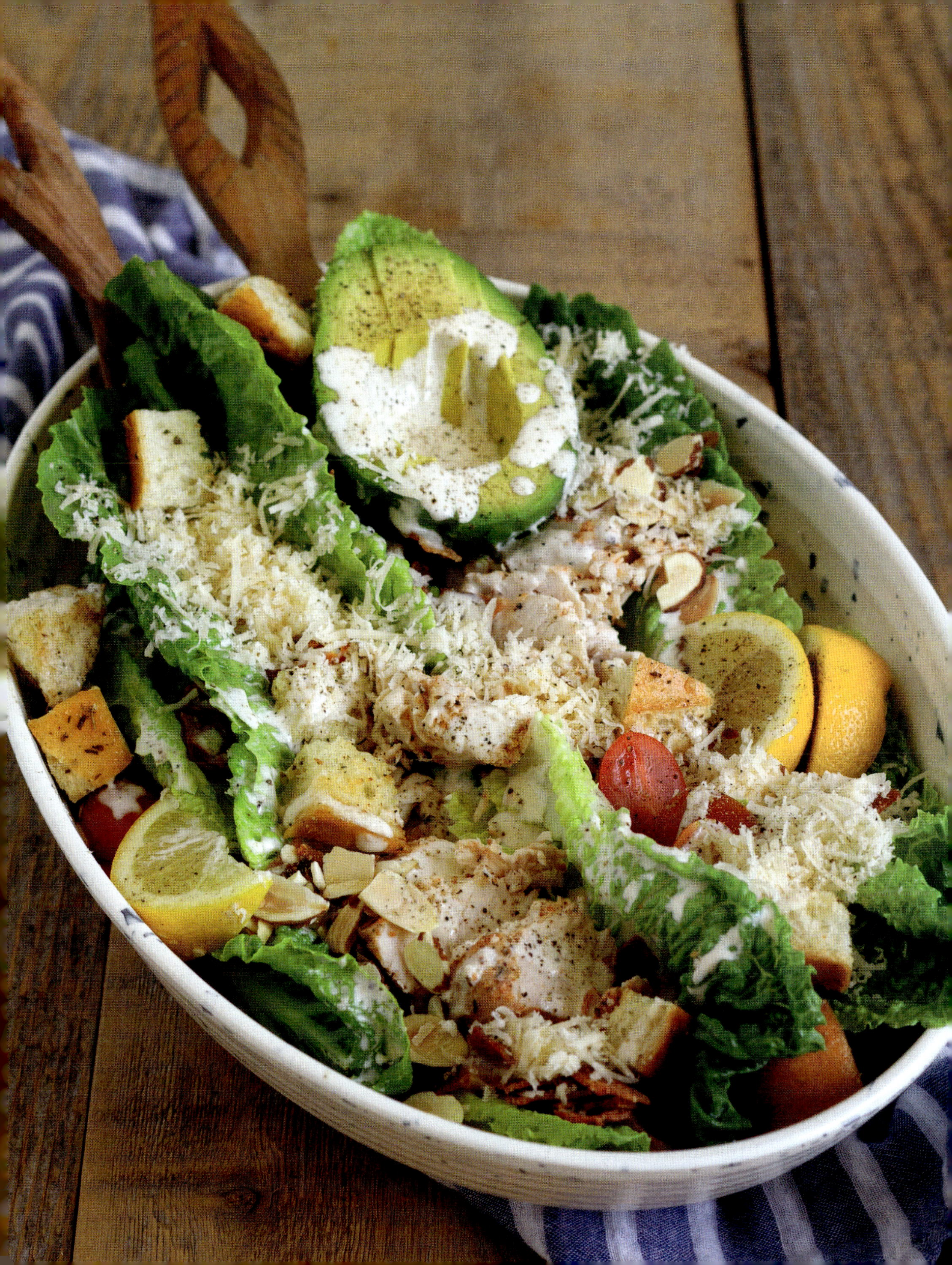

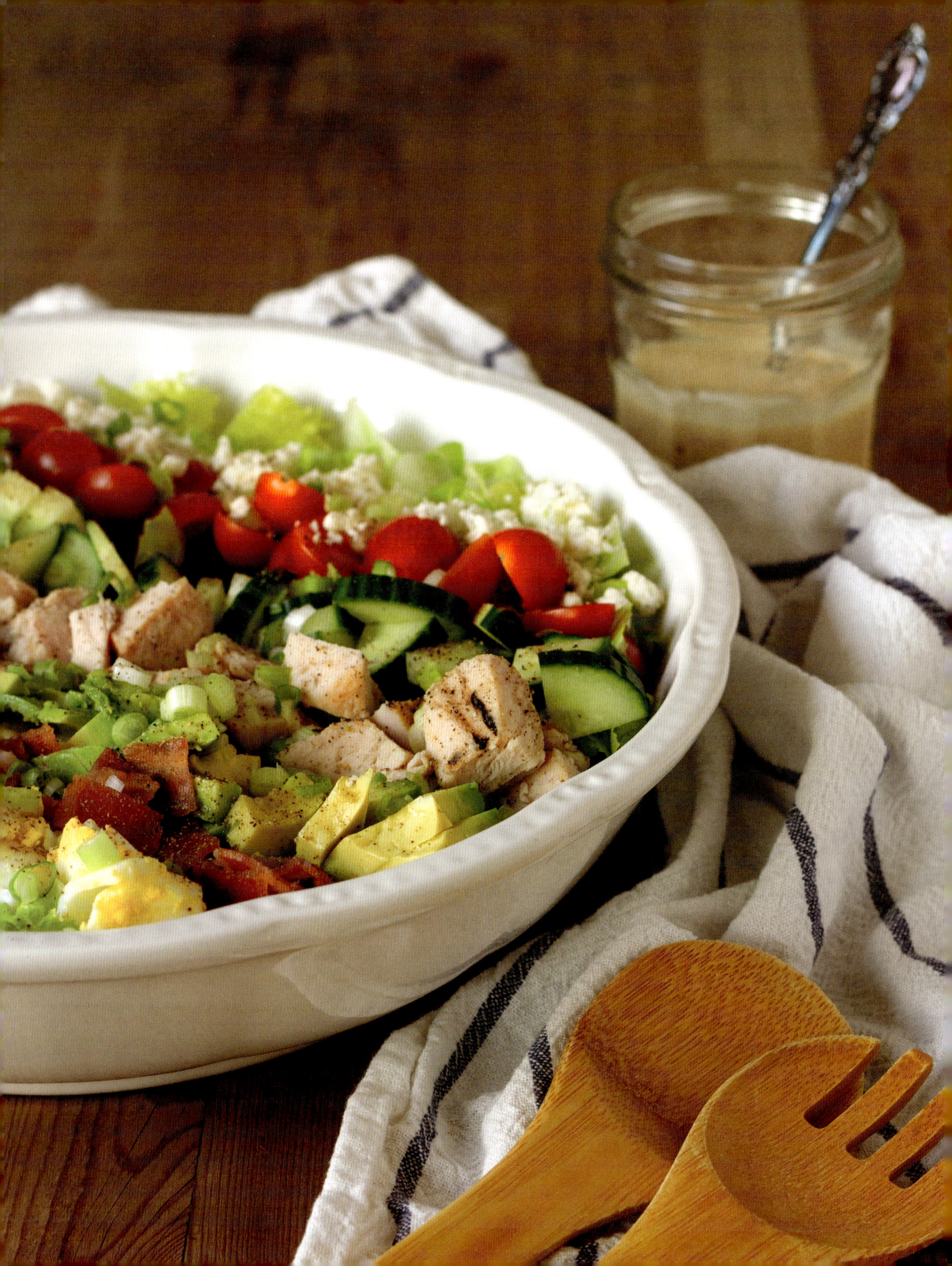

Classic Cobb Salad with Lemon-Shallot Vinaigrette

I love a big salad for dinner, especially when the weather is warm or when we've been eating lots of heavy foods and need a break. I think the bright, fresh flavors of the lemon-shallot vinaigrette in this Cobb salad really make everything sing and are such a nice contrast to some of the richer salad ingredients like avocado, bacon, and egg. If you are lucky enough to have leftovers, they make a very quick, very delicious lunch the day after.

Prep: 20 minutes | Cook: 0 minutes | Total: 20 minutes | Serves 4

FOR THE LEMON-SHALLOT VINAIGRETTE

Juice of 1 lemon

2 tablespoons minced shallot

1 tablespoon Dijon mustard

1 teaspoon minced garlic, or 1 garlic clove, minced

5 tablespoons light-tasting oil, such as vegetable, canola, or extra-light olive oil

1 teaspoon honey

A pinch of kosher salt

Freshly ground black pepper

FOR THE SALAD

2 romaine lettuce hearts, chopped into bite-size pieces

1 bunch green onions, white and light green parts only, finely chopped

4 hard-boiled eggs, halved, chopped, or sliced

1 cup cherry tomatoes, halved

1 thin-skinned cucumber, halved or quartered and thinly sliced

8 bacon slices, cooked and crumbled

1 pound chopped grilled chicken (see bonus recipe on page 70)

1 large or 2 small avocados, peeled, pitted, and sliced

Crumbled blue cheese

continued

1. To make the vinaigrette, combine all of the dressing ingredients in the bowl of a food processor and process until smooth. Alternatively, you can combine all of the ingredients in a small jar with a tight-fitting lid and shake until the dressing comes together. Cover and refrigerate until needed.

2. To prepare the salad, put the chopped lettuce in the bottom of a large salad bowl or on a large platter (with curved edges so that ingredients don't fall off). Put the remaining ingredients on top of the lettuce in stripes, with one big stripe for each ingredient.

3. Serve immediately with the dressing on the side.

SHORTCUTS & NOTES

- Pre-minced garlic (frozen cubes, or a jar or squeeze tube)

- Store-bought hard-boiled eggs

- Pre-cooked bacon (We like the black package from Costco.)

- Your favorite already-cooked chicken (rotisserie chicken works, and Costco has some grilled chicken bites that we love.)

Bonus Recipe! I have a couple of go-to marinades for grilled chicken. The first is this Honey-Dijon-Ranch Marinade: Whisk ⅓ cup extra-virgin olive oil, ⅓ cup orange juice, 2 tablespoons Dijon mustard, 2 tablespoons honey, 1 teaspoon kosher salt, and 1 (1-ounce) packet ranch dressing mix in a large bowl until combined. Add about 1½ pounds uncooked chicken, toss gently to coat, cover, and refrigerate for at least 30 minutes. Place the chicken on a preheated grill, season with salt and pepper, and cook with the cover down until the chicken is cooked through, turning as necessary. Remove from the heat, let cool slightly, then slice and serve.

Bonus Recipe! The second is Soy & Citrus Marinade: Combine ½ cup soy sauce, 2 tablespoons Worcestershire sauce, ¾ cup lemon-lime soda, ½ bunch green onions, chopped, and 3 garlic cloves, minced, in a large bowl. Add 1½ pounds uncooked chicken, toss gently to coat, cover, and refrigerate for at least 30 minutes. Place the chicken on a preheated grill, season with salt and pepper, and cook with the cover down until the chicken is cooked through, turning as necessary. Remove from the heat, let cool slightly, then slice and serve.

Emily's South Lane Chopped Salad with Cilantro-Lime Vinaigrette

My sister, Emily, lives in a very charming small town in New England. It has a green in the center of town that is surrounded by tall trees, old homes, city buildings, shops, and restaurants. We love walking around the green when we visit. This yummy salad is Emily's go-to order at her favorite restaurant on the green. It makes a delicious dinner salad that is filling without being heavy.

Prep: 15 minutes | Cook: 5 minutes | Total: 20 minutes | Serves 6

FOR THE VINAIGRETTE

¼ cup fresh lime juice

2 tablespoons white vinegar

½ bunch fresh cilantro

1 tablespoon brown sugar

1 teaspoon minced garlic, or 1 garlic clove, minced

¼ teaspoon salt

1 tablespoon spicy brown mustard

¾ cup extra-virgin olive oil or your favorite neutral cooking oil

FOR THE SALAD

1 (10-ounce) container mixed greens

1 pound shredded rotisserie chicken

1 avocado, peeled, pitted, and sliced

1 (10-ounce) bag frozen sweet corn, cooked according to package directions and cooled

1 pint grape tomatoes, halved

Shredded Monterey jack cheese

continued

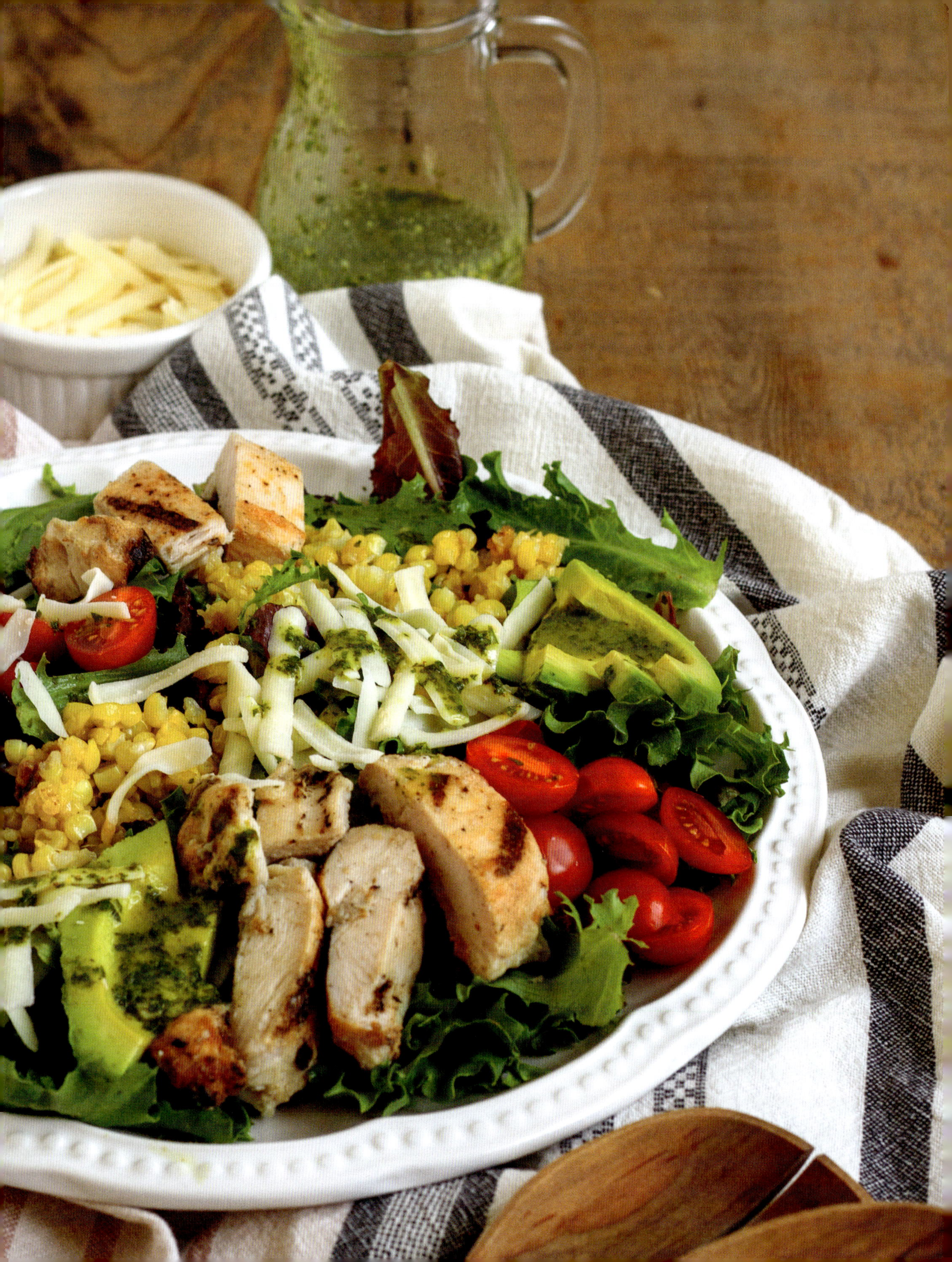

1. To make the vinaigrette, combine all of the dressing ingredients in a blender, and blend on the highest setting until well combined and mostly smooth.

2. To make the salad, layer the greens, chicken, sliced avocado, corn, tomatoes, and cheese either in one large serving dish or on six individual plates. Top with the dressing and serve.

SHORTCUTS & NOTES

- Pre-minced garlic (frozen cubes, or a jar or squeeze tube)

- Pre-shredded Monterey jack cheese

- My sister always serves this with grilled, marinated chicken instead of rotisserie chicken. Just marinate 1 pound of chicken breasts in your favorite marinade, grill it, and chop it up. See two of my favorite marinade recipes on page 70.

- In the summer, she also likes to grill fresh corn on the cob and cut the kernels off instead of using frozen corn. She uses 2 or 3 ears of corn.

- Coincidentally, one of our favorite local restaurants in Oregon used to serve a salad almost exactly like this one from the East Coast! The Oregon additions include pickled red onion, crumbled cotija, and fried tortilla strips.

SALADS 73

Harvest Salad with Creamy Herb-Dijon Vinaigrette

I love this hearty salad so much that I eat it regularly for lunch. It reminds me of a French Niçoise salad thanks to the tomatoes, green beans, and hard-boiled eggs, and it has a delicious, herby, homemade vinaigrette dressing that has just a hint of sweetness.

Prep: 15 minutes | Cook: 5 minutes | Total: 20 minutes | Serves 6

FOR THE DRESSING

½ cup mayonnaise

2 tablespoons plus 1 teaspoon natural or unseasoned rice vinegar

2 teaspoons Dijon mustard

1 teaspoon water

1 teaspoon honey

1 teaspoon dried basil

1 teaspoon fresh thyme

¼ teaspoon salt

Freshly ground black pepper

FOR THE SALAD

1 (10-ounce) container mixed greens

12 ounces green beans, steamed or roasted (see page 144)

1 pound chopped grilled chicken (see page 70)

6 ounces white cheddar, cut into small cubes

1 (10-ounce) bag frozen sweet corn, cooked according to package directions and cooled

1 pint grape tomatoes, halved

3 to 6 hard-boiled eggs, halved

1. To make the dressing, combine all of the ingredients in a blender or small jar with a tight-fitting lid. Run the blender or vigorously shake the jar until the ingredients are well combined, 30 seconds to 1 minute. Cover and chill until ready to serve.

2. To make the salad, layer all of the salad ingredients either in one large serving dish or on six individual plates. Top with the dressing and serve.

SHORTCUTS & NOTES

- Frozen, steam-in-the-bag whole green beans

- Your favorite already-cooked chicken (Rotisserie chicken works, and Costco has some grilled chicken bites that we love.)

- Pre-cubed white cheddar

- Store-bought hard-boiled eggs

- If you only have seasoned rice vinegar (which is flavored with sugar and salt), you can substitute it for the natural rice vinegar. Just omit the honey from the recipe and add salt to taste. The dressing will be a little sweeter than usual.

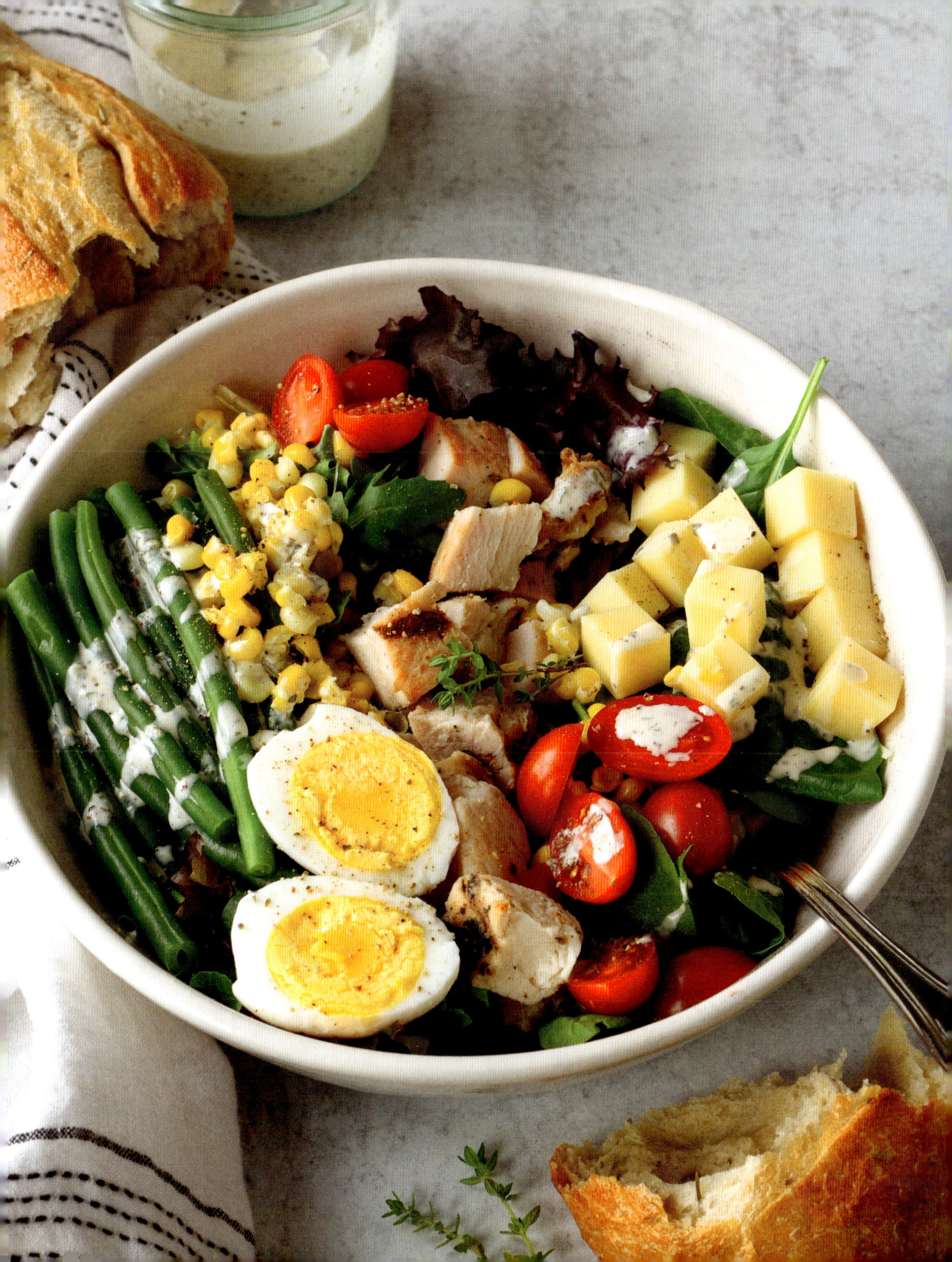

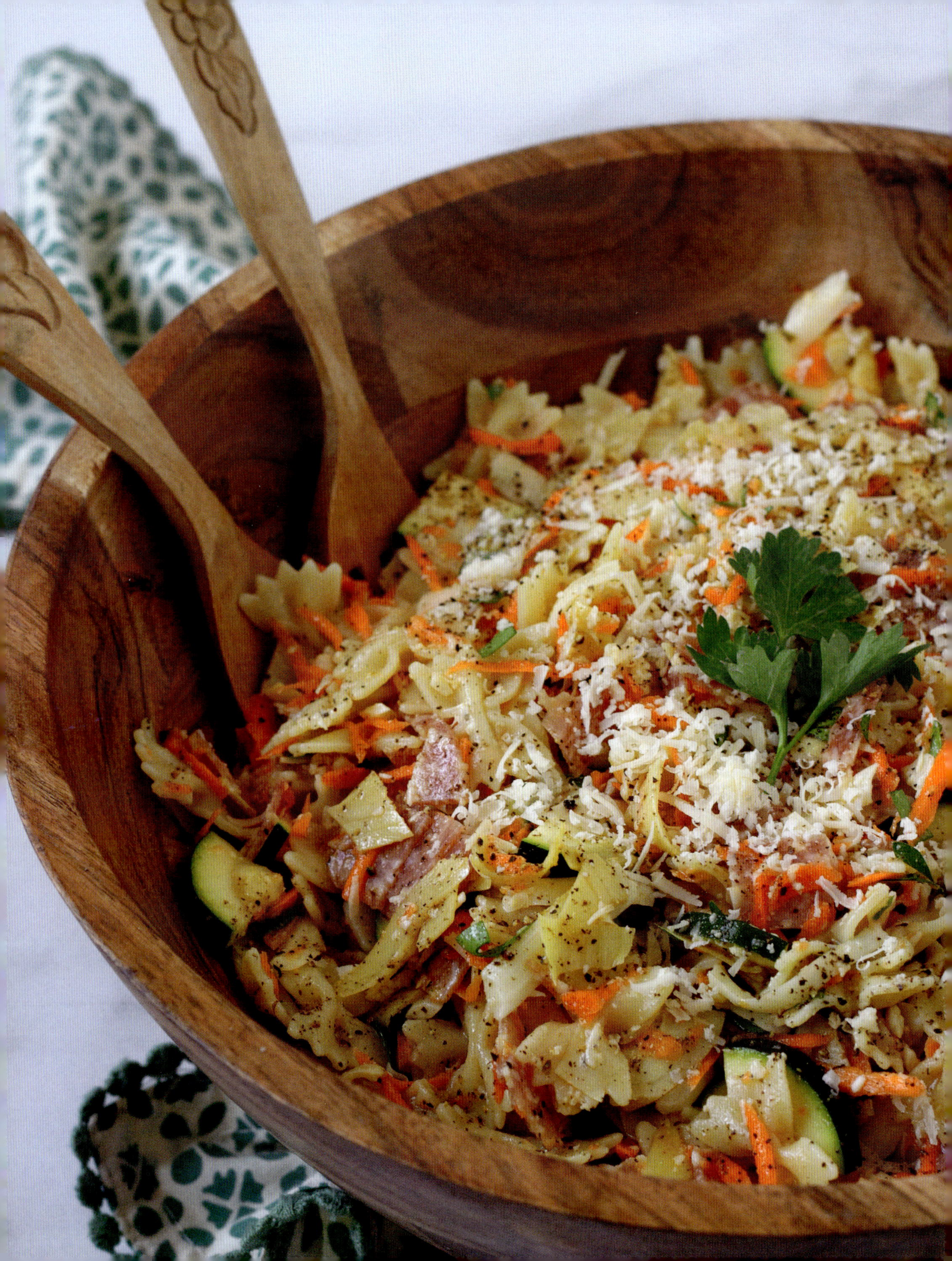

Italian Pasta Salad

My friend Marcelle introduced me to this pasta salad many years ago, and it has been my favorite pasta salad ever since. Some pasta salads have ingredients I want to pick through or ingredients that fall off your fork, but all of the components of this one go together so beautifully, and every forkful of salad is perfectly delicious. This salad makes a great cookout or sandwich side dish but can also be more of a main dish if you serve it with some hearty sides.

Prep: 30 minutes | Cook: 8 minutes | Total: 38 minutes | Serves 6 to 8

6 ounces mini bow tie pasta

1 (6-ounce) jar marinated artichoke hearts

2 tablespoons extra-virgin olive oil or your favorite neutral cooking oil

2 tablespoons white wine vinegar

1 teaspoon minced garlic, or 1 garlic clove, minced

¾ teaspoon dry mustard

½ teaspoon dried oregano

½ teaspoon dried basil

1 small zucchini, quartered and cut into ¼-inch slices

1 large carrot, peeled and shredded

4 ounces salami, diced

1 cup shredded mozzarella cheese

2 tablespoons shredded Parmesan cheese

1. Bring a large pot of salted water to a boil. Cook the pasta according to the package directions until tender. Drain the pasta and rinse it under cold water until cool. Set aside.

2. While waiting for the water to boil and the pasta to cook, prepare the rest of the salad. Pour the liquid from the marinated artichoke hearts into a medium bowl. Add the olive oil, white wine vinegar, minced garlic, dry mustard, oregano, and basil. Whisk and set aside.

3. Chop the artichoke hearts and place them in a large bowl. Add the zucchini, carrot, salami, and both cheeses. Add the cooled pasta and dressing, and toss to combine. Enjoy!

SHORTCUTS & NOTES

- Pre-minced garlic (frozen cubes, or a jar or squeeze tube)

- Pre-sliced zucchini (just be sure to quarter those slices)

- Pre-shredded carrots (Although they have a thicker texture than if you shred them yourself, they'll still work.)

- Pre-shredded mozzarella cheese

- This is one of the few times I think the store-bought, pre-shredded Parmesan cheese works just fine.

Toasted Ramen Noodle Salad

I cannot remember a time in my life when I didn't love this salad. We only had it on special occasions when I was growing up, so it has always felt fancy to me, despite the humble list of ingredients. The vegetables are fresh, crunchy, and piquant, the dressing is a little sweet and a little savory, and the buttery, toasted topping is so good you'll want to eat it with a spoon.

Prep: 15 minutes | Cook: 15 minutes | Total: 30 minutes | Serves 6 to 8

¼ cup butter

1 (3-ounce) package chicken-flavored ramen noodles

½ cup slivered almonds

½ cup shelled sunflower seeds

1 (2-pound) Napa cabbage, cored

1 bunch green onions, white and light green parts only

1 bunch radishes

½ cup neutral-flavored oil, such as vegetable or canola

5 tablespoons granulated sugar

¼ cup rice vinegar

1 tablespoon soy sauce

1. Preheat the oven to 350°F. When the oven is fully preheated, put the butter on a rimmed baking sheet and place it in the oven. Let the butter melt.

2. While the butter is melting, open the ramen noodle package and set the seasoning packet aside. Crush the ramen noodles into small pieces.

3. When the butter is melted, add the broken ramen noodles, almonds, and sunflower seeds to the baking sheet and gently toss everything together with a spatula until the butter evenly coats all the pieces. Toast for 10 to 12 minutes, until golden, then remove from the oven and set aside to cool.

4. While the noodle mixture is cooking, chop the cabbage, and thinly slice the green onions and radishes and toss them in a large bowl.

5. In a pint-size mason jar with a tight-fitting lid, combine the oil, sugar, vinegar, soy sauce, and ramen seasoning packet. Put the lid on the jar and shake vigorously to combine.

6. If you are going to eat the entire salad immediately, go ahead and add the cooled topping and the dressing to the cabbage mixture, toss, and serve. If you aren't going to eat the whole salad now, plate up individual portions of cabbage, then top each serving with a couple of tablespoons of dressing and toasted noodles.

SHORTCUTS & NOTES

- The leftovers of all of the individual parts will keep well for 3 to 4 days in airtight containers in the refrigerator as long as they aren't mixed together.

- This is a very light, refreshing salad. If you'd like to make it heartier, you can add some cooked chicken breast or salmon.

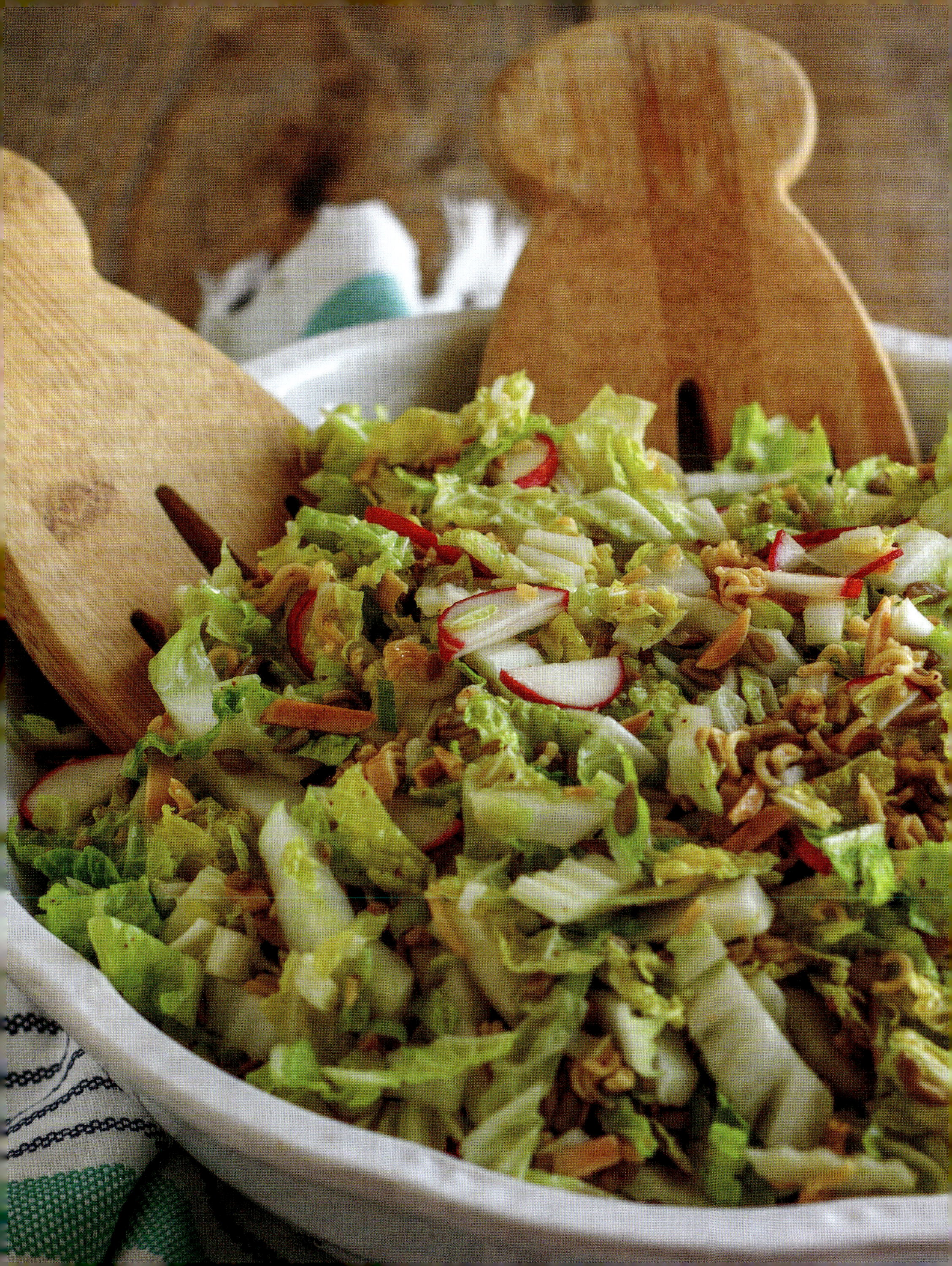

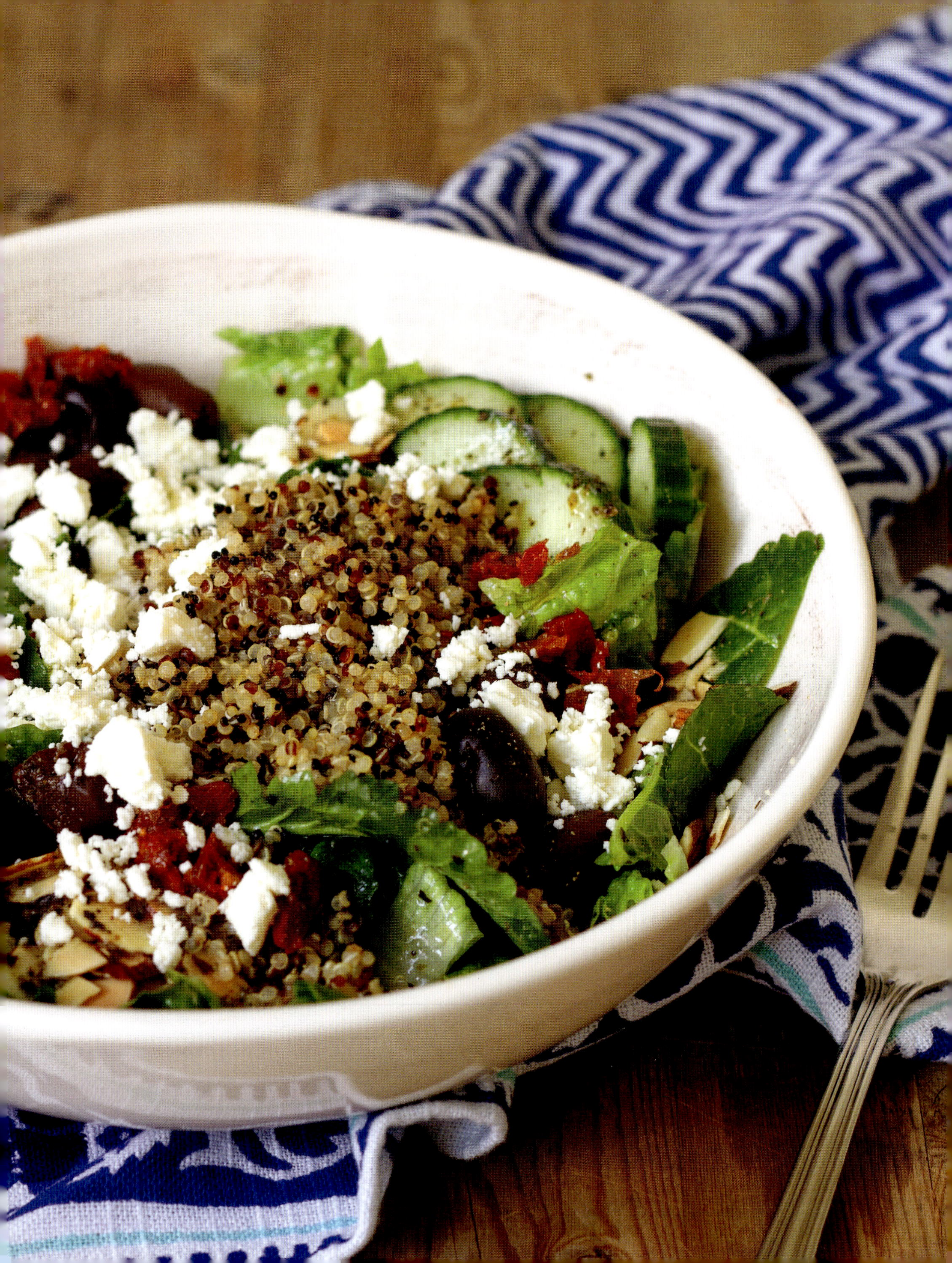

Mediterranean Quinoa Salad

One of the fast-casual soup/salad/sandwich places we get takeout from makes a salad like this, and I figured out how to make it at home so that we can have it whenever we want. Thanks to the quinoa, it's really filling without being heavy, and it's a great option for a meatless meal.

Prep: 10 minutes | Cook: 20 minutes (just for the quinoa) | Total: 30 minutes | Serves 4

FOR THE GREEK DRESSING

¾ cup extra-virgin olive oil

¾ cup red wine vinegar

2 teaspoons garlic powder

2 teaspoons dried oregano

2 teaspoons dried basil

1½ teaspoons freshly ground black pepper

1½ teaspoons salt

1½ teaspoons onion powder

1½ teaspoons Dijon mustard

FOR THE SALAD

4 cups chopped romaine lettuce

4 cups baby kale

1 thin-skinned cucumber, diced

2 cups cooked and cooled quinoa

Kalamata olives

Finely minced sun-dried tomatoes

Roasted, sliced almonds

Crumbled feta cheese

1. Combine all of the dressing ingredients in a pint-size mason jar with a tight-fitting lid. Shake vigorously until dressing is combined. Shake as needed before serving.

2. To make the salad, layer the ingredients on a plate in the order listed. Where no amount is given, add as much or as little of the ingredients as you wish. Drizzle with the Greek dressing and enjoy!

SHORTCUTS & NOTES

- Pre-cooked quinoa

- Roasted sliced almonds from the produce section, usually near the croutons

Taco Salad

Taco salad is a dinnertime classic! It's one of those dishes that always gets two thumbs up from everyone at home when it shows up on the dinner menu. People can make it as hearty or as light as they want, or if they're anything like my kids, they can leave out the lettuce entirely and make nachos!

Prep: 15 minutes | Cook: 10 minutes | Total: 25 minutes | Serves 6

1 pound ground beef

1 (1-ounce) packet taco seasoning (see page 140)

1 head iceberg or romaine lettuce, washed and chopped into bite-size pieces

1 (15.5-ounce) can kidney, black, or pinto beans, drained and rinsed

Diced white or red onions

Diced green onions, white and light green parts only

Diced tomatoes

Sliced olives

Guacamole (page 154) or diced avocado

Shredded cheddar, Monterey jack, or pepper jack cheese

Crumbled cotija

Grilled corn, cut off the cob

Salsa

Tortilla chips, Fritos, or Doritos

Ranch dressing (see page 139)

1. In a large skillet, brown the ground beef. Drain any excess grease, then follow the directions on the taco seasoning packet to add it and the required amount of water to the ground beef. Set aside.

2. At this point, I put all of the ingredients out and let people build their own salads.

SHORTCUTS & NOTES

- Pre-chopped onions
- Pre-made guacamole (if you have one you like)
- Pre-shredded cheese

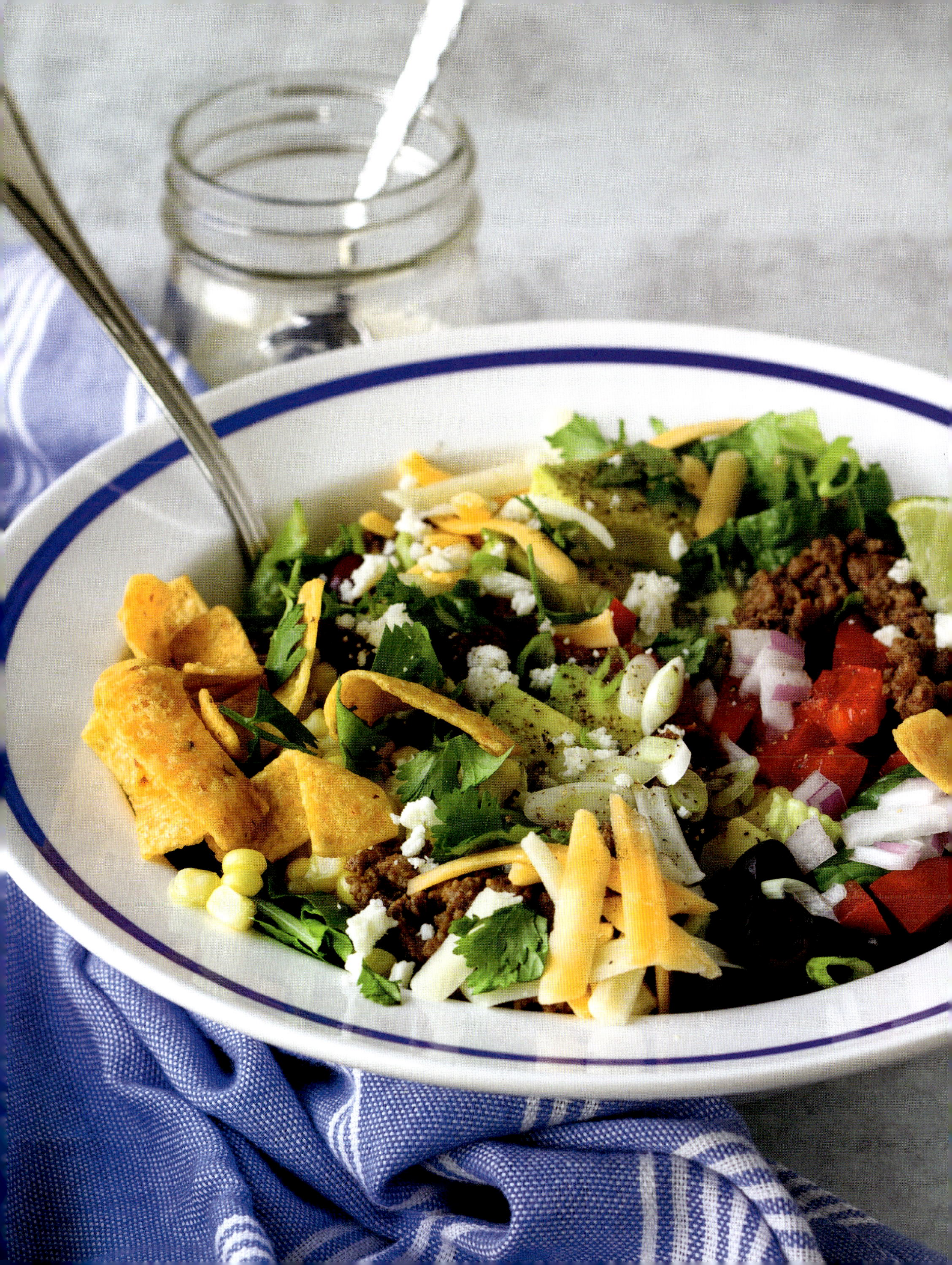

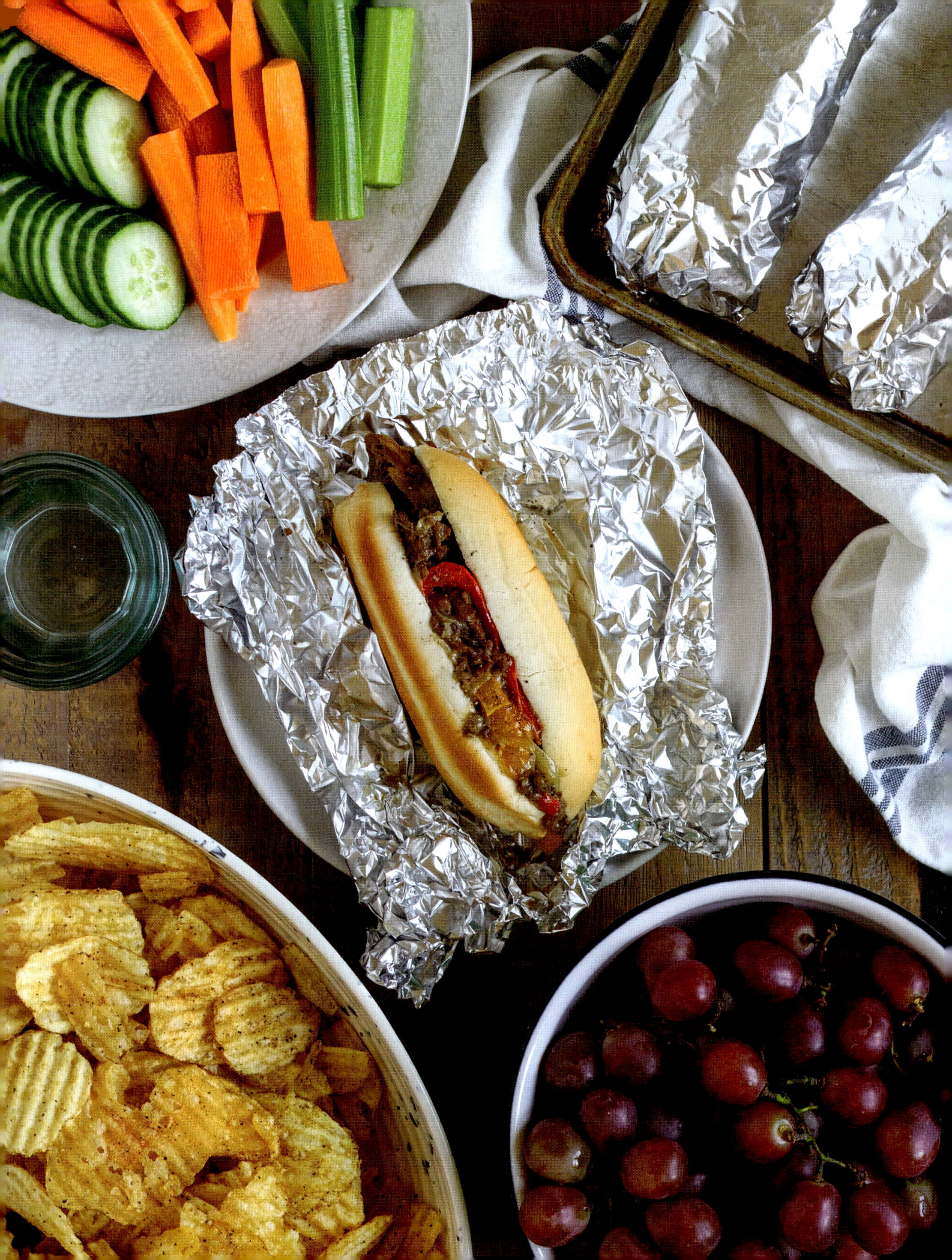

SANDWICHES

WE HAVE SANDWICHES on the dinner menu pretty regularly at our house. It's really easy to make them one at a time if the whole household isn't able to sit down for dinner at the exact same time. And they're always easy to make, full of flavor, and very hearty. They're also one of the very quickest dinner options; if you glance through the chapter and read the total time for each sandwich recipe, you'll notice that they are incredibly quick. Even the hot sandwiches only require a few minutes of work.

Round these dinners out by serving them with:

A GREEN SALAD (PAGES 61–83) OR FRESH VEGGIES

FRESH FRUIT

CHIPS

A SIDE OF SOUP

DILL PICKLE SPEARS

Green Goddess Veggie Sandwiches

Veggie sandwiches can sometimes skew a little bland and boring. Thanks to a flavorful, herby green goddess spread, generous salt and pepper, and a few piquant ingredients, those two words will be far from your mind when you eat these veggie sandwiches. You won't miss the meat!

Prep: 20 minutes | Cook: 0 minutes | Total: 20 minutes | Makes 4 sandwiches

FOR THE GREEN GODDESS SPREAD

1 (8-ounce) brick cream cheese

¼ cup mayonnaise

¼ cup sour cream

2 green onions, white and light green parts only

½ cup fresh parsley

2 tablespoons chopped fresh chives

1 tablespoon dried basil

1 tablespoon dried dill

Zest of 1 lemon

1 teaspoon minced garlic, or 1 garlic clove, minced

Kosher salt

Freshly ground black pepper

FOR THE VEGGIE SANDWICHES

8 whole-grain bread slices

1 thin-skinned cucumber, thinly sliced

Alfalfa sprouts

4 to 8 leaves green leaf or romaine lettuce

2 cups loosely packed baby spinach

1 large or 2 small avocados, peeled, pitted, and thinly sliced

1 large tomato, thinly sliced

1 red onion, thinly sliced

Kosher salt

Freshly ground black pepper

continued

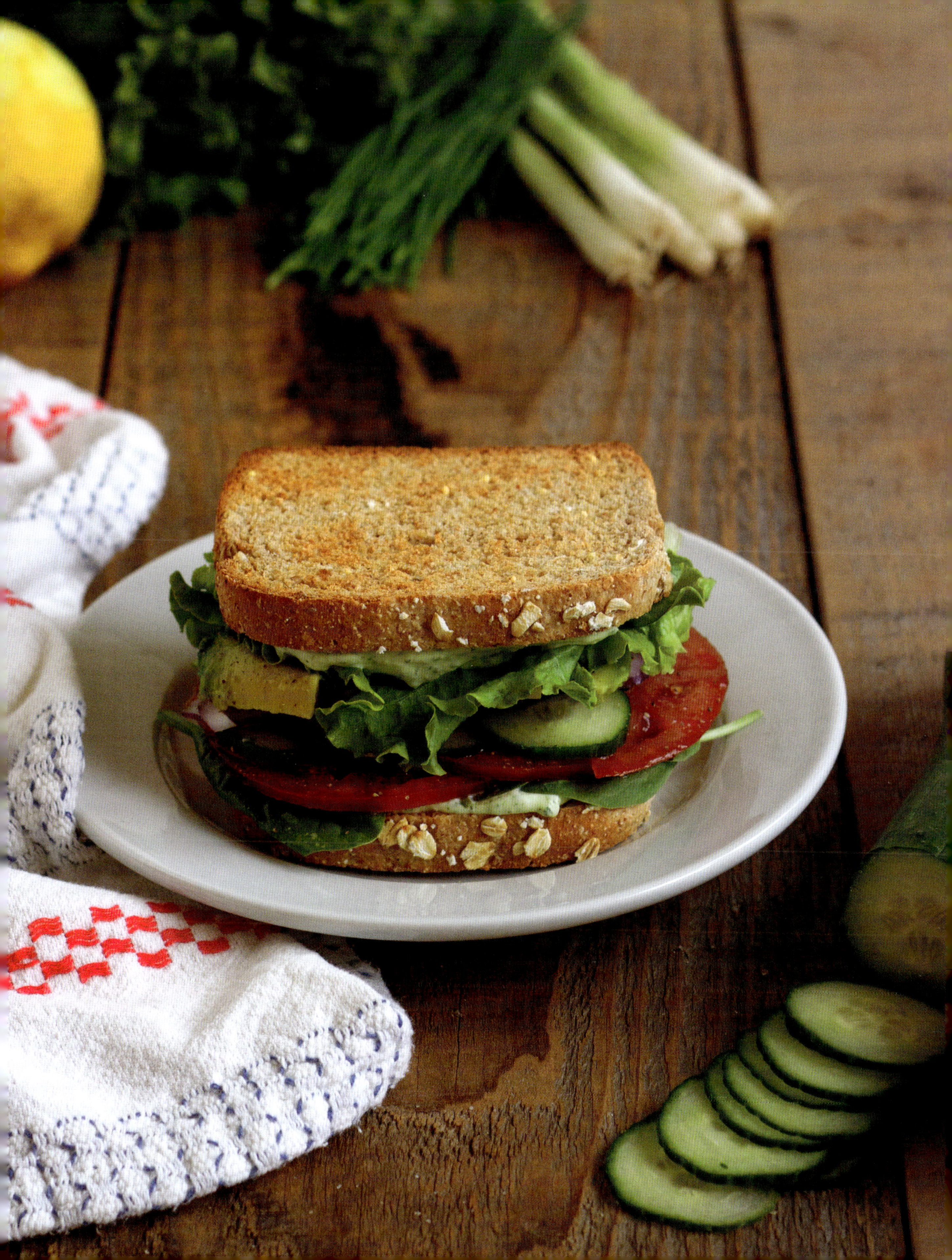

1. To make the green goddess spread, in the bowl of a food processor, combine all of the spread ingredients. Process the ingredients until the spread is mostly smooth, with only small bits of green visible. No big chunks. Set aside.

2. To make the veggie sandwiches, lightly toast the bread and set all pieces on a work surface or on individual plates.

3. Spread 1 to 2 tablespoons of green goddess spread on each slice of bread. You can do this to taste; I like a lot of spread.

4. Pile all of the remaining ingredients on 4 of the bread slices. Feel free to lightly season some of the veggie layers with kosher salt and freshly ground black pepper. The avocado and tomato layers are really well suited to this because they're a little wet and the seasonings will stick. Top each sandwich with one of the remaining pieces of bread. Serve immediately!

SHORTCUTS & NOTES

- Pre-minced garlic (frozen cubes, or a jar or squeeze tube)

- I have not included an exhaustive list of veggies you can add to your sandwich, so feel free to throw on those thinly sliced bell peppers or carrot ribbons or whatever else you particularly love.

- The green goddess spread also makes a really tasty dip for fresh veggies.

Slow Cooker Barbecue Chicken Sandwiches

I love a good BBQ sandwich, and this hearty chicken version is one of my faves. You can absolutely just dump the chicken, onions, garlic, and barbecue sauce in your slow cooker without the extra step of browning things first, but this really only takes a few minutes and makes the sandwiches taste extra amazing. I think it is worth the 15 minutes of work and takes already delicious sandwiches up a notch.

Prep: 15 minutes | Cook: 4 hours | Total: 4 hours 15 minutes | Serves 6

2½ pounds boneless, skinless chicken breasts (not frozen)

Kosher salt

Freshly ground black pepper

2 tablespoons extra-virgin olive oil or your favorite neutral cooking oil, divided

½ large onion, thinly sliced

4 teaspoons minced garlic, or 4 garlic cloves, minced

2 tablespoons water

16 ounces barbecue sauce

6 large hamburger buns

Softened butter, optional

Coleslaw, for serving (see bonus recipe on page 90)

1. Season the chicken breasts with salt and pepper on both sides. On the stove, warm 1 tablespoon of oil in a large skillet over medium heat. Add the chicken breasts and cook until lightly browned on both sides, 3 to 5 minutes per side. Remove the chicken from the skillet and set it in the bottom of a slow cooker.

2. Add the remaining 1 tablespoon of oil, sliced onion, and garlic to the skillet and sauté until the onion is translucent and tender, about 5 minutes. Pour the water into the skillet and use a spatula to scrape up any browned bits from the bottom. Pour the onion mixture over the chicken in the slow cooker.

3. Top the chicken and onions with the barbecue sauce. Cover and cook on low for 4 hours, until the chicken is tender and shreds easily. Add salt and pepper to taste.

continued

4. Optional step: Just before assembling the sandwiches, butter the inside of the hamburger buns and griddle them butter-side down over medium heat until golden. Place the griddled buns butter-side up on a cooling rack to cool.

5. Serve the shredded chicken on the buns, with coleslaw on the sandwiches or on the side.

SHORTCUTS & NOTES

- Pre-sliced onions

- Pre-minced garlic (frozen cubes, or a jar or squeeze tube)

Bonus Recipe! Our very favorite coleslaw recipe can also be found in *Farmhouse Weekends*. It's so easy and so good, it's the only coleslaw recipe I ever make. In a large bowl, whisk ½ cup mayonnaise, ⅓ cup granulated sugar, ¼ cup milk, ¼ cup buttermilk, ¼ cup apple cider vinegar, ½ teaspoon salt, and some freshly ground black pepper. Add 1 (14-ounce) bag of shredded cabbage (usually labeled "coleslaw") from the produce section of the grocery store. Toss and chill until ready to serve.

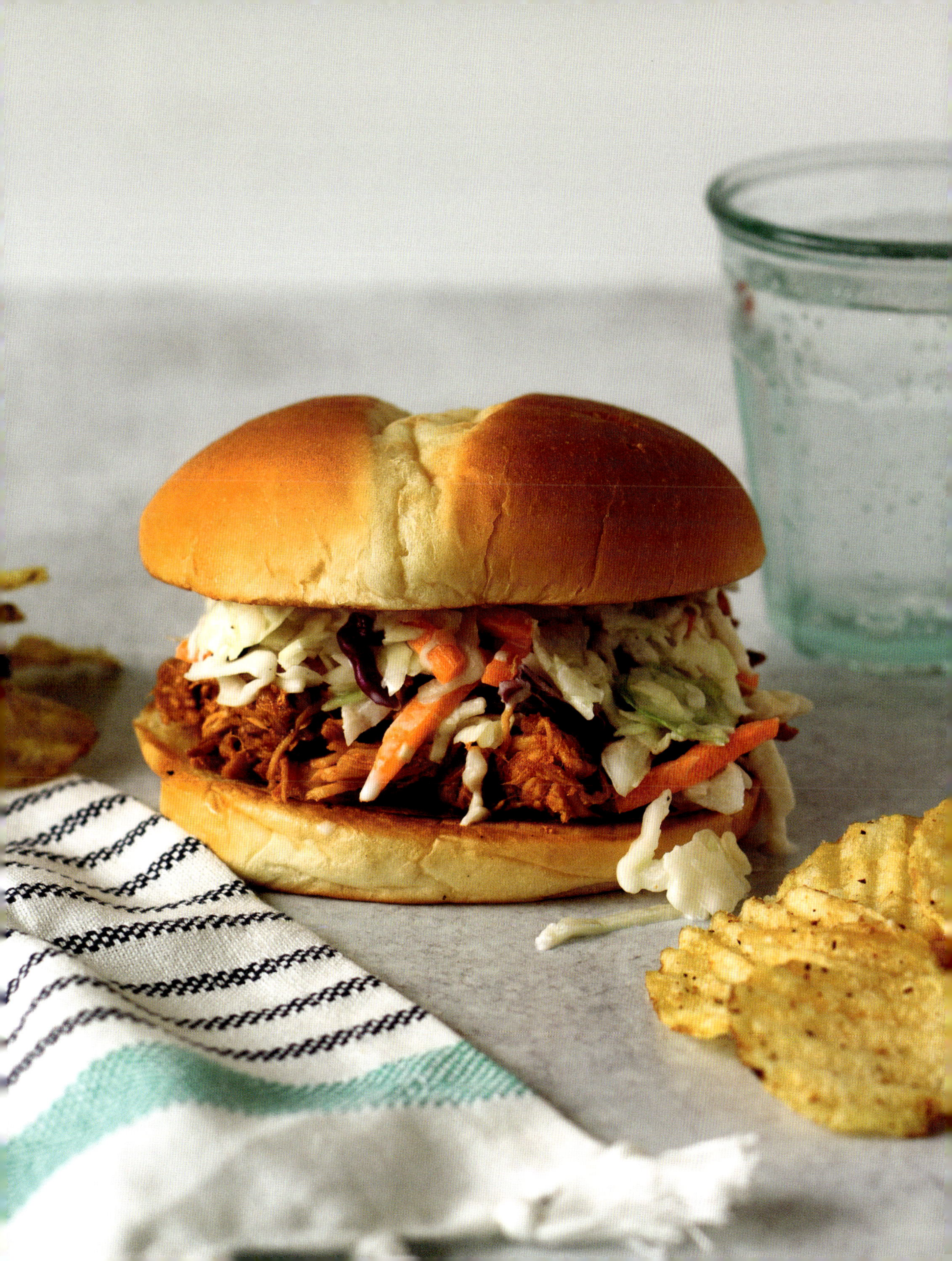

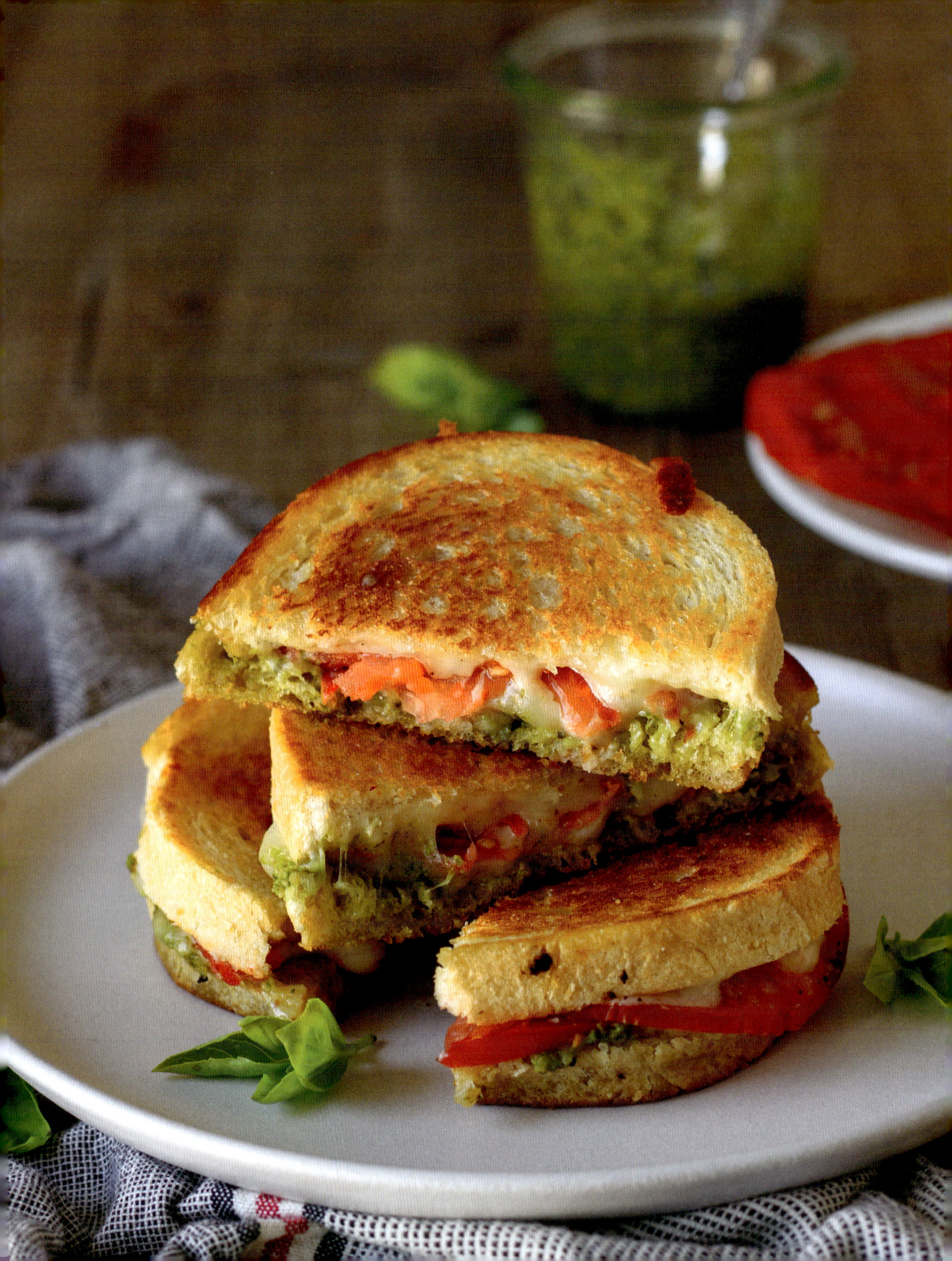

Caprese Grilled Cheese Sandwiches

The only thing better than a grilled cheese sandwich is a fancy grilled cheese sandwich! Okay, maybe "better" isn't the right word. Let's try "just as fabulous"! These caprese grilled cheeses are super easy to make and taste so good. We love the fresh burst of garden-fresh tomato flavor, the mild, melty mozzarella, and the aromatic basil pesto. They are a fun, fast way to turn grilled cheese night into something new.

Prep: 5 minutes | Cook: 10 minutes | Total: 15 minutes | Makes 4 sandwiches

8 slices sourdough bread

½ cup pesto

2 cups shredded mozzarella cheese

2 big tomatoes, thinly sliced

Garlic salt

Freshly ground black pepper

Softened butter

Balsamic vinegar, for serving, optional

1. Preheat a big griddle over medium-low heat.

2. Butter 1 side of 4 slices of sourdough bread and lay them butter-side down on a large cutting board or baking sheet. Divide the pesto evenly among the 4 slices of bread, spreading 1 to 2 tablespoons of pesto on each piece, all the way to the edges. Next place a layer of cheese on the 4 slices of bread. Use ¼ to ⅓ cup of shredded cheese per slice of bread. Divide the tomato slices among the 4 slices of sourdough and season the tomato slices with garlic salt and black pepper. Divide the remaining cheese among the 4 sandwiches. Butter 1 side of the remaining pieces of bread, and place them butter-side up on top of each sandwich.

3. Use a large spatula to lift each buttery sandwich and place it on the hot griddle. Grill the sandwiches for about 5 minutes, until the cheese is beginning to melt and the bottoms of the sandwiches are dark golden brown, then flip and cook for another 5 minutes. If you have any big stock pot or saucepan lids, you can put one over the sandwiches to help the cheese melt faster. I sometimes use a rimmed baking sheet flipped upside down. If your sandwiches aren't quite golden after 5 minutes per side, that's okay. You can keep cooking and flipping until the cheese is melted all the way through and both sides of the sandwiches are golden. Serve immediately with balsamic vinegar for dipping or drizzling on top, if desired.

SHORTCUTS & NOTES

- Store-bought pesto (We like the one from Costco.)
- Pre-shredded mozzarella cheese

Chicken Pesto Paninis

I got the idea for this tasty sandwich from a beloved local grocery store. They have a big pizza oven in the deli section and bake up fresh pizzas and a couple of different kinds of hot sandwiches. This one with tender chicken and flavorful pesto is my favorite. I treat myself to one if I'm at the store around lunchtime, but they're super simple to make at home, too. All of the different sandwich ingredients lend something special to the finished product: sharpness from the red onion, sweetness from the tomato, that delicious peppery flavor from the arugula. Focaccia is the best option for bread, so use it if you can find it.

Prep: 10 minutes | Cook: 3 to 5 minutes | Total: 15 minutes | Makes 1 sandwich

2 pieces thick-sliced sourdough, or 1 piece of focaccia, halved like a hamburger bun

1 tablespoon mayonnaise

1 tablespoon pesto

1 ounce sliced mozzarella or provolone cheese

2½ ounces shredded rotisserie chicken

Baby arugula

Thinly sliced red onion

Thinly sliced tomato

SHORTCUTS & NOTES

- Store-bought pesto (We like the one from Costco.)
- Pre-sliced cheese
- If you don't have a panini press, you can still enjoy this sandwich—just give it the grilled cheese treatment! Lightly butter the outside of both pieces of bread and cook it in a skillet or on a griddle over medium heat until each side is golden and the cheese is melty.

1. Preheat your panini maker.

2. Lay both pieces of bread out on a plate or cutting board. Spread the mayonnaise on both halves, then drizzle with the pesto. On 1 of the pieces of bread, layer the cheese, chicken, baby arugula, onion, and tomato. Top the sandwich with the remaining piece of bread.

3. Cook in the panini press for 3 to 5 minutes, until the bread is golden and crusty.

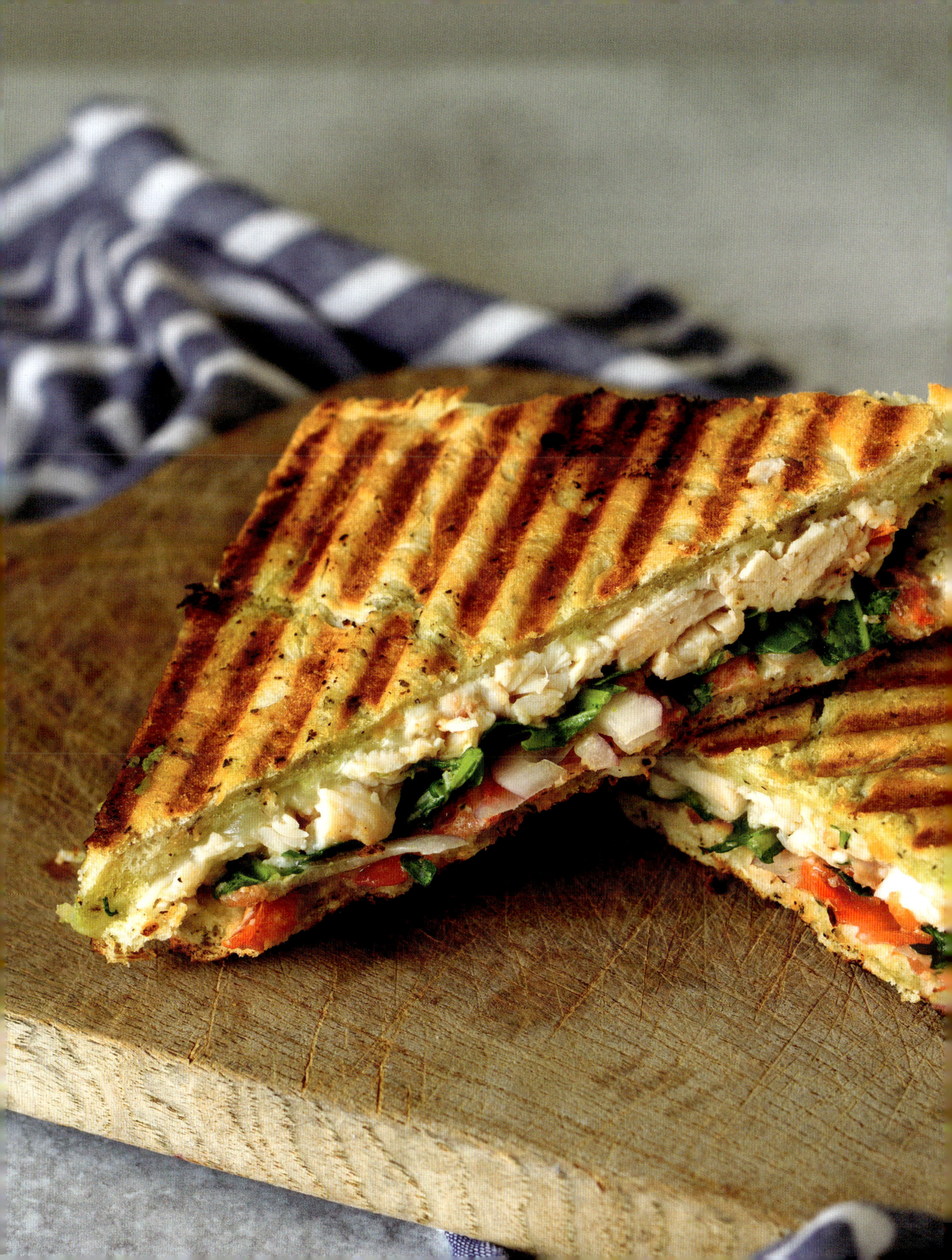

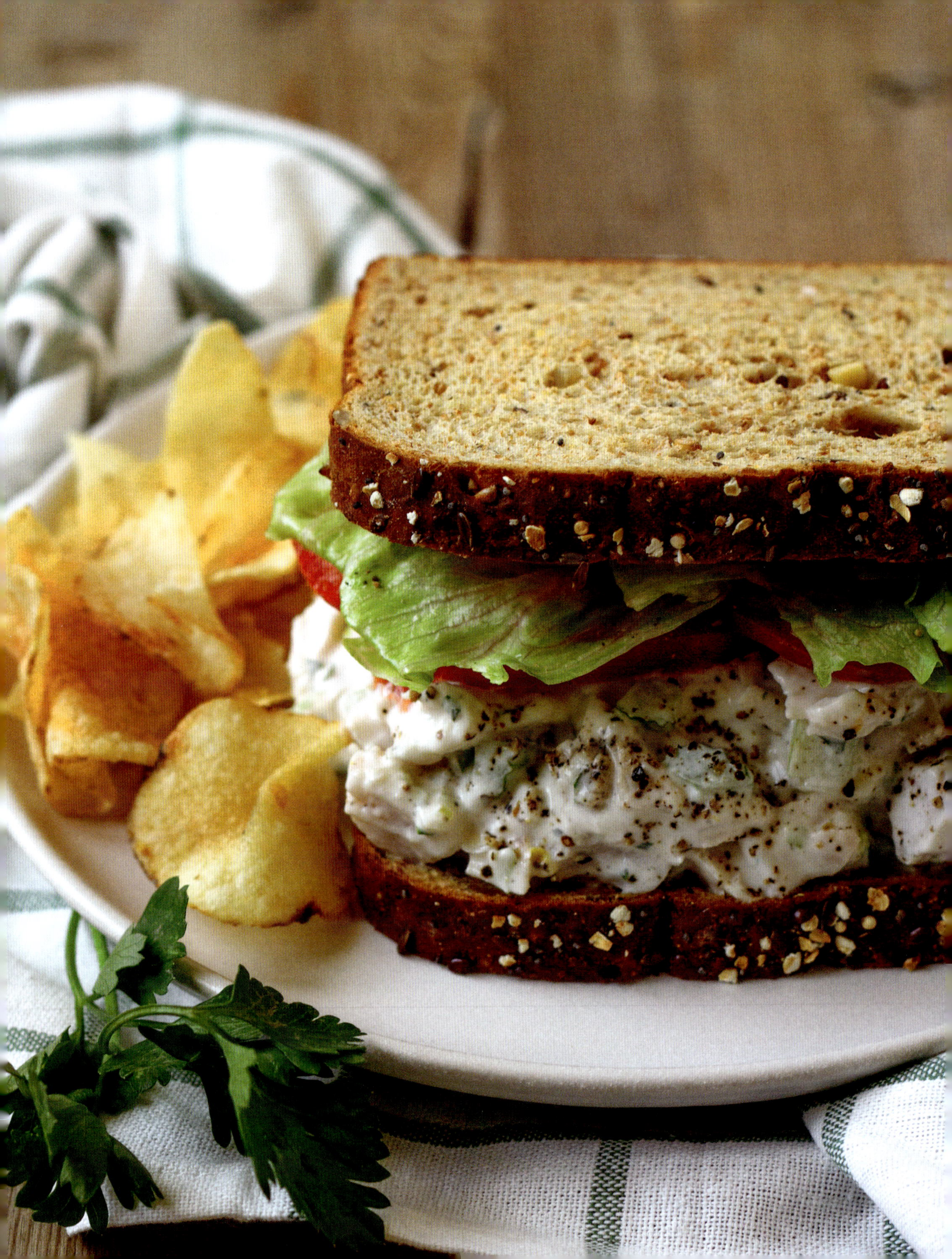

Chicken Salad Sandwiches

Chicken salad sandwiches have always been one of my favorites, even as a kid. They're super easy to make and customize, they're hearty enough to make a filling dinner, and they're nice and cool during heat waves. This recipe is a mash-up of several favorites. It's light, bright, and full of fresh, herby flavors.

Prep: 20 minutes | Cook: 0 minutes | Total: 20 minutes | Serves 10 to 12

1½ cups mayonnaise

⅔ cup sour cream

1 tablespoon ranch dressing powder

Zest and juice of 1 small lemon

Freshly ground black pepper

2½ pounds cooked chicken breast, chopped or shredded

2 cups minced celery

2 bunches green onions, white and light green parts only, minced

Up to ¼ cup minced fresh herbs, optional (I like parsley, chives, and thyme)

Sandwich bread, of choice

Lettuce and thinly sliced tomatoes, for serving, optional

1. In a large bowl, combine the mayonnaise, sour cream, ranch dressing powder, lemon zest and juice, and pepper. Whisk until smooth.

2. Add the chicken, celery, green onions, and fresh herbs. Stir until combined, then serve immediately or cover and chill until ready to serve.

3. Make into sandwiches using your favorite bread, lettuce, and thinly sliced tomatoes, if desired.

SHORTCUTS & NOTES

- Chopped or shredded rotisserie chicken

- Pre-chopped celery

- Different members of my family appreciate different things in their chicken salad, so this serves as a base recipe. Try adding quartered red or green grapes or diced apple with toasted, chopped almonds or pecans. Or try stirring in chopped dill pickles or some pickle relish. One of my personal favorites includes shredded cheddar cheese, minced white onion, and chopped cashews.

- Growing up, we had chicken salad in pita pockets a lot. That's where I first developed my undying love of chicken salad, and it is so nostalgic for me!

- For an entirely different variation, we like making open-faced chicken salad melts. Add 12 ounces of shredded cheddar cheese to the chicken salad. Divide the chicken salad evenly among 8 to 10 slices of your favorite bread (we like sourdough), place the sandwiches on a rimmed baking sheet, and bake at 350°F for 8 to 10 minutes, or until the cheese is melted and bubbly. Let cool slightly before eating so you don't burn the roof of your mouth.

Turkey-Bacon-Avocado Clubs

Can you resist a club sandwich? I've never been able to. If I see a club sandwich on the menu somewhere, I'm utterly powerless to do anything but order it. This homemade version is just as irresistible, and it's easy to customize for all household members. Serve them with a side of chips or, for a real restaurant vibe, serve them with a side of fries or tots.

Prep: 10 minutes | Cook: 10 minutes | Total: 20 minutes | Makes 4 sandwiches

8 bacon slices

8 sandwich bread slices

Mayonnaise

Yellow mustard, Dijon mustard, or spicy brown mustard

1 pound thinly sliced oven-roasted deli turkey

8 slices cheese, of choice

4 to 8 leaves green leaf or romaine lettuce

1 large, ripe avocado, peeled, pitted, and sliced

1 large tomato, thinly sliced

Pickle slices (I love dill pickles, but you can use your fave.)

Thinly sliced red onion

1. Cook the bacon. Place on a paper towel-lined plate and set aside.

2. Lightly toast the slices of bread, then lay them out on a work surface.

3. Spread a thin layer of mayonnaise and mustard on each piece of bread. Divide the turkey and cheese evenly among 4 of the slices of bread, then divide all other toppings as desired. Close and eat!

SHORTCUTS & NOTES

- Pre-sliced cheese

- Pre-cooked bacon (We like the black package from Costco.)

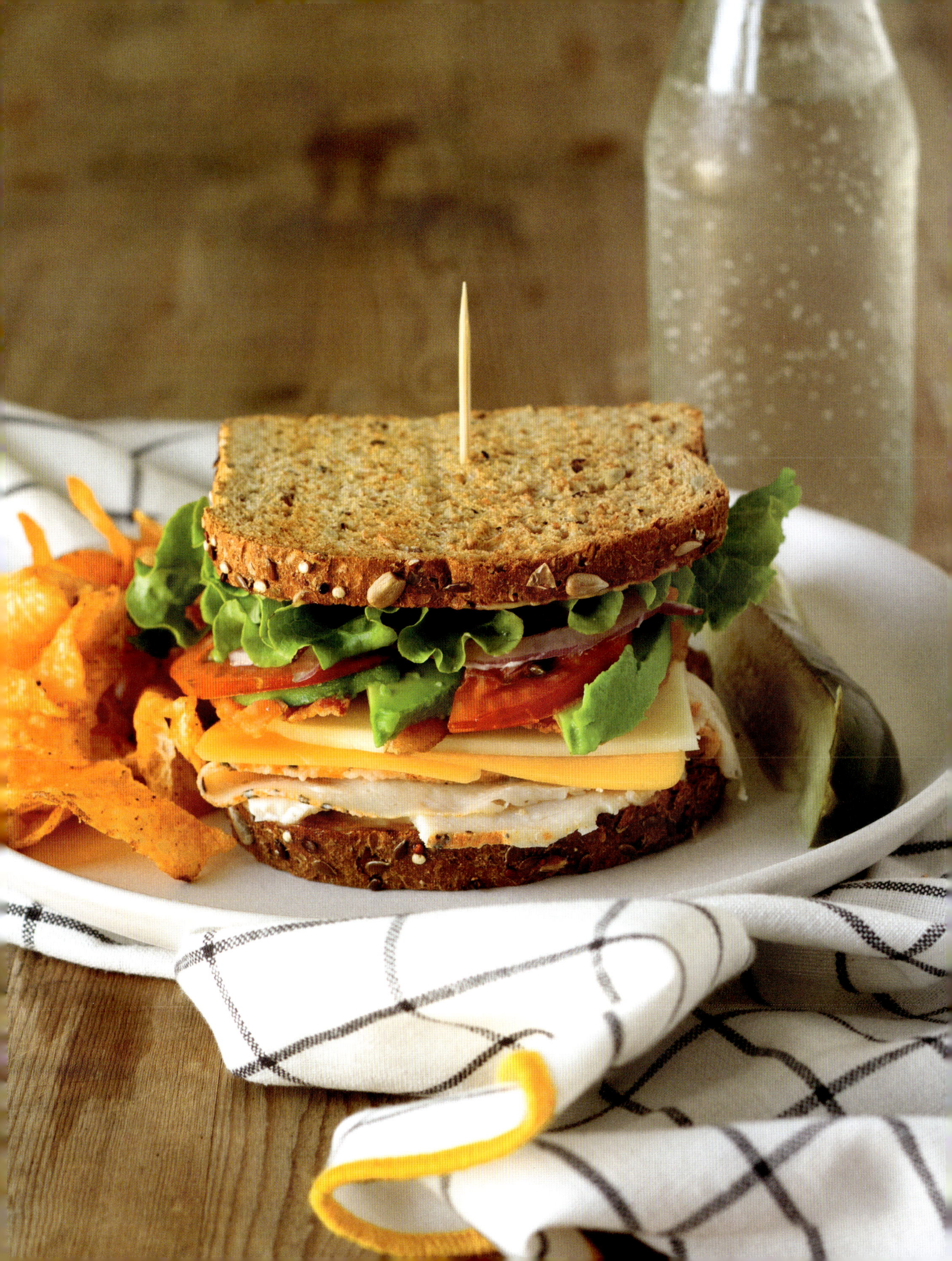

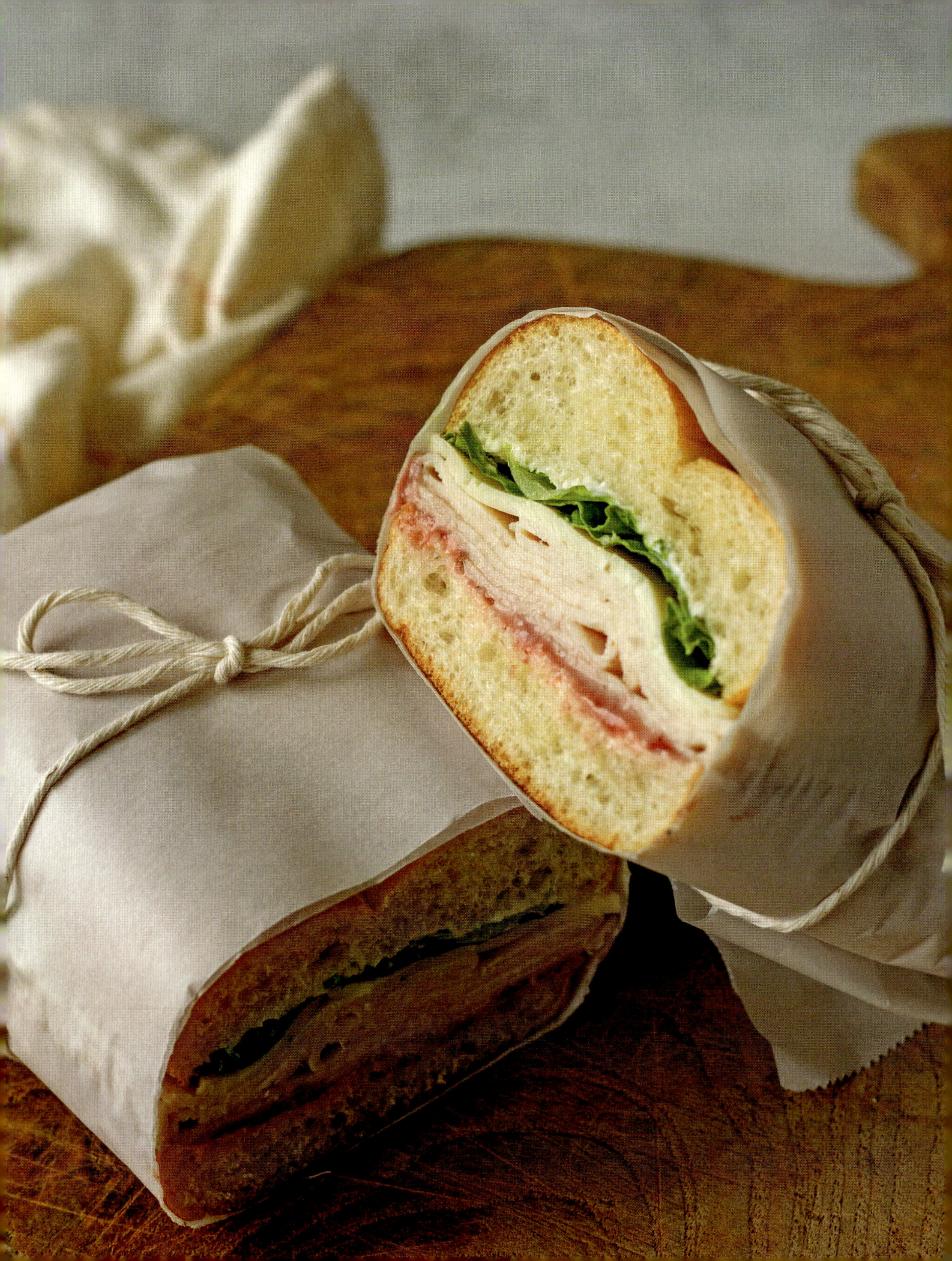

Turkey & Cranberry Plymouth Rock Sandwiches

Cranberry and turkey are a match made in heaven, whether it's on the Thanksgiving table or the dinner table on any old weeknight. My husband and I used to order these turkey and cranberry sandwiches from the deli counter of our local grocery store when we were first married. For a slightly different (and even more savory) variation on the turkey and cranberry sandwich, check the recipe notes.

Prep: 10 minutes | Cook: 0 minutes | Total: 10 minutes | Makes 6 sandwiches

6 hoagie rolls

⅓ cup mayonnaise

¾ cup jellied cranberry sauce

1½ pounds thinly sliced oven-roasted deli turkey

12 slices Havarti cheese

6 to 12 leaves green leaf lettuce

1. Split the hoagie rolls in half if they're not already cut, and lay them open on a work surface.

2. Spread a thin layer of mayonnaise on each cut side of each hoagie roll. Spread 1 to 2 tablespoons of cranberry sauce on one side of each hoagie roll. Divide the turkey evenly among the hoagie rolls. Place 2 slices of cheese and 1 or 2 leaves of lettuce on each sandwich. Close and eat!

SHORTCUTS & NOTES

• Pre-sliced Havarti cheese

Bonus Recipe! There are so many great turkey and cranberry sandwich variations. This one is a homemade version of the Bobbie Sandwich from Capriotti's. The original Las Vegas location was close to my dad's office when I was a kid, and the sandwiches always felt like a special treat. Prepare 1 (6-ounce) box of herb stuffing according to the instructions on the box. Set it aside to cool. Spread mayonnaise and cranberry sauce on 6 hoagie rolls, then divide up the stuffing evenly among the hoagie rolls along with the turkey. So good!!

Meatball Subs

Meatball subs are a Top 5 dinner at our house. They are very easy to make and everyone adores them. They're basically perfect for everything from busy weeknights to big, family dinners to special occasions like birthdays.

Prep: 5 minutes | Cook: 25 minutes | Total: 30 minutes | Makes 4 sandwiches

4 hoagie rolls

Softened butter

Garlic bread seasoning, optional

4 to 8 slices provolone cheese, halved

24 frozen meatballs

16 ounces marinara sauce

1. Preheat the oven to 425°F. If the hoagie rolls aren't already split, halve them. Lay them open-side up on a rimmed baking sheet. Spread the cut surfaces with butter and sprinkle with garlic bread seasoning, if desired.

2. While the oven is preheating, combine the meatballs and marinara sauce in a medium saucepan, cover, and cook over medium heat until the sauce is simmering and the meatballs are heated through, 15 to 20 minutes.

3. Once the oven is preheated and the meatballs are ready, toast the rolls for about 4 minutes, until the butter has melted. Place 2 to 4 half slices of provolone on each bun and continue baking until the cheese is melted, about 2 minutes.

4. Put the meatballs on the cheesy, toasted hoagie rolls and enjoy immediately!

SHORTCUTS & NOTES

- Pre-sliced provolone cheese

- Our favorite store-bought marinara is Rao's.

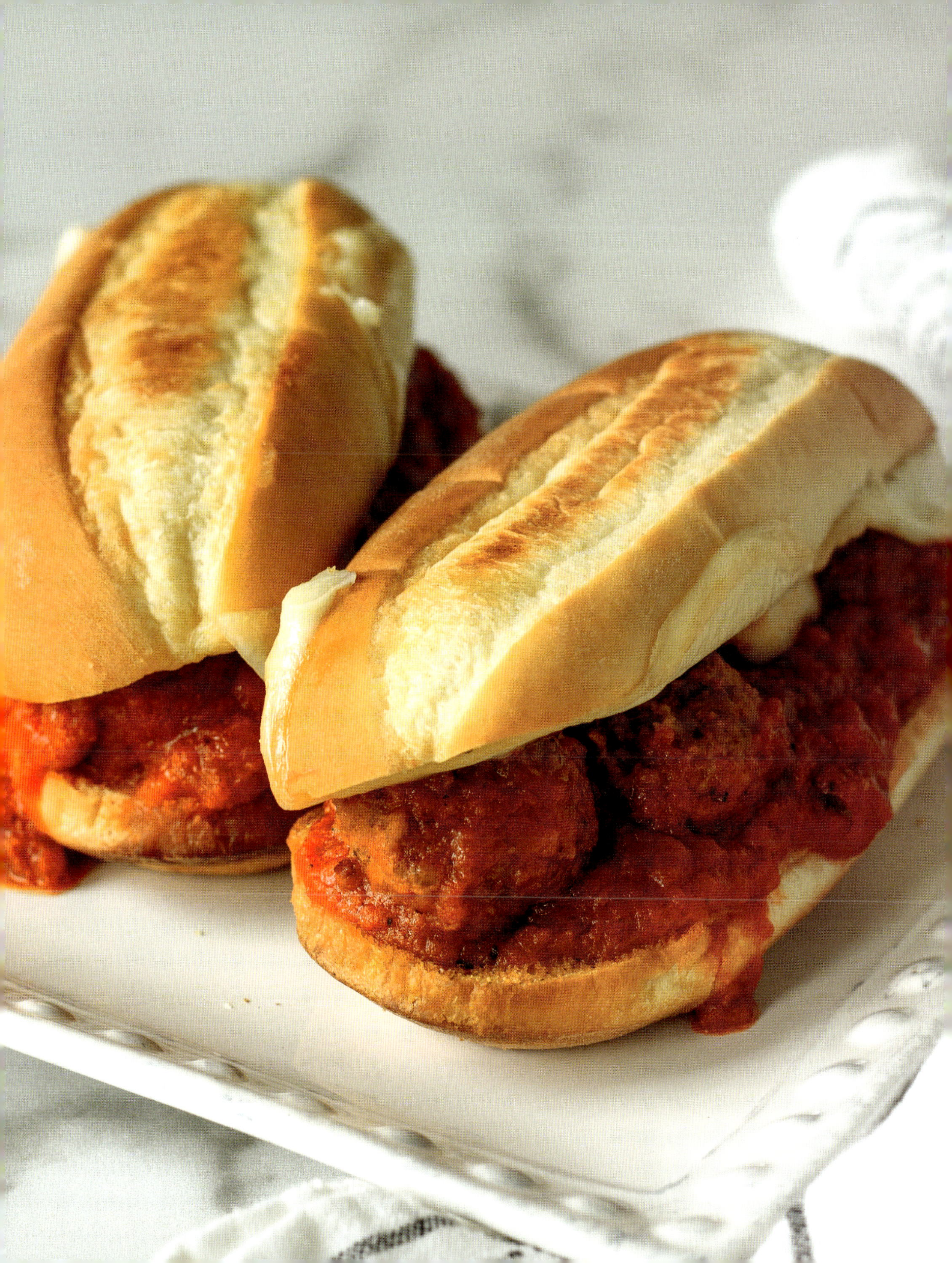

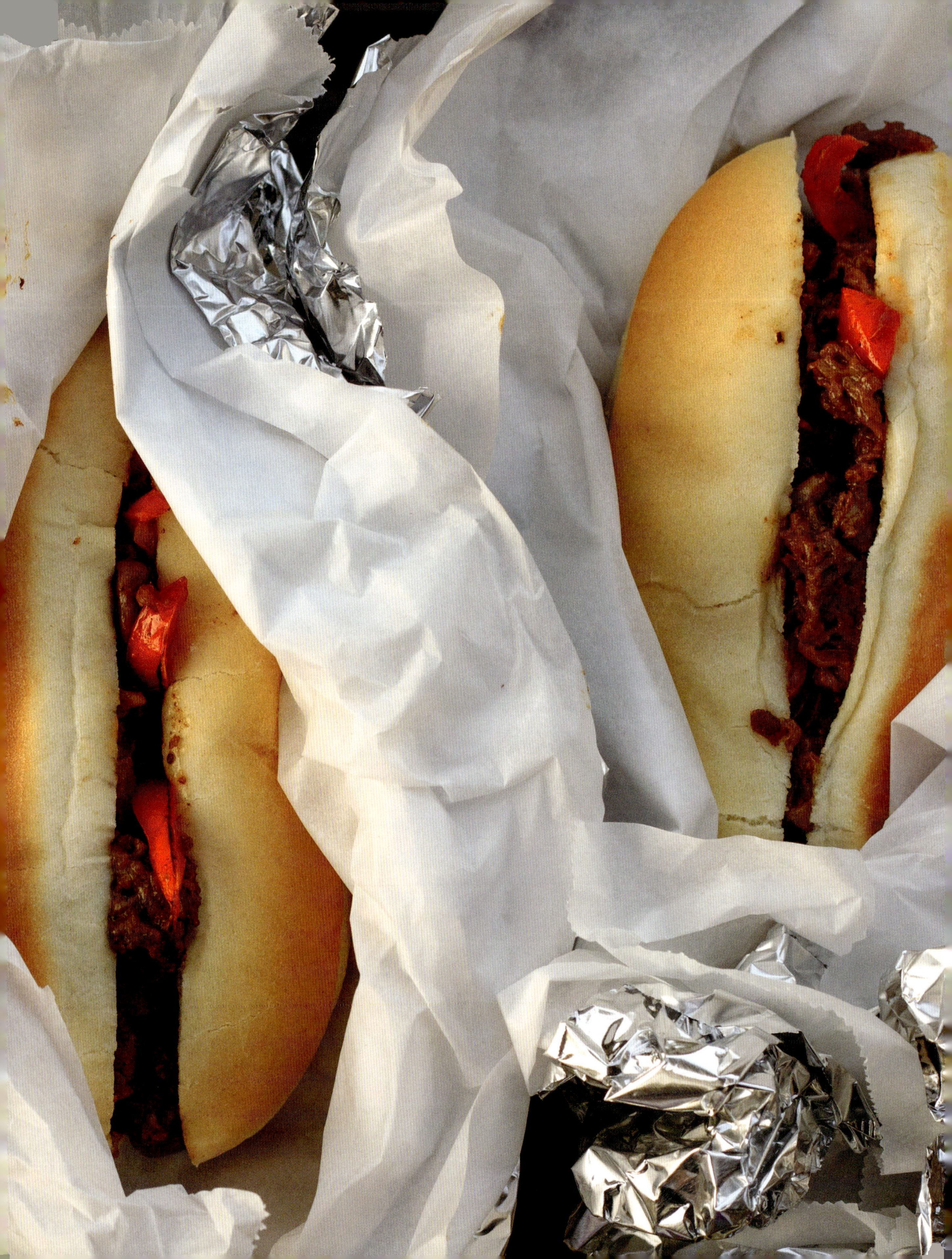

Philly Cheesesteaks

My parents lived in Philadelphia when they were first married and starting a family. My mom picked up a few cheesesteak-making tips from the sandwich shops they frequented and has been making delicious Philly cheesesteaks for my entire life. When I was a kid and a much pickier eater than I am now, I liked them with just three ingredients: bread, meat, and cheese. I happily enjoy them full of sautéed peppers and onions now, but they are really easy to customize for any choosier eaters in your household—an all-ages family favorite.

Prep: 5 minutes | Cook: 25 minutes | Total: 30 minutes | Makes 6 sandwiches

2 red bell peppers, thinly sliced

1 onion, thinly sliced

2 tablespoons extra-virgin olive oil or your favorite neutral cooking oil, plus more as needed

Kosher salt

Freshly ground black pepper

2 teaspoons minced garlic, or 2 garlic cloves, minced

2 (14-ounce) packages shaved beef or beef-shaved steak

6 ounces sliced white American cheese (from the deli)

6 hoagie rolls

1. Preheat the oven to 425°F. Prepare 6 large pieces of aluminum foil and set them on a work surface.

2. In a large skillet over medium heat, sauté the bell peppers and onion in the oil for 8 to 10 minutes. Season with a pinch of kosher salt and freshly ground black pepper. Add the garlic and sauté for 1 minute. Add the beef and sauté until brown and cooked through, 4 to 5 minutes. Season to taste with kosher salt and black pepper.

3. Remove from the heat. Add the cheese and cover, allowing the cheese to melt, about 5 minutes. Stir until the cheese is evenly distributed.

4. Divide the meat mixture evenly among the 6 split hoagie rolls. Wrap each sandwich in foil and place in the oven for 3 to 5 minutes. Serve hot!

SHORTCUTS & NOTES

- Pre-sliced peppers and onions

- Pre-minced garlic (frozen cubes, or a jar or squeeze tube)

- The shaved beef has become really easy to find prepackaged in the meat department of regular grocery stores. If you can't find it, however, there are a few easy, great-tasting substitutions. My mom always used Steak-umm to make Philly cheesesteaks when I was growing up. Steak-umm is a box of paper-thin slices of beef, frozen with a layer of parchment paper between each slice. If you can find it, it'll be in the freezer section. And if you can't find either shaved beef or Steak-umm, we have used really rare, really thin-sliced deli roast beef in a pinch. Just coarsely chop it on a cutting board before you cook it.

Slow Cooker Sausage & Pepper Sandwiches

When I was growing up, my mom made these amazing kielbasa sandwiches she'd gotten the recipe for from her sister, my aunt Kari. Even though I was kind of a picky eater as a kid, these sandwiches were so delicious, filled with onions and peppers and a yummy tomato sauce, that I couldn't resist them. And I still love them now! I've tinkered with the recipe a little, adding a few herbs and spices along the way. I've also lightened the sauce a bit; my husband was fond of calling the original version "heartburn sandwiches"!

Prep: 10 minutes | Cook: 4 hours | Total: 4 hours 10 minutes | Serves 6 to 8

2 (12-ounce) packages kielbasa or smoked sausage, sliced in 2-inch sections, then sliced in half lengthwise

2 bell peppers, any color but green, seeded and thinly sliced

1 large onion, thinly sliced

2 teaspoons minced garlic, or 2 garlic cloves, minced

1 teaspoon dried oregano

1 teaspoon dried basil

1 bay leaf

1 teaspoon kosher salt

Freshly ground black pepper

¼ cup tomato paste

¼ cup low-sodium chicken broth

1 (14.5-ounce) can petite diced tomatoes

6 to 8 kaiser rolls, for serving

1. Place the sliced kielbasa in the bottom of a slow cooker, then top with the sliced peppers, onion, and garlic. Sprinkle with the oregano, basil, bay leaf, kosher salt, and some freshly ground black pepper.

2. In a medium bowl or a large glass measuring cup, combine the tomato paste, chicken broth, and diced tomatoes with their liquid. Pour the tomato mixture into the slow cooker.

3. Put the lid on the slow cooker and cook for 4 hours over low heat, stirring once halfway through cooking.

4. Serve the sausage, peppers, and onions on kaiser rolls and eat immediately.

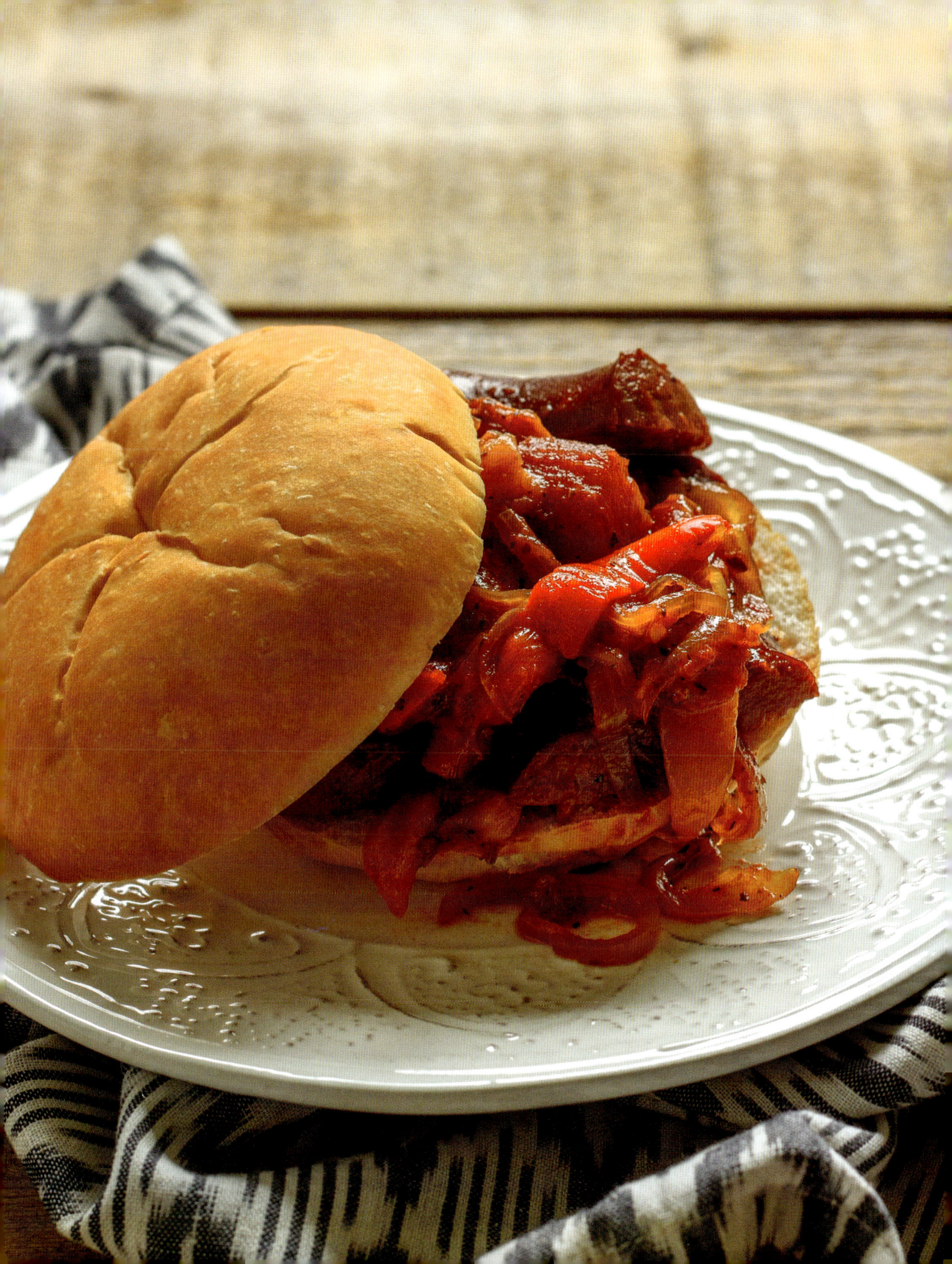

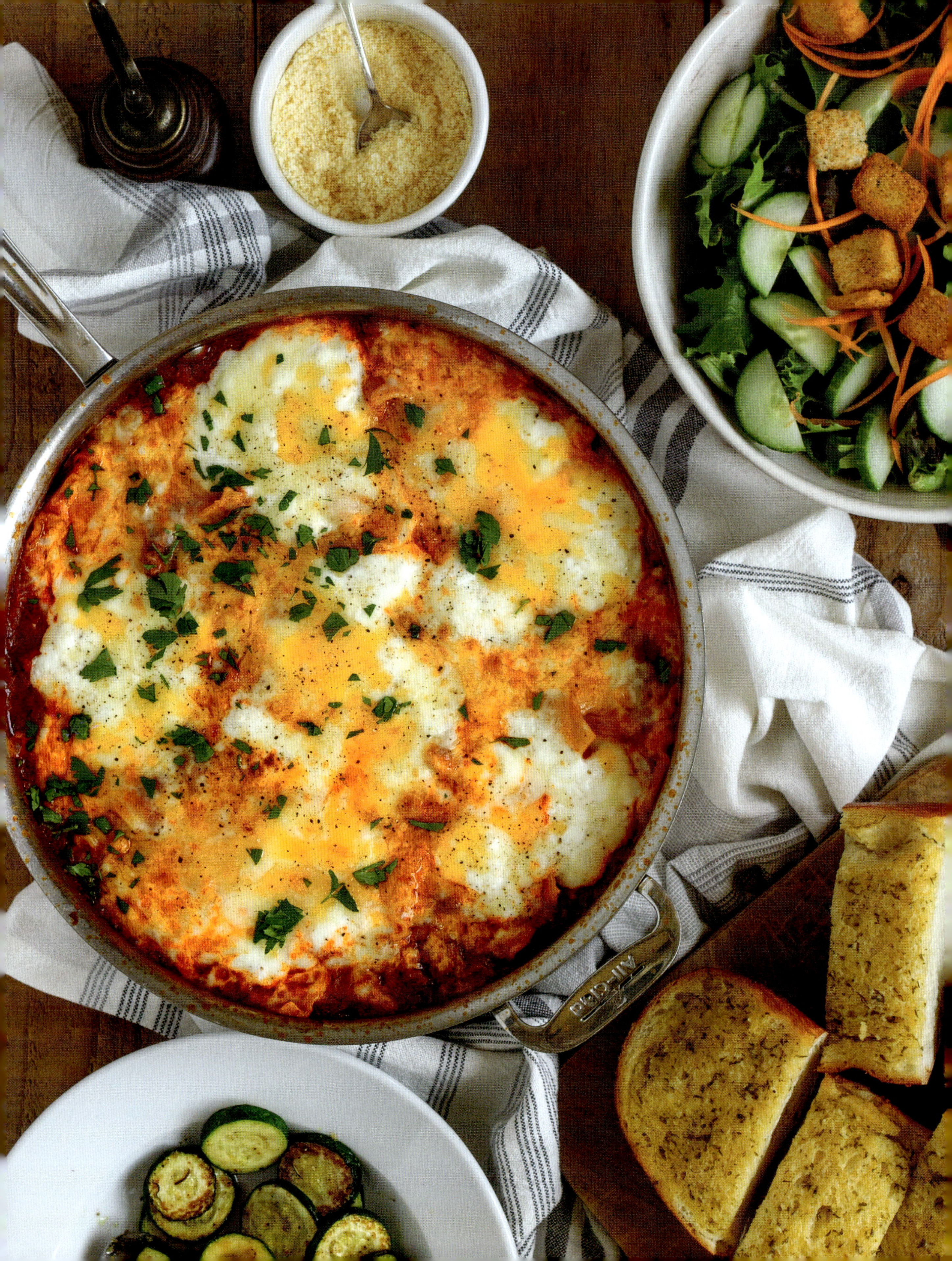
All-Clad

PASTAS

PASTA DINNERS ARE PERFECTLY SUITED for busy nights. It's easy to have a stash of dried pasta in the pantry that you can cook up at a moment's notice, and sauces can range from store-bought to simple to fancy, all while being both tasty and easy to make. Pasta dishes are a natural fit for Meatless Mondays thanks to lots of veggies and cheeses, but pastas with chicken, beef, seafood, or other meats are deliciously hearty. Pastas are the reigning rulers of mouthwatering versatility.

Round these dinners out by serving them with:

A GREEN SALAD (PAGES 61–83)

FRENCH BREAD FROM THE GROCERY STORE BAKERY, CORNBREAD, MUFFINS, DINNER ROLLS, HAWAIIAN ROLLS, OR GARLIC BREAD

SAUTÉED, STEAMED, OR ROASTED VEGGIES (SEE OUR FAVE GREEN BEANS ON PAGE 144)

Cheese Tortellini with Pesto & Veggies

I've been making some version of this recipe for three decades! I started making tortellini with pesto and chopped tomatoes in college. At some point, I stopped using a packet of dried pesto mix and started using real pesto. Then I started roasting or sautéing the tomatoes. Then I decided to add pine nuts. Then I threw in some zucchini. Then I added summer corn cut straight off the cob. In all of its many stages, this pasta recipe has been a favorite, and I think this current version is the absolute best.

Prep: 5 minutes | Cook: 25 minutes | Total: 30 minutes | Serves 6 to 8

1 (20-ounce) package refrigerated cheese tortellini

½ cup pine nuts

1 tablespoon extra-virgin olive oil or your favorite neutral cooking oil

1 (10-ounce) package grape tomatoes, halved

2 medium zucchini, cut into ¼-inch slices and halved

1 (10-ounce) package frozen sweet corn

Garlic salt

Italian seasoning

Freshly ground black pepper

¾ cup pesto

Fresh Parmesan cheese, for topping

Fresh basil, for garnishing, optional

1. Bring a large pot of salted water to a boil. Cook the tortellini according to the package directions. Drain and set aside.

2. While the water is coming to a boil and the tortellini is cooking, put the pine nuts in a large, dry skillet over medium heat. Cook, stirring gently, until the nuts are fragrant and golden, 3 to 5 minutes. Pour the pine nuts onto a plate and set aside. Wipe the skillet clean with a paper towel.

3. Drizzle the olive oil into the skillet and return it to medium heat. Add the halved tomatoes and cook for 5 minutes. Add the zucchini and corn and sauté until the zucchini is tender and the corn is cooked through, about 10 minutes. Season the vegetables lightly with garlic salt, Italian seasoning, and pepper.

4. Add the toasted pine nuts, cooked tortellini, and pesto to the vegetables, and toss to combine. Serve topped with fresh Parmesan cheese and basil if using.

SHORTCUTS & NOTES

- Pre-sliced zucchini (It's already sliced, but quarter it as well.)

- Store-bought pesto (We like the one from Costco.)

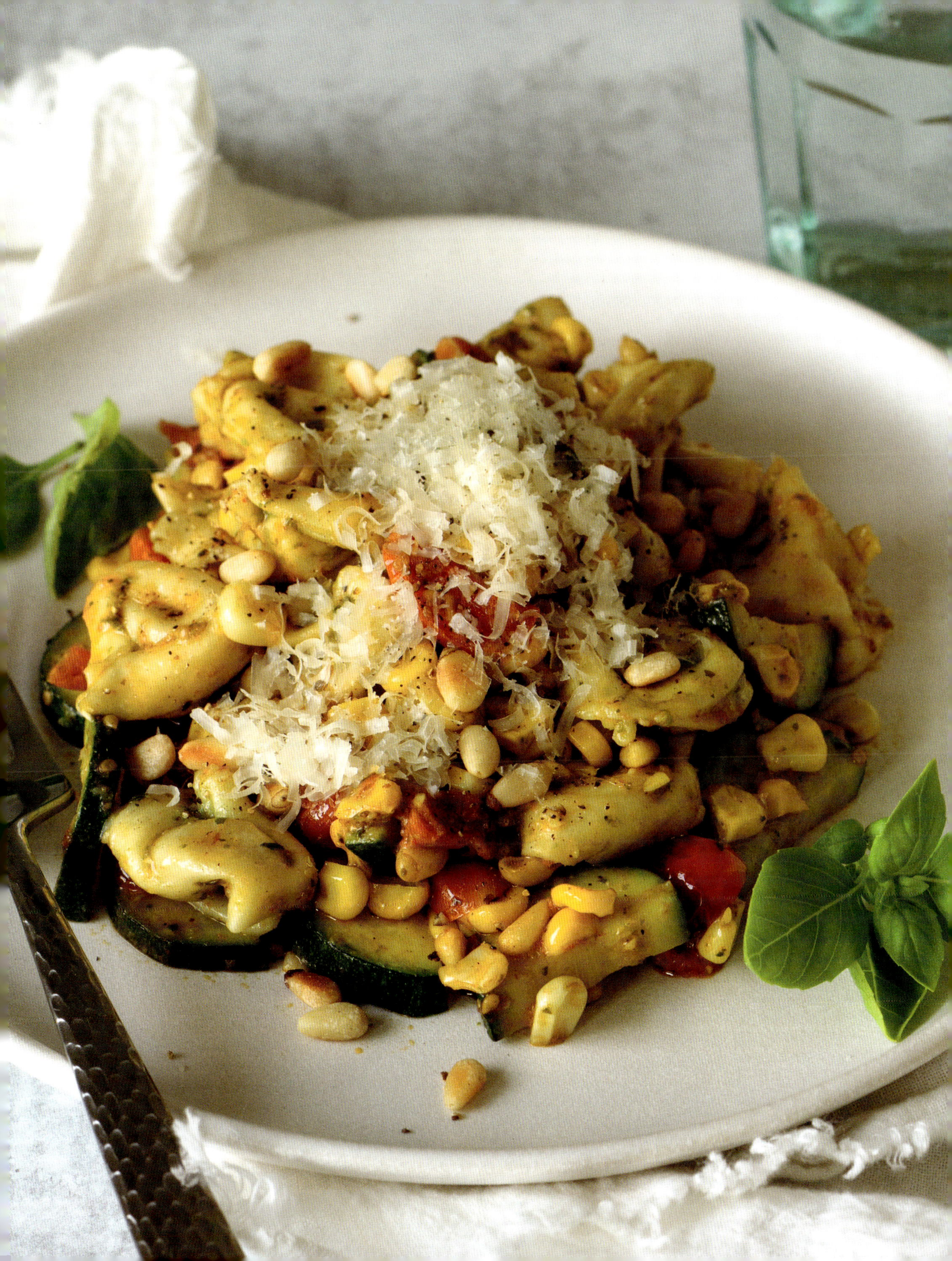

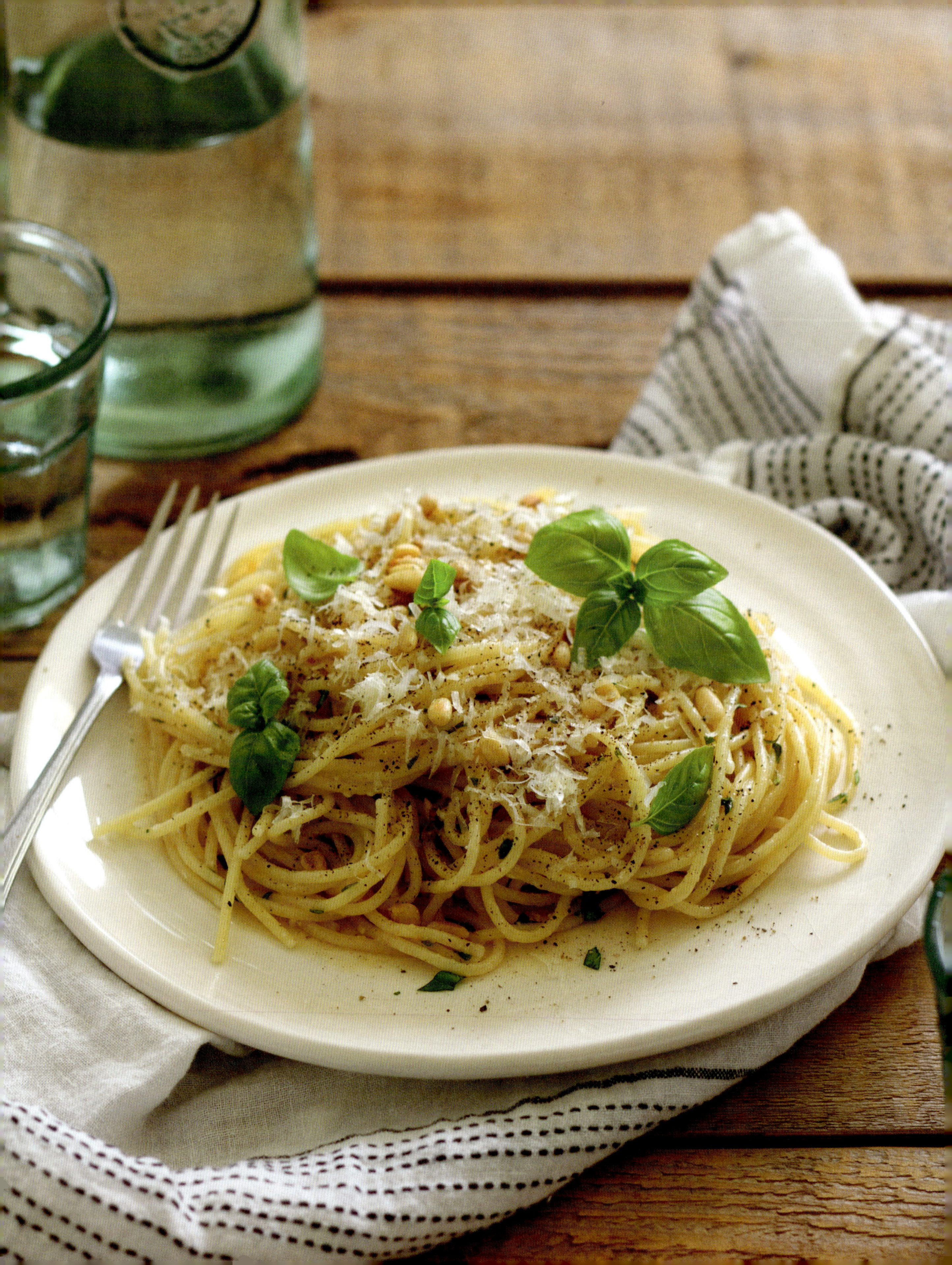

Lemon Garlic Spaghetti

Lemon garlic spaghetti is one of our very favorite dinners for a couple of reasons: It's absolutely delicious, and it's incredibly easy to make. Other than the basil, which is easy to get from the grocery store or the summer garden, we usually have all of the ingredients in our pantry and refrigerator, and every ingredient on the list adds something wonderful to the finished dish.

Prep: 10 minutes | Cook: 10 minutes | Total: 20 minutes | Serves 6 to 8

1 pound dried spaghetti

½ cup pine nuts

3 tablespoons extra-virgin olive oil or your favorite neutral cooking oil

4 teaspoons minced garlic, or 4 garlic cloves, minced

¼ cup finely minced fresh basil, plus more for garnishing

1 cup freshly shredded Parmesan cheese, plus more for topping

¼ cup fresh lemon juice, plus more as needed

Kosher salt

Freshly ground black pepper

1. Bring a large pot of salted water to a boil. Add the dried pasta and cook according to the package instructions, stirring occasionally to prevent it from sticking.

2. While the spaghetti is cooking, toast the pine nuts in a small skillet over medium heat until golden, stirring gently, 3 to 4 minutes. Watch them carefully; when they're toasted, put them on a small plate or in a small bowl and set aside.

3. Add the olive oil and garlic to the skillet, turn the heat to low, and cook until golden, 2 to 3 minutes.

4. When the pasta is done cooking, drain it, reserving about ½ cup of pasta water.

5. Return the pasta to the pot and add the toasted pine nuts, garlic and olive oil, fresh basil, shredded Parmesan cheese, and ¼ cup of fresh lemon juice. Add salt, pepper, and more lemon juice to taste. If the pasta seems too dry, add the reserved pasta water a little at a time over low heat, stirring the pasta continuously, until your desired consistency is reached. This is not a saucy pasta, just a delicious pasta. Serve immediately, topped with more shredded Parmesan cheese and lots of freshly ground black pepper. Garnish with some basil leaves.

SHORTCUTS & NOTES

- Pre-minced garlic (frozen cubes, or a jar or squeeze tube)

Chicken Tetrazzini

Chicken tetrazzini is family-friendly comfort food at its finest. Tender noodles and succulent chicken in an easy, from-scratch white sauce with a hint of salty Parmesan cheese. This is a recipe my husband grew up eating. It was a favorite in his family, and is still a favorite at our house today.

Prep: 5 minutes | Cook: 40 minutes | Total: 45 minutes | Serves 8 to 10

1 pound dried spaghetti

¼ cup butter

½ cup all-purpose flour

2 cups whole or 2-percent milk

2 cups chicken broth

¼ cup sherry

¼ teaspoon ground nutmeg

Freshly ground black pepper

½ cup plus 2 tablespoons grated Parmesan cheese, divided (nothing fancy, just the one in the plastic shaker jar)

Salt

4 cups chopped cooked chicken

1. Preheat the oven to 350°F. Lightly grease a 9 x 13-inch baking dish with nonstick cooking spray.

2. Bring a large pot of salted water to a boil and cook the spaghetti according to package directions. Drain and set aside.

3. While the spaghetti is cooking, melt the butter in a large, heavy-bottom Dutch oven or saucepan over medium heat. Whisk in the flour and cook for 1 minute. Slowly add the milk, broth, and sherry, whisking constantly to avoid lumps. Add the nutmeg, black pepper, and ½ cup of grated Parmesan cheese. Add salt to taste. Stir in the chicken and cooked spaghetti.

4. Pour the tetrazzini into the prepared baking dish and sprinkle the remaining 2 tablespoons of Parmesan cheese evenly over the top.

5. Bake for 10 to 15 minutes, until the topping begins to turn golden brown and the sauce is bubbling.

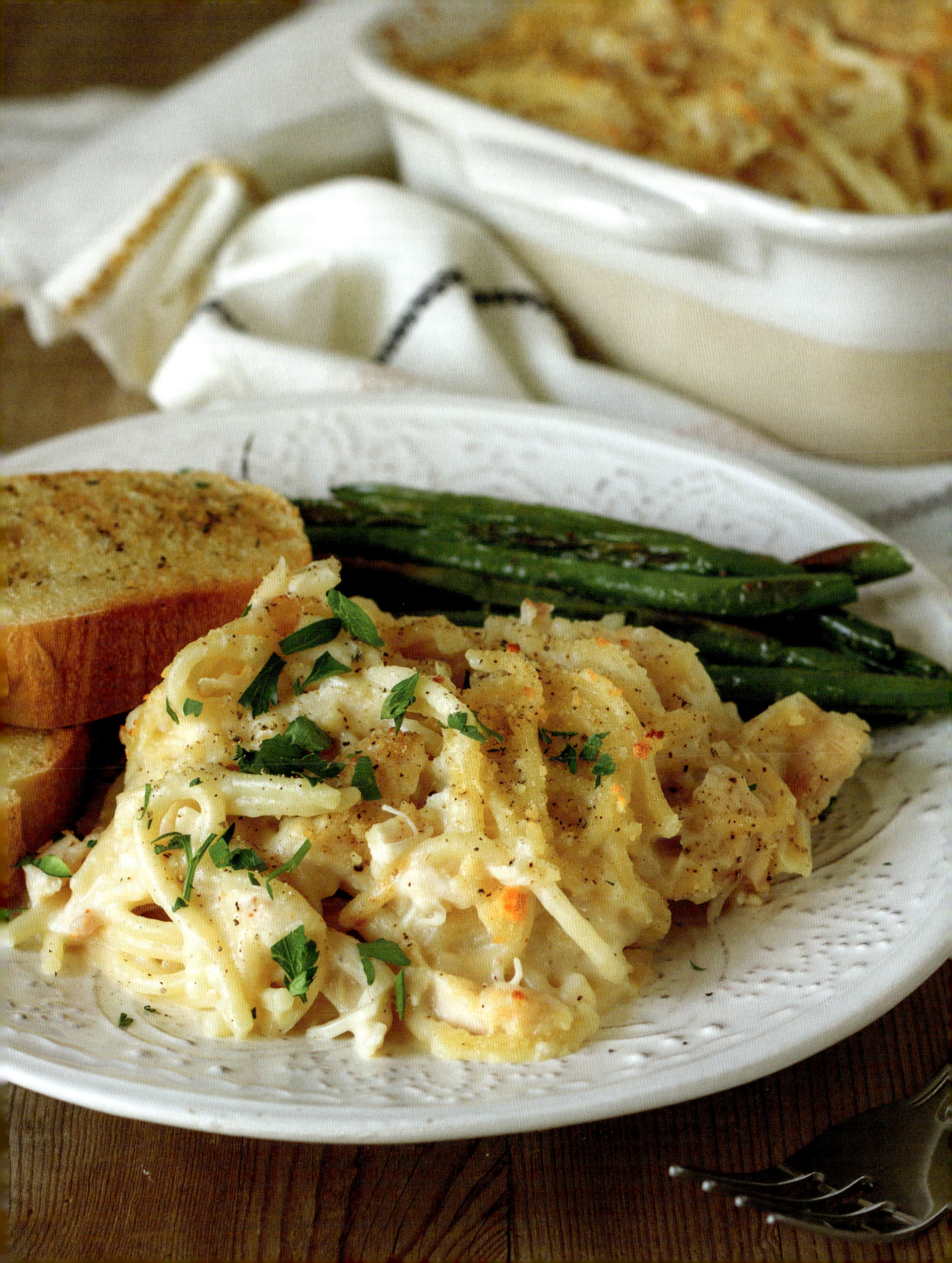

One-Pan Weeknight Lasagna

Lasagna is so delicious, but I almost never make it—and certainly not in the middle of a busy week—because it takes so long to make and gets so many dishes dirty. This recipe solves both of those problems! Everything cooks in the same large skillet in under an hour, so you can enjoy hearty, flavorful, comforting lasagna without any of the usual mess or hassle.

Prep: 10 minutes | Cook: 45 minutes | Total: 55 minutes | Serves 6

1 pound ground beef

1 cup diced onion

Kosher salt

Freshly ground black pepper

1 (28-ounce) jar marinara or spaghetti sauce

1 (14.5-ounce) can chicken broth

8 ounces lasagna noodles, broken into bite-size pieces

½ cup water

1 cup cottage cheese

2 tablespoons grated Parmesan cheese, divided (nothing fancy, just the one in the plastic shaker jar)

¾ cup shredded mozzarella cheese

¾ cup shredded cheddar cheese

Minced fresh parsley, for garnishing

1. In an oven-safe, deep, 12-inch skillet, crumble the ground beef. Add the onion, season lightly with kosher salt and pepper, and sauté over medium heat until the ground beef is brown and cooked through, about 10 minutes. Drain off any excess grease and return the pan to medium heat.

2. Add the marinara sauce and chicken broth, turn the heat up, and bring to a boil. Stir in the lasagna noodle pieces, making sure they are fully submerged. Reduce the heat so that the sauce is simmering gently. Cook until the noodles are tender, 20 to 22 minutes. Stir frequently to make sure the noodles aren't sticking to the bottom of the pan, and make sure you tuck them back under the sauce after stirring each time. If the sauce is getting too dry before the noodles are tender, add the water and continue cooking.

3. While the noodles are cooking, combine the cottage cheese, 1 tablespoon of Parmesan cheese, and a pinch of kosher salt and pepper in a medium bowl. Set aside.

4. Also while the noodles are cooking, turn the oven on to the broil setting and put one of the racks in the top third of the oven.

5. Once the noodles are tender, mix the sauce one last time, then dollop the cottage cheese mixture on top in small spoonfuls evenly spaced out. Sprinkle the mozzarella and cheddar evenly on top, then sprinkle on the remaining 1 tablespoon of Parmesan cheese. Cover, turn off the heat, and let the lasagna sit for about 4 minutes.

6. Take the cover off the skillet and place the lasagna under the broiler just until the cheese gets bubbly and has brown spots, about 1 minute. Remove from the oven, sprinkle with parsley, and serve.

SHORTCUTS & NOTES

· Pre-chopped onions

· Our favorite store-bought marinara is Rao's.

· Pre-shredded mozzarella and cheddar cheeses

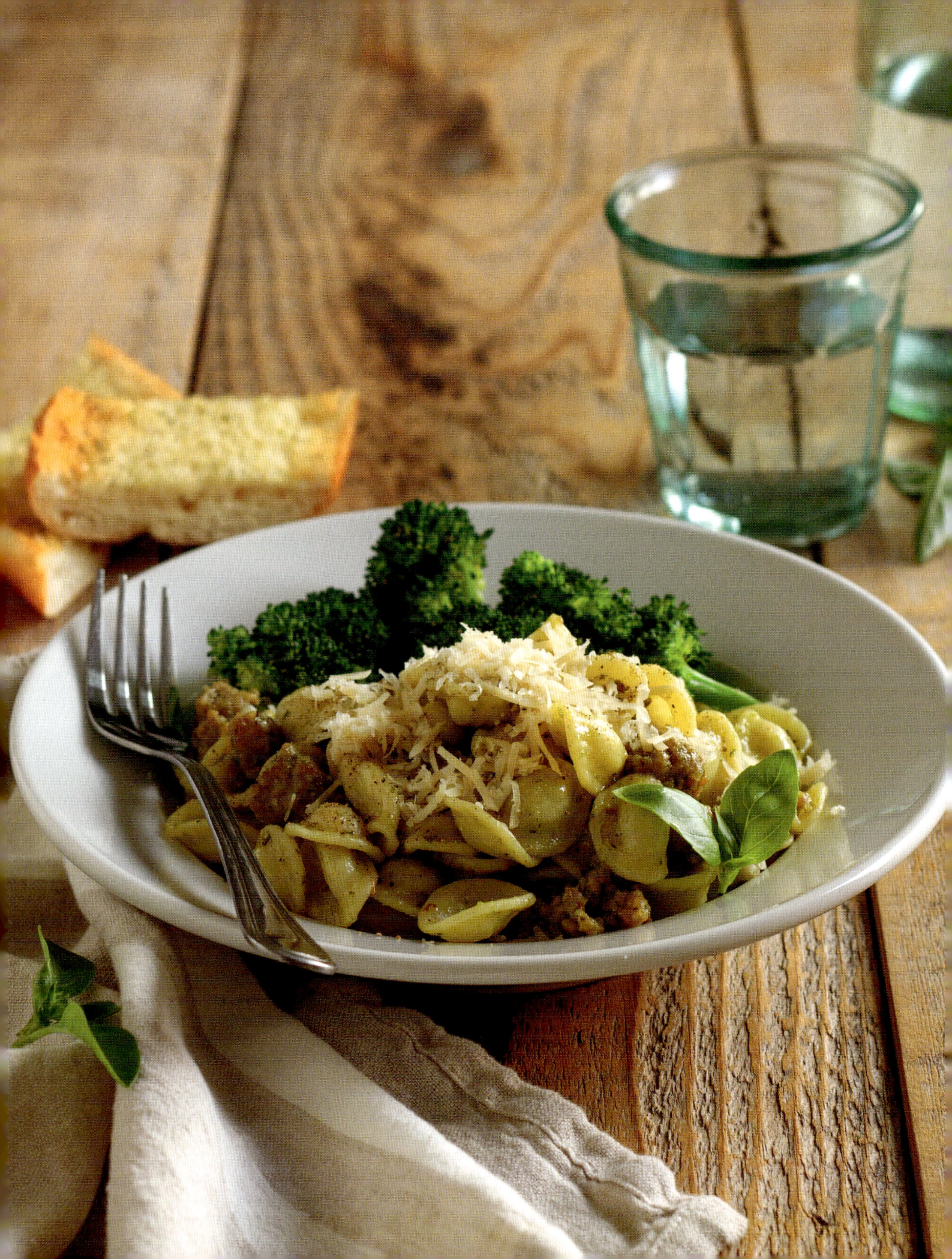

Sausage & Pesto Pasta

This tasty dinner might also be one of the easiest to make. Brown up your favorite Italian sausage (we like sweet, but you can certainly go hot if you like), and add cooked pasta, pesto, and Parmesan. That's it! I'm forever grateful to my little sister for sharing this family fave with us.

Prep: 5 minutes | Cook: 20 minutes | Total: 25 minutes | Serves 6 to 8

---

1 pound orecchiette pasta (or another small to medium pasta shape)

1 pound ground Italian sausage

⅔ cup pesto

½ cup freshly shredded Parmesan cheese, plus more for topping

Kosher salt

Freshly ground black pepper

1. Bring a large pot of salted water to a boil. Cook the pasta according to the package directions. Drain and set aside.

2. While waiting for the water to boil and the pasta to cook, brown the Italian sausage in a large skillet over medium heat, about 10 minutes. Drain off any excess grease.

3. Add the drained pasta to the skillet, then toss with the pesto and Parmesan cheese. Stir until well mixed. Add salt and pepper to taste, then serve topped with more Parmesan cheese.

SHORTCUTS & NOTES

- Store-bought pesto (We like the one from Costco.)

Bonus Recipe! My parents and siblings love pasta with sausage and sautéed peppers, but the recipe is so similar to this one that it made more sense to just make it a variation instead of its own recipe. Add 2 diced red, orange, or yellow bell peppers to the pan when you start cooking the sausage. After draining the grease, add ½ cup chicken broth and sauté for 5 minutes. Add the cooked pasta, top with lots of fresh Parmesan cheese, and serve. No pesto needed. My mom always uses bow tie pasta or mini bow ties for this.

Shrimp Scampi

My husband spent a lot of time waiting tables in college. At one of the restaurants, at the end of the night shift, the chef would whip up something delicious for my husband to eat while he did end-of-shift paperwork. This shrimp scampi was his very favorite, and the chef taught him how to make it as a present when he graduated. My husband has made it for us a lot over the years. We love the silky sauce flavored with tomatoes, garlic, and pineapple. It tastes luxurious but is easy enough for regular, old weeknights. Thank you, Chef!

Prep: 20 minutes | Cook: 15 minutes | Total: 35 minutes | Serves 4

---

6 tablespoons butter

3 tablespoons minced garlic, or 9 garlic cloves, minced

¾ cup white wine

9 ounces fresh pineapple, diced

9 ounces grape tomatoes, halved

¾ cup heavy cream

1 teaspoon kosher salt

Freshly ground black pepper

A dash of cayenne pepper

12 ounces shrimp

3 tablespoons snipped fresh chives

8 ounces dried or 12 ounces fresh linguine, cooked according to package directions

Toasted baguette slices for serving (see recipe notes)

1. In a large skillet over medium heat, melt the butter. Add the minced garlic and sauté until fragrant and lightly browned, about 2 minutes. Add the white wine, pineapple, and tomatoes, return to a simmer, and cook for 2 minutes. Add the heavy cream, salt, black pepper, and cayenne pepper and cook for 2 minutes. Add the shrimp and cook for 1 minute per side.

2. Add the chives, toss to combine, and serve over the cooked linguine with toasted baguette slices on the side.

SHORTCUTS & NOTES

- Pre-minced garlic (frozen cubes, or a jar or squeeze tube)

- Pre-chopped pineapple from the produce section (just dice it a little smaller)

- You can easily substitute 12 ounces of diced chicken breast for the shrimp. Add the chicken when you add the garlic. Everything else remains the same.

- My husband always makes a batch of toasted garlic butter baguette slices to go with this meal. Preheat the oven to 350°F, slice a baguette into ¼-inch-thick rounds, and lay the slices on a rimmed baking sheet. Spread softened butter on each slice and sprinkle with your favorite garlic bread seasoning, then toast for 10 minutes.

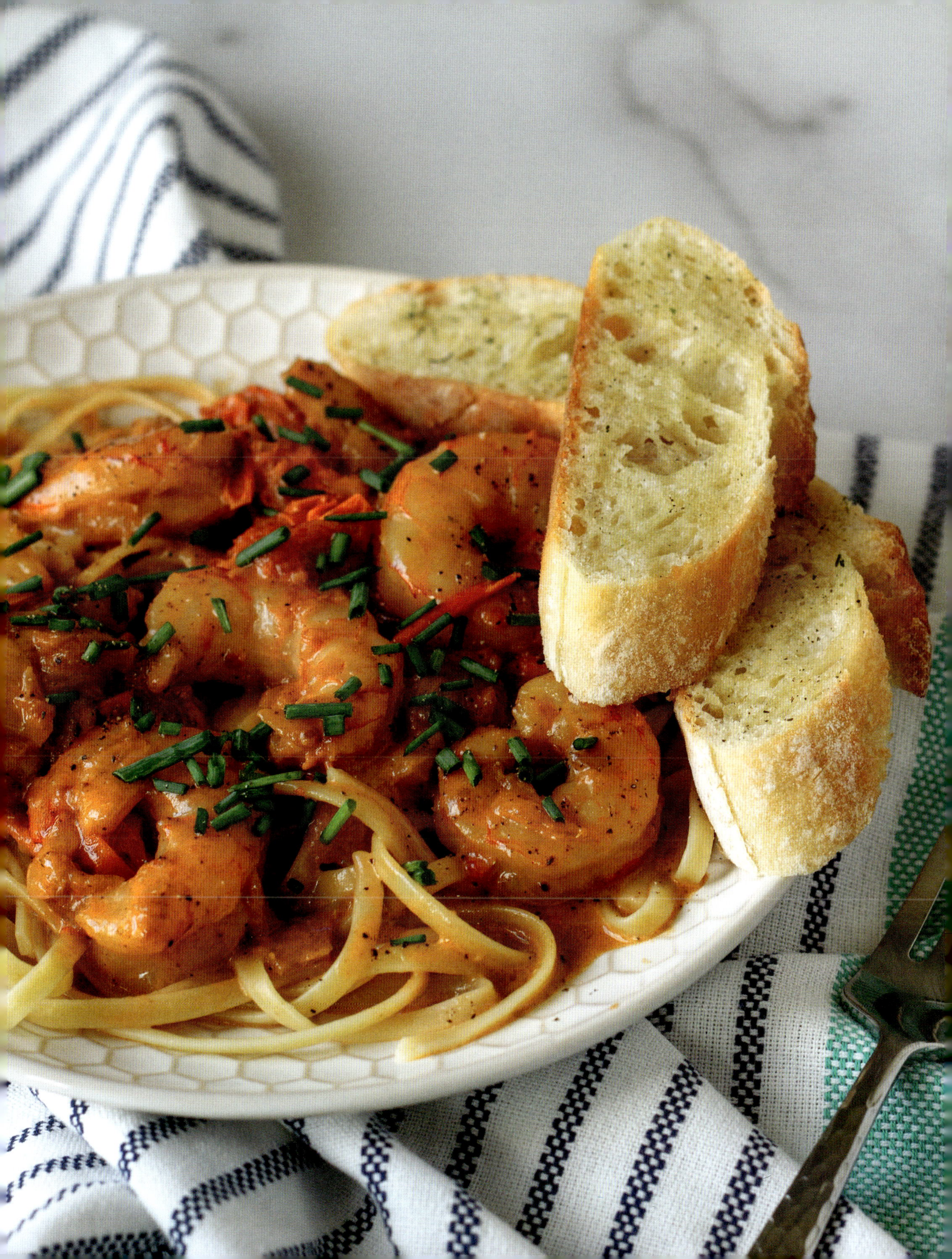

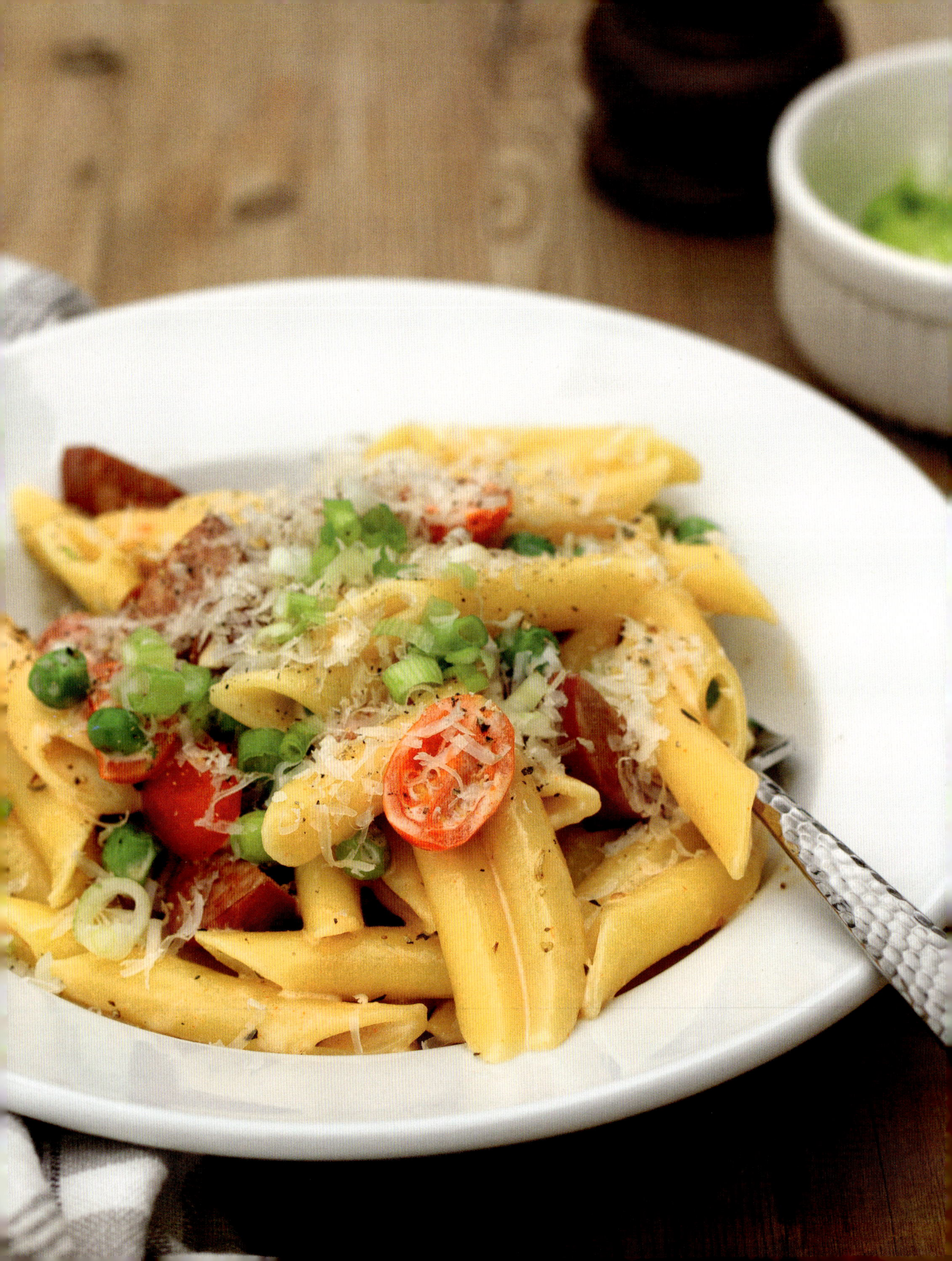

Cajun Alfredo Pasta with Kielbasa

My mom found a version of this recipe online many years ago, and everyone who lived at home at the time loved it. As one does with great new recipe discoveries, my mom shared it with the rest of us, and it quickly became a go-to dinner for my whole family. The creamy Parmesan sauce and smoky kielbasa add great flavor to this easy pasta favorite. This is my sister's version, full of juicy tomatoes and sweet peas, and topped with fresh, savory green onions. We love it served with French bread from the grocery store bakery or homemade cornbread.

Prep: 10 minutes | Cook: 25 minutes | Total: 25 minutes | Serves 6

12 ounces dried penne pasta (or any medium shape you like)

1 (12-ounce) package kielbasa or smoked sausage, cut into ½-inch slices and then halved (so they look like half circles)

1 cup heavy cream

1 cup half-and-half

2 teaspoons Cajun seasoning

1 cup grape tomatoes, halved lengthwise

1 cup frozen peas

½ cup freshly shredded Parmesan cheese, plus more for topping

Kosher salt

Freshly ground black pepper

4 green onions, white and light green parts only, minced, for serving

1. Put a large pot of salted water on high heat, bring to a boil, and cook the pasta according to the package directions. When cooked, drain and set aside.

2. While you are waiting for the water to boil and for the pasta to cook, sauté the kielbasa in a large, deep skillet over medium heat until golden brown, 5 minutes.

3. Add the heavy cream, half-and-half, and Cajun seasoning to the kielbasa. Turn the heat up to high and bring the sauce to a boil, then reduce the heat enough to keep the sauce at a simmer. Cook for 3 to 4 minutes.

4. Add the grape tomatoes and peas and continue simmering for 3 more minutes, until the peas are heated through.

5. Remove the sauce from the heat and stir in the Parmesan cheese. Add the cooked, drained pasta. Add salt and pepper to taste. Serve topped with green onions and more Parmesan.

SHORTCUTS & NOTES

- The longest step of this recipe is the first. I put the water on to boil and then slice the kielbasa, tomatoes, and green onions. The sauce should end up being done at just about the same time as the pasta finishes cooking.

Mac & Cheese with Toasted, Buttered Breadcrumbs

My mom got the original version of this recipe from an issue of *Yankee* magazine when my oldest was a baby. We had just moved from an apartment a few blocks from my parents' house to one in an entirely different state a plane ride away. My mom came to visit us often during those first few months of living far away, and on one of the trips that fall, she shared this recipe with me. I've changed lots of little things about it over the years, but it is still a favorite and our go-to mac & cheese recipe. And it always reminds me of my mom.

Prep: 5 minutes | Cook: 40 minutes | Total: 45 minutes | Serves 4 to 6

8 ounces small dried pasta (elbows, ditalini, small shells, etc.)

6 tablespoons butter, divided

½ cup panko breadcrumbs

4 tablespoons flour

2 cups milk

¼ teaspoon salt

¼ teaspoon freshly ground black pepper

¼ teaspoon garlic powder

⅛ teaspoon mustard powder

⅛ teaspoon paprika

2 cups shredded sharp cheddar cheese

1. Preheat the oven to 350°F. Lightly grease an 8-inch square baking dish with nonstick cooking spray.

2. Bring a large pot of salted water to a boil. Add the pasta and cook according to the package directions until al dente. Drain and set aside.

3. While the water is boiling and the pasta is cooking, melt 2 tablespoons of butter over medium heat in a medium saucepan. Add the breadcrumbs and cook until golden brown. Scoop the toasted breadcrumbs onto a small plate or bowl, wipe out the saucepan if necessary, and return to the heat.

4. Melt the remaining 4 tablespoons of butter. Whisk in the flour and cook for 1 minute. Add the milk, salt, pepper, garlic powder, mustard powder, and paprika, whisking constantly. Add the cheese, again whisking constantly. When the sauce has thickened and the cheese has melted, add the drained pasta and stir to combine.

5. Pour the mac & cheese into the prepared baking dish. Spread the toasted breadcrumbs evenly over the top and bake for 20 minutes. Serve and enjoy!

SHORTCUTS & NOTES

- This is a case where it sometimes pays to shred the cheese yourself. Freshly shredded cheese generally melts a little better and more smoothly than pre-shredded cheese. But I've done both with success!

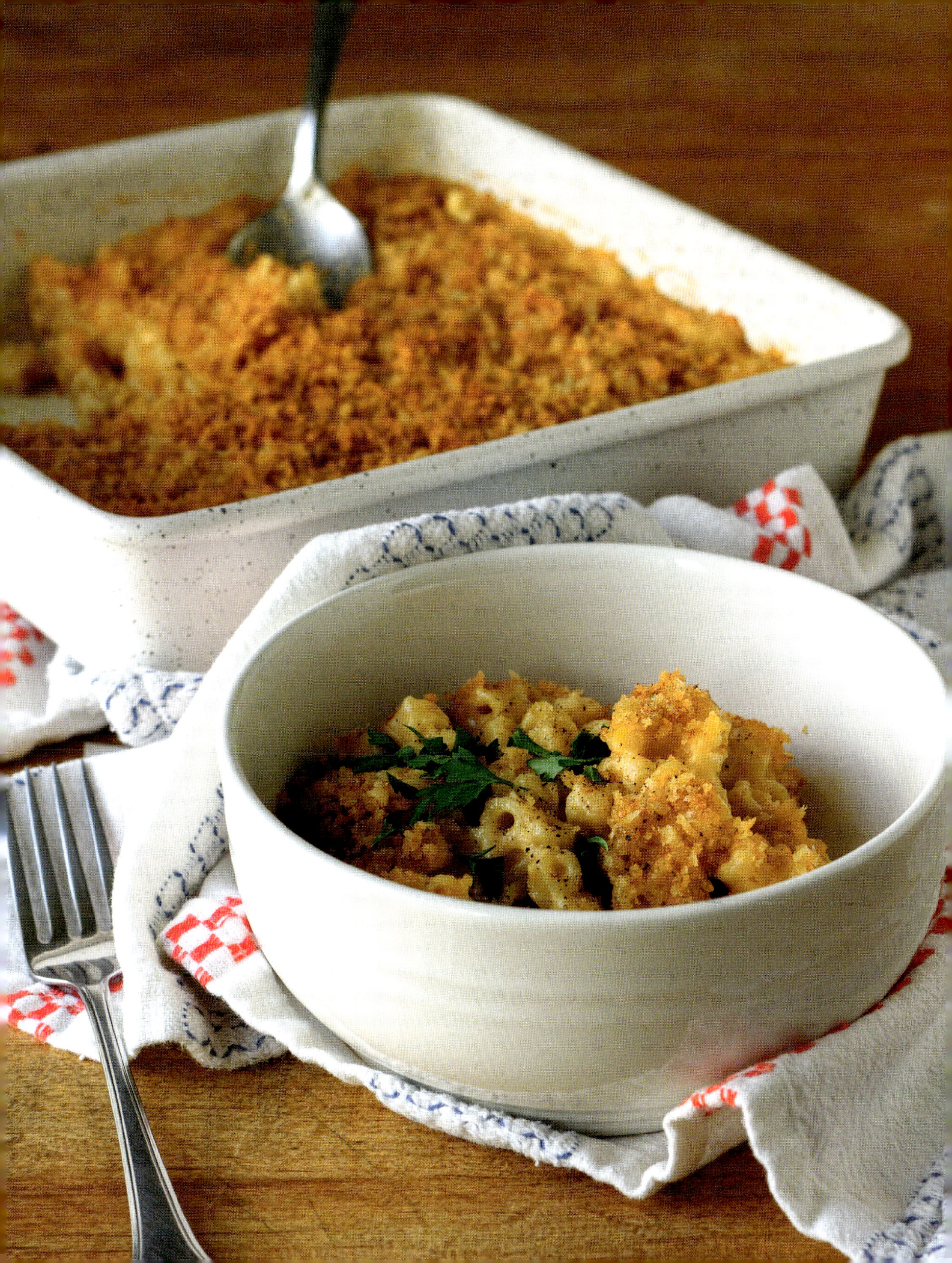

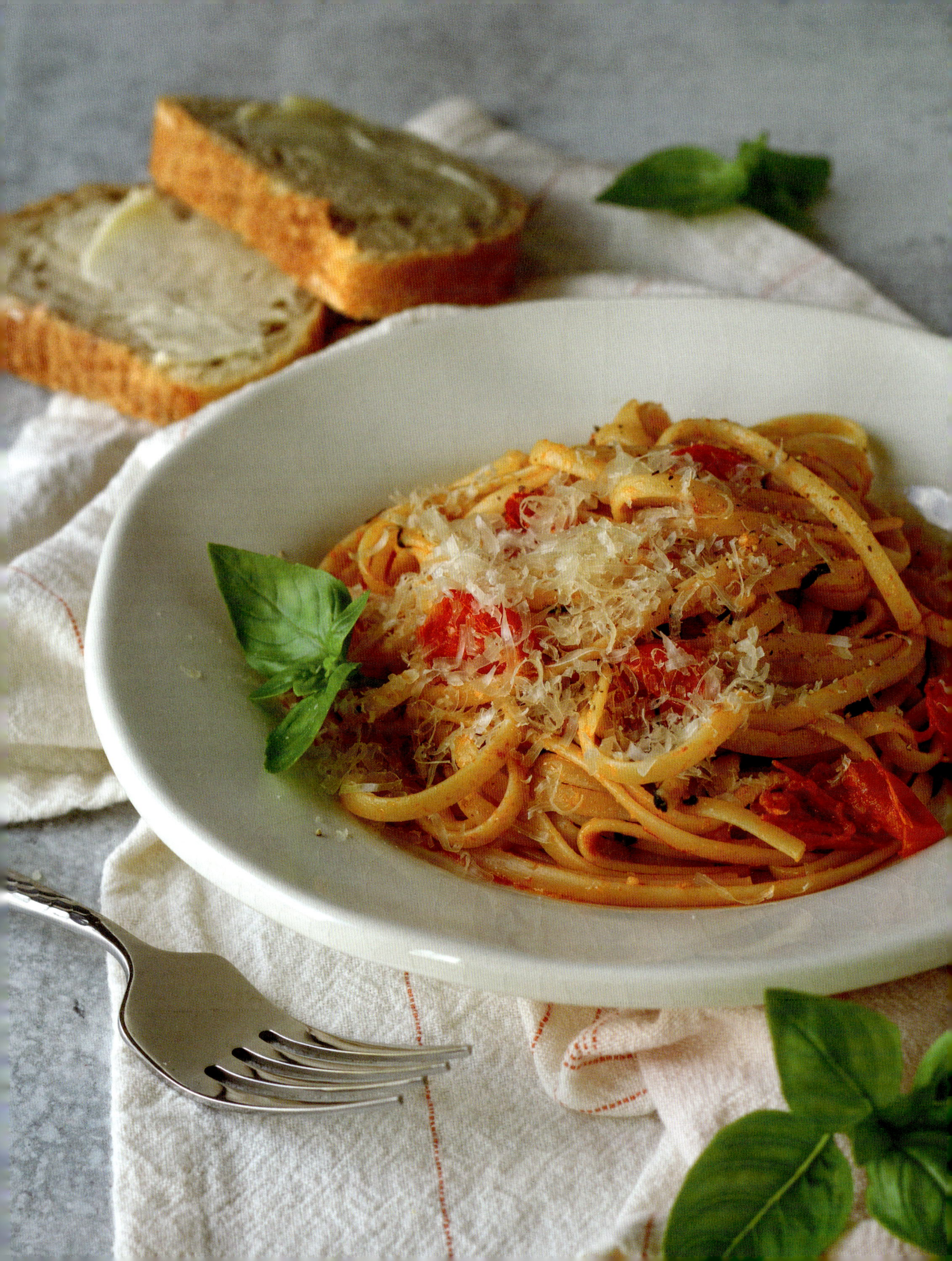

Stella Blues' Pasta

When my family was on vacation in Maui many years ago, we ate at a really tasty restaurant called Stella Blues. And then we ate there again a few days later! More than one family member ordered and loved their angel hair pasta with tomatoes, basil, and garlic, and as soon as we got home, my mom wrote down the recipe. We've all been making "Stella Blues" ever since!

Prep: 10 minutes | Cook: 20 minutes | Total: 30 minutes | Serves 6 to 8

1 pound dried angel hair or linguine

3 tablespoons extra-virgin olive oil or your favorite neutral cooking oil

8 teaspoons minced garlic, or 8 garlic cloves, minced

2 (10-ounce) packages grape tomatoes, halved

A pinch of kosher salt

Freshly ground black pepper

½ cup basil leaves, very thinly sliced, plus more for garnish

1 tablespoon butter

Fresh Parmesan cheese, for topping

1. Bring a large pot of salted water to a boil. Cook the pasta according to package directions until al dente. Drain, reserving 1 cup of pasta water. Set noodles and pasta water aside.

2. In a large skillet, heat the olive oil over low heat. Add the minced garlic and sauté until fragrant, sizzling, and just barely turning golden, about 5 minutes. Add the tomatoes, salt, and pepper and turn the heat up to medium. Sauté for 5 minutes, then add the basil. Continue cooking until the tomatoes are saucy, another 5 minutes.

3. Add the drained noodles and the butter, then toss to combine. If the pasta seems too dry, add a little bit of pasta water at a time until you get a lightly saucy consistency. I usually only add a couple of tablespoons. Serve immediately, topped with plenty of fresh Parmesan cheese, and basil leaves for garnish.

SHORTCUTS & NOTES

- Pre-minced garlic (frozen cubes, or a jar or squeeze tube)

Weeknight Beef Stroganoff

We have been making this recipe for beef stroganoff for two decades now, and it is one of the most popular dinners in our home. When people get to choose a homemade dinner for their birthday or to celebrate something special, the odds are good that they'll say "Beef stroganoff!" I've tinkered with it pretty extensively over the years to make it weeknight friendly, and it's both delicious and ready quickly. We love it, and I think you'll love it too!

Prep: 0 minutes | Cook: 40 minutes | Total: 40 minutes | Serves 8

2 pounds ground beef

6 tablespoons butter, divided

6 tablespoons all-purpose flour

½ teaspoon salt, plus more

¼ teaspoon garlic powder

Freshly ground black pepper

2 cups water

1 (10.5-ounce) can cream of mushroom soup

1 (10.5-ounce) can French onion soup

1 pound egg noodles

1 cup sour cream

Minced fresh parsley, for garnishing

1. In a large skillet or Dutch oven, crumble and cook the ground beef until brown, about 10 minutes. Drain any excess grease.

2. Add 4 tablespoons of butter to the pan and allow it to melt. Add the flour, salt, garlic powder, and black pepper. Stir until the flour and seasonings are completely mixed in and the flour is no longer visible. Slowly stir in the water. Stir in both cans of soup and bring to a simmer. Cover and cook for 15 minutes, stirring every few minutes to prevent sticking.

3. While the sauce is simmering, bring a large pot of salted water to a boil and cook the egg noodles according to the package directions. Drain the noodles, put them back in the pot, and stir in the remaining 2 tablespoons of butter. Season lightly with salt and black pepper.

4. After the sauce has simmered for 15 minutes, add the sour cream and continue cooking just until heated through. Serve the sauce over the buttered egg noodles and garnish with parsley.

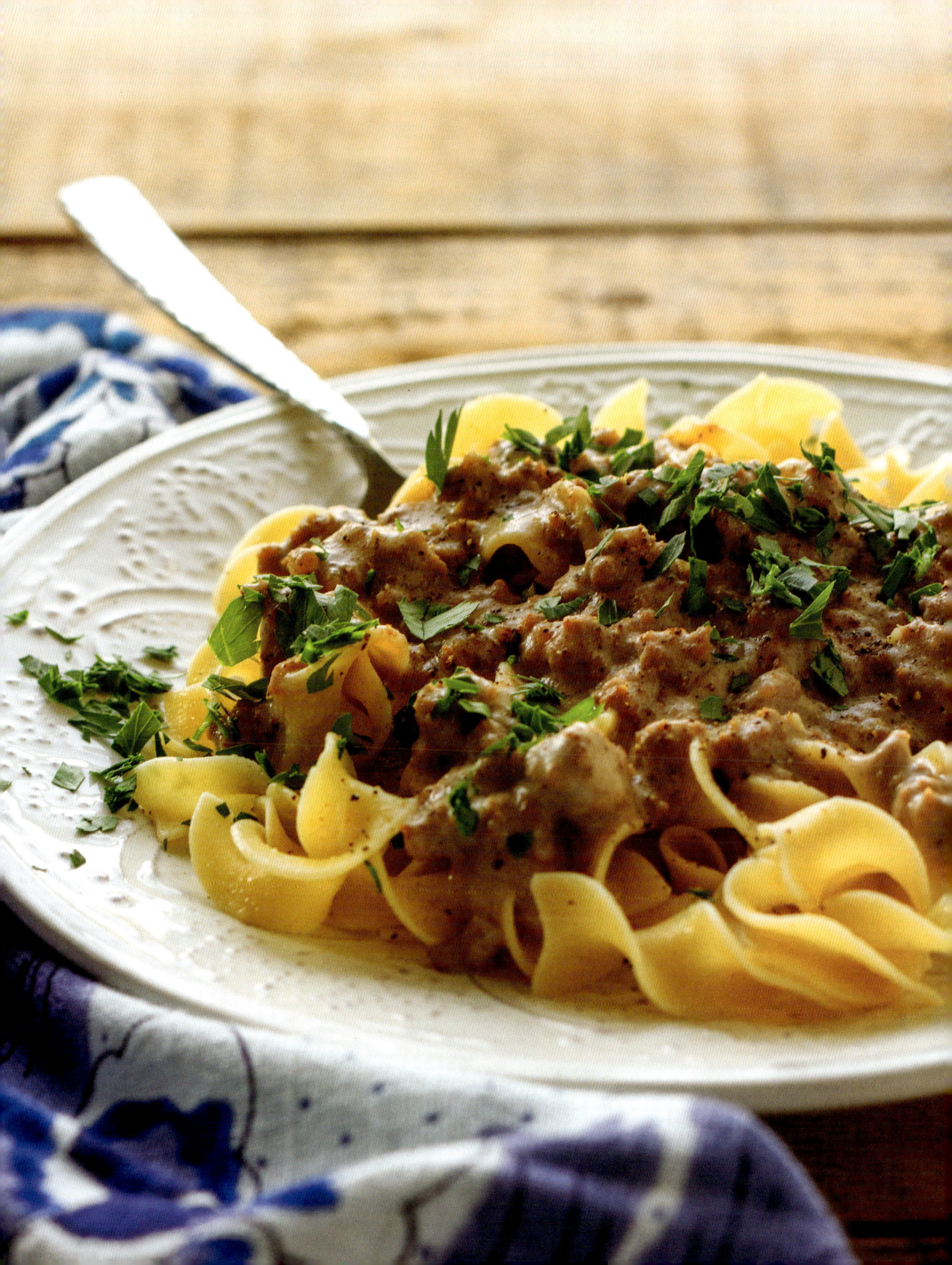

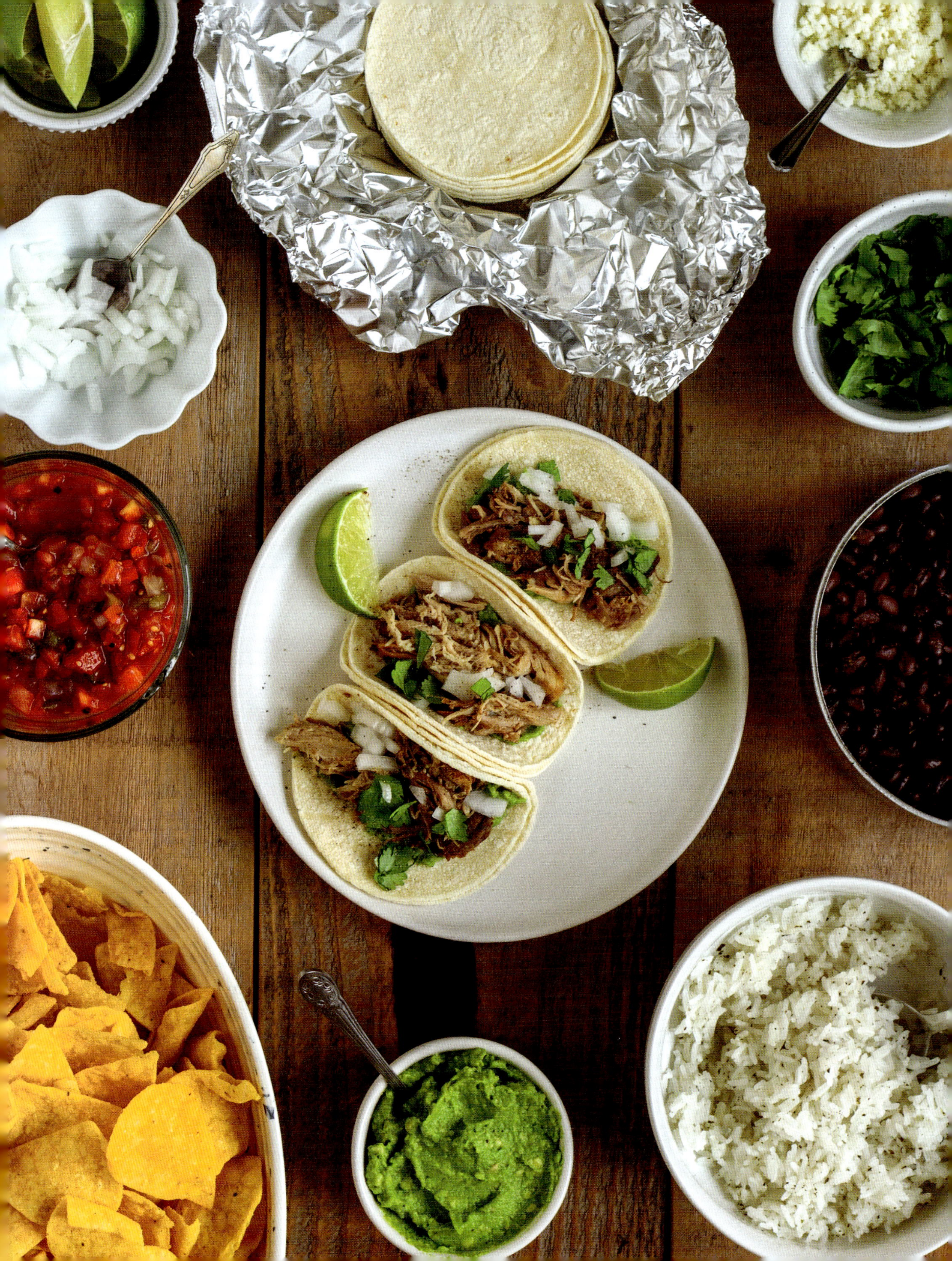

SLOW COOKER ENTRÉES

SLOW COOKER RECIPES are lifesavers on the busiest days. They usually have minimal prep and hours of completely hands-off cooking. They make dinner so easy that lots of things we tend to think of as weekend dinners, like pot roast, are suddenly made accessible to us no matter the day.

These dinners are a little more varied than some of the previous chapters, so I've created a couple of subgroups for serving suggestions.

Round these dinners out by serving them with:

A GREEN SALAD (PAGES 61–83)

FRENCH BREAD FROM THE GROCERY STORE BAKERY, CORNBREAD, MUFFINS, DINNER ROLLS, HAWAIIAN ROLLS, OR GARLIC BREAD

SAUTÉED, STEAMED, OR ROASTED VEGGIES (OUR FAVE GREEN BEANS ARE ON PAGE 144)

MASHED POTATOES, PASTA, OR STEAMED WHITE RICE

or

MEXICAN RESTAURANT-STYLE RICE OR LIME-CILANTRO RICE

BLACK BEANS (PAGE 154)

A GREEN SALAD (PAGES 61–83)

FRESH FRUIT

CHIPS AND GUACAMOLE (PAGE 154)

Easy Pot Roast

This is the pot roast I grew up eating on lots and lots of Sundays, either at home or at my nana's house. It's really easy to make (five minutes of prep) and turns out so good. The gravy it makes is my absolute favorite and tastes great on a side of mashed potatoes. We often eat the leftover pot roast in sandwiches, served over rice with gravy and shredded cheese, or even rolled up in flour tortillas and fried to make chimichangas. It's a very versatile recipe and couldn't be easier or more delicious.

Prep: 5 minutes | Cook: 8 hours | Total: 8 hours 5 minutes | Serves 10 to 12

4 to 5 pounds boneless chuck or round roast

2 (0.7-ounce) packets Good Seasons Italian Dressing mix

1½ pounds baby potatoes

1½ pounds baby carrots

Kosher salt

Freshly ground black pepper

Minced fresh parsley, for garnishing

1. Place the roast in a slow cooker. Sprinkle 1 packet of Italian dressing mix evenly over the meat. Add the baby potatoes and baby carrots, then sprinkle the second packet of Italian dressing mix evenly over the top.

2. Put the lid on the slow cooker and cook on low for 8 hours.

3. Remove the meat and slice or shred it, then return it to the slow cooker for serving. Add salt and pepper to taste, and serve with a sprinkle of parsley.

SHORTCUTS & NOTES

- If you use true baby carrots and the tiny, bite-size potatoes, you won't have to chop anything.

- You can substitute 2 packets of Lipton's Onion Soup mix for the Italian dressing mix in a pinch. It doesn't taste exactly the same, but it is also delicious and works well.

- If you'd like to make gravy out of the cooking liquid (it's so good it'll blow your mind!), pour the liquid into a medium saucepan and put it over medium heat. In a measuring cup, whisk 1 tablespoon cornstarch and 2 tablespoons cold water for every cup of cooking liquid. Whisk that mixture into the saucepan, then whisk gently while the gravy comes to a boil and thickens. Adjust the seasoning if necessary with salt and pepper.

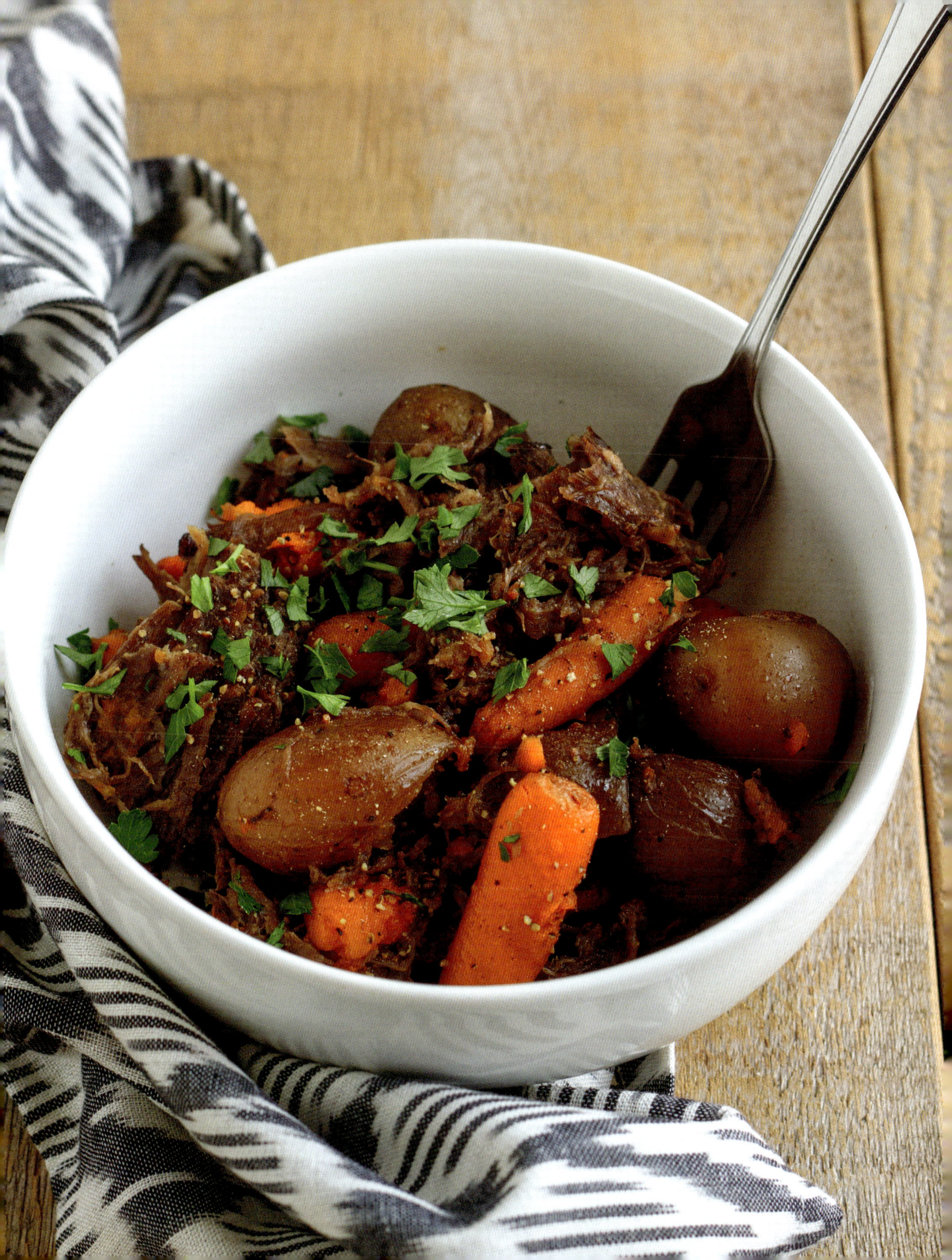

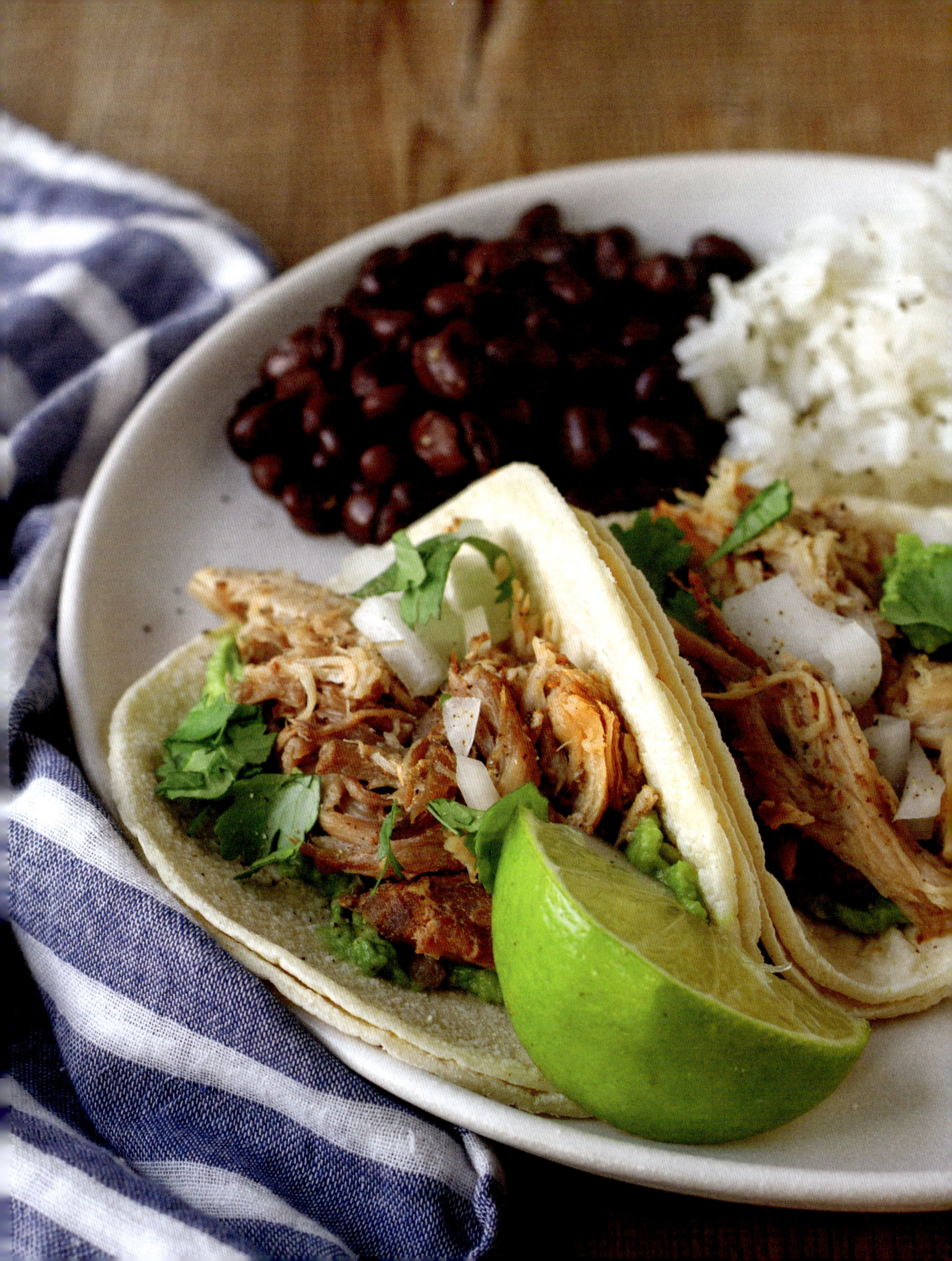

Carnitas

Of all the meat options in Mexican food, carnitas is hands-down my favorite. What do I want in my tacos? Carnitas. What kind of burrito bowl would I like? Carnitas. What's the best kind of fajita? Carnitas. So flavorful, so tender, so versatile, carnitas is hard to beat. And thanks to this slow cooker method, making carnitas is really easy, too.

Prep: 10 minutes | Cook: 8 hours | Total: 8 hours 10 minutes | Serves at least 8

1 large onion, halved

½ cup orange juice

¼ cup fresh lime juice (from 3 or 4 limes)

1 heaping tablespoon minced garlic, or 3 large garlic cloves, minced

1 tablespoon chili powder

1 tablespoon kosher salt

1 teaspoon ground cumin

1 teaspoon ground coriander

1 teaspoon dried oregano

Freshly ground black pepper

4 pounds boneless pork shoulder or pork butt

1. Place the onion halves in the bottom of a slow cooker. Pour the orange and lime juices on top.

2. In a medium bowl, combine the minced garlic, chili powder, kosher salt, cumin, coriander, oregano, and pepper.

3. Pat the pork dry with paper towels. Rub the spice mixture all over all sides of the pork. Place the pork in the slow cooker on top of the onions and citrus juices. Cover and cook on low for 8 hours.

4. Remove the onion halves from the slow cooker and discard them. Shred the pork with two forks, season with salt and pepper as necessary, and serve.

SHORTCUTS & NOTES

- Pre-minced garlic (frozen cubes, or a jar or squeeze tube)

- If you have a few extra minutes, just before serving, put the shredded carnitas on a rimmed baking sheet, ladle about ½ cup of cooking liquid over the top, and broil for a few minutes in the oven until the meat just begins to get crispy and brown on the edges. It's completely optional, but it gives the carnitas some great caramelization!

- For regular tacos, serve in corn or fajita-size flour tortillas with your favorite taco toppings: guacamole (page 154), salsa, pico de gallo, sour cream, shredded Monterey jack, or crumbled cotija cheese. Serve with beans (page 154) and rice.

- For street tacos, serve in tiny corn tortillas (warmed on a griddle) with chopped onion, chopped cilantro, and avocado slices or guacamole.

- Carnitas is also good in burritos, burrito bowls, enchiladas, huevos rancheros, and taco salad.

Smothered Pork Chops

When I was about ten, my grandma moved from another state to a house just a mile from ours. We started having dinner together every Sunday, sometimes at our house and sometimes at hers. Having dinner with Nana every Sunday taught us all how to do important things like set a proper table and bake a quick dessert. These easy smothered pork chops popped up often on the Sunday dinner menu in those days, and they're still a favorite in my family all these years later.

Prep: 5 minutes | Cook: 6 hours in the slow cooker plus 10 minutes | Total: 6 hours 15 minutes | Serves 8

1 tablespoon extra-virgin olive oil or your favorite neutral cooking oil

8 (1-inch-thick) pork chops (boneless or bone-in work equally well)

Kosher salt

Freshly ground black pepper

Seasoned salt

1 large onion, thinly sliced into rings

1 (10.5-ounce) can cream of chicken or cream of mushroom soup

Mashed potatoes, for serving

1. Drizzle the olive oil in the bottom of a large skillet over medium-high heat. Place as many of the pork chops as will fit in the skillet and sprinkle lightly with kosher salt and black pepper. Let cook for about 5 minutes, until browned on the bottom, then flip and repeat.

2. Place half of the seared pork chops in the bottom of a slow cooker. Sprinkle with seasoned salt and more black pepper, then top with half the onion slices. Repeat layers.

3. Spread the cream of chicken soup evenly over the top with a rubber spatula. Place the lid on the slow cooker and cook on low for 6 hours, until the pork chops are very tender. Add salt and pepper to taste and serve with mashed potatoes.

SHORTCUTS & NOTES

• Pre-sliced onions

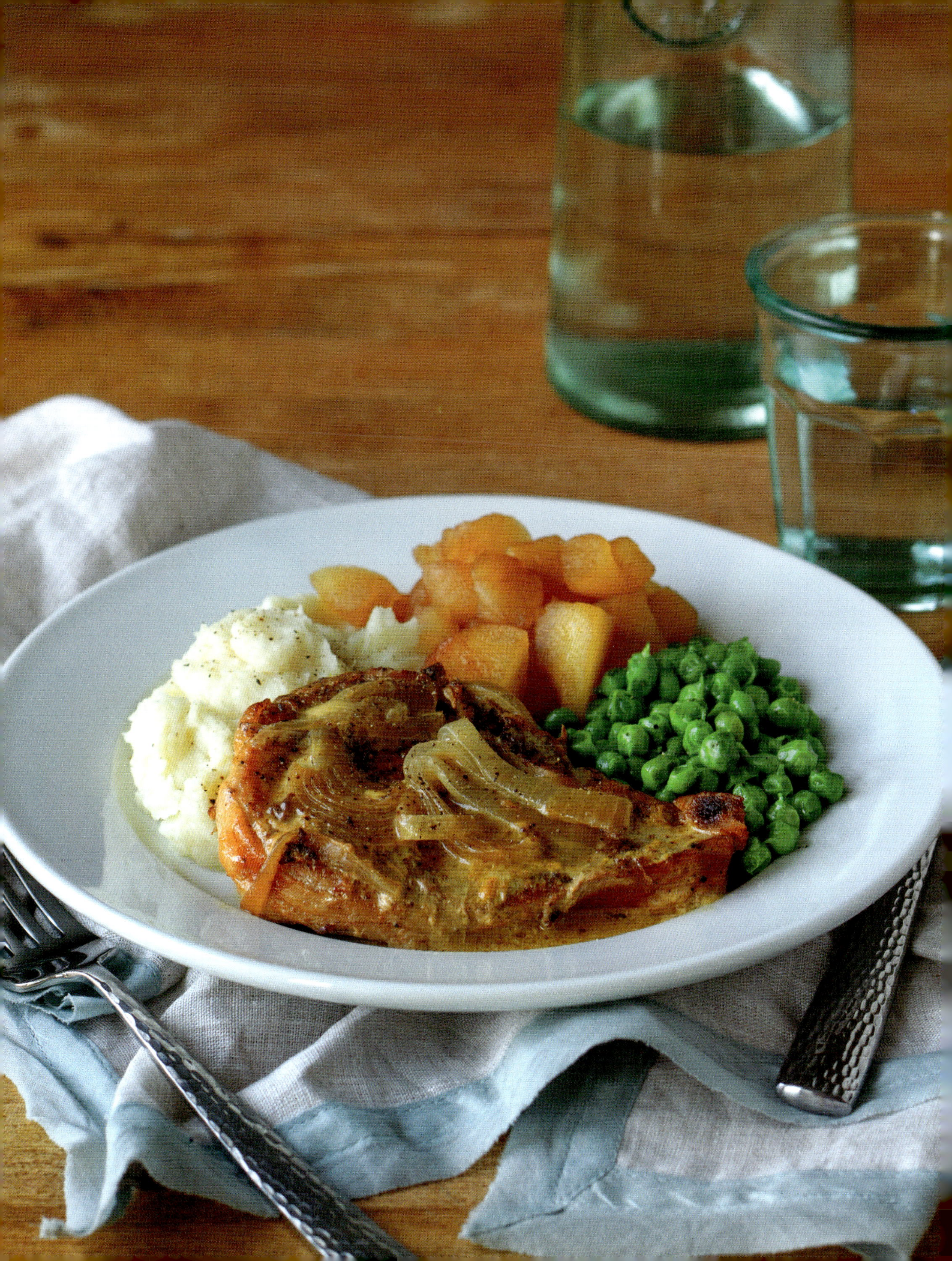

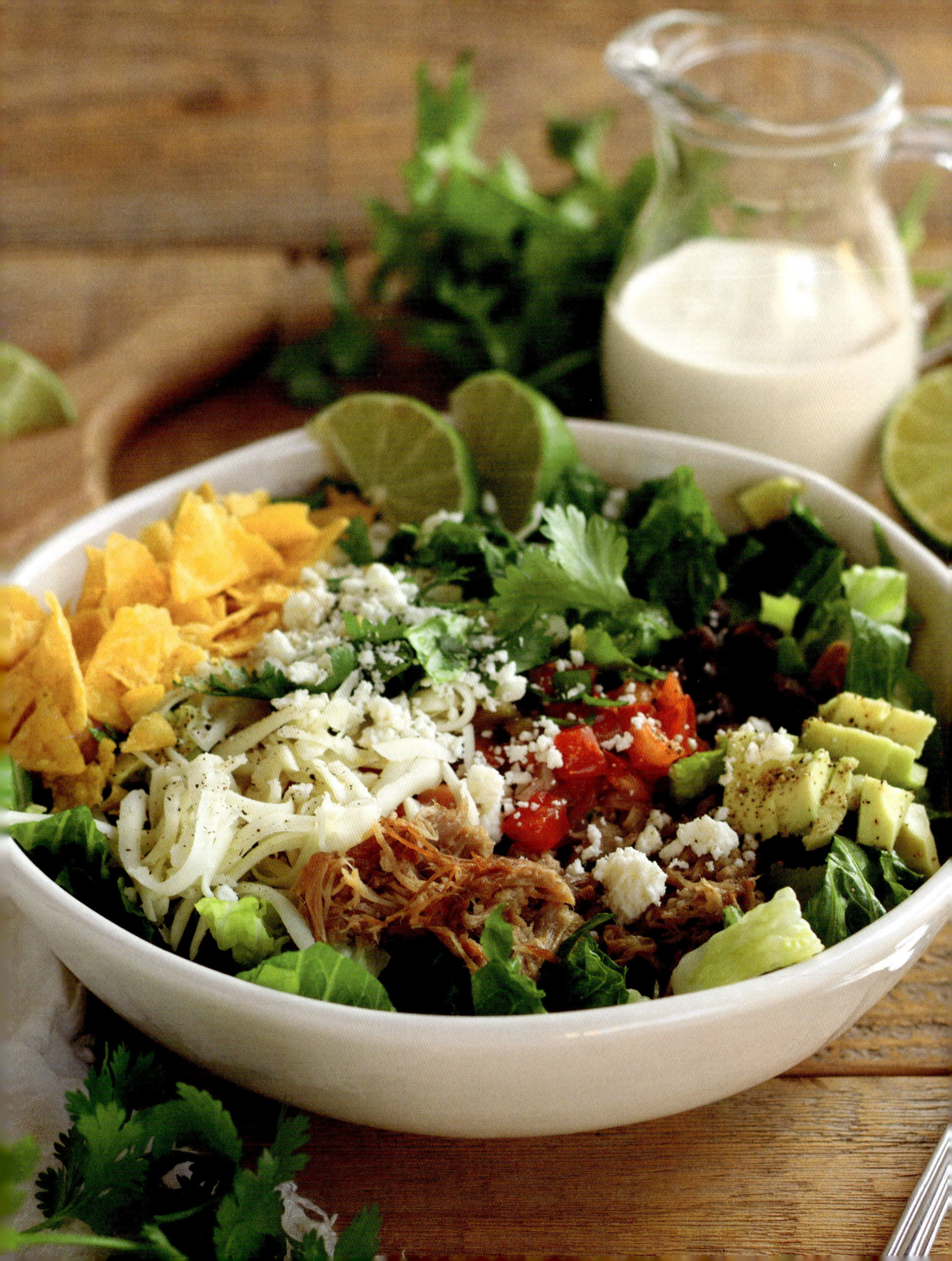

Sweet Shredded Pork

You might be wondering if a cookbook needs two different recipes for slow cooker shredded pork. The recipe for savory, citrusy carnitas is just a few pages before this one, after all. But I'm a big fan of both that recipe and this one for a sweeter, slightly smoky shredded pork. I love them both and refuse to choose! This one is a copycat for the sweet pork at a very well-known fresh Mex restaurant that I fell in love with in college and still can't get enough of. We like it in cheesy enchiladas, giant rice-and-bean-stuffed burritos, and fresh salads topped with a tangy cilantro buttermilk ranch.

Prep: 15 minutes | Cook: 8 hours | Total: 8 hours 15 minutes | Serves 8 to 10

3 pounds boneless pork butt or pork shoulder

1 cup brown sugar, divided

1 teaspoon kosher salt

1 teaspoon chili powder

½ teaspoon onion powder

4 or 5 good shakes Worcestershire sauce

Freshly ground black pepper

1 (10-ounce) can mild green chile enchilada sauce

½ cup apple juice

Juice of 1 lime

1. Put the pork in the bottom of a slow cooker.

2. In a small bowl, combine ½ cup of brown sugar, the salt, chili powder, onion powder, Worcestershire sauce, and black pepper to make a wet spice rub. Rub the mixture evenly over all sides of the pork.

3. Pour the enchilada sauce carefully over the pork and pour the apple juice around the pork but not on top.

4. Put the lid on the slow cooker and cook on low heat for 7½ hours.

5. Add the remaining ½ cup of brown sugar and continue cooking for another 30 minutes on low heat. Remove the meat from the slow cooker, shred it, and toss with the lime juice.

SHORTCUTS & NOTES

- We love this sweet pork in tacos, enchiladas, burritos, burrito bowls, taco salads, quesadillas, tostadas, huevos rancheros, and more. You can swap it into any of the recipes in this book that make use of Carnitas (page 135) or Taco Chicken (page 140).

Bonus Recipe! My sister makes an amazing salsa verde ranch dressing that is great on sweet pork salads. Prepare a buttermilk ranch packet from the grocery store according to the package directions, but reduce the amount of buttermilk to ¾ cup and add ¼ cup green salsa. Throw it in the blender with a handful of chopped cilantro, 1 teaspoon minced garlic, and a lot of freshly ground black pepper. Blend until smooth and refrigerate until needed.

Taco Chicken

Taco chicken deserves to win the weeknight dinner MVP award. It is one of the easiest recipes in my playbook (the prep time is listed as 5 minutes, but it's actually more like 2) and is incredibly versatile. We use taco chicken for soft tacos, crunchy tacos, burritos, taco salad, enchiladas, burrito bowls, nachos, and more. It's truly a gold medal recipe.

Prep: 5 minutes | Cook: 4 hours | Total: 4 hours 5 minutes | Serves 8

3 pounds boneless skinless chicken breasts or thighs, not frozen

16 ounces salsa of choice

1 (1-ounce) packet taco seasoning

1. Combine all ingredients in a slow cooker. Cover and cook on low for 4 hours. Shred the chicken with two forks and serve.

SHORTCUTS & NOTES

- Use red salsa for tomato-based taco chicken or salsa verde for a tangier tomatillo flavor. I honestly like them both equally well. And I use mild salsa because that's what my family likes, but use whatever level of spice you want.

Bonus Recipe! I know enchiladas should be easy to make, but I tried so many recipes that didn't work. And then I started following this easy method, and it's been nothing but delicious enchiladas ever since: (1) Get all of your ingredients and a 9 x 13-inch baking pan prepped, and build just one enchilada at a time. (2) Heat a very thin layer of a neutral cooking oil in the bottom of a skillet over low heat. Cook a corn tortilla just until it has softened and become pliant. (3) Set the tortilla on your work surface and sprinkle about 1 tablespoon of shredded cheese down the center of the tortilla, followed by 2 to 3 tablespoons of chicken. (4) Roll up the enchilada and place it seam-side down against one edge of the baking pan. (5) Repeat until you've assembled as many enchiladas as you want. I aim for 2 per person. (6) Pour 2 (10-ounce) cans of red or green enchilada sauce evenly over the top of the enchiladas, top with 2 cups of shredded cheese, cover with foil, and bake at 350°F until the cheese is melted and everything is hot and bubbly, about 20 minutes. Serve with sour cream, guacamole (page 154), minced green onions, cilantro, etc.

Bonus Recipe! Don't want to buy taco seasoning at the store? Make your own! In a pint jar with a tight-fitting lid, combine ½ cup plus 2 tablespoons chili powder; 2½ teaspoons garlic powder; 2½ teaspoons onion powder; 2½ teaspoons red pepper flakes (full disclosure: I skip this!); 2½ teaspoons dried oregano leaves; 5 teaspoons of paprika; ¼ cup plus 1 tablespoon ground cumin; 1½ tablespoons salt; and 3 tablespoons plus 1 teaspoon freshly ground black pepper. Shake to combine. 2 tablespoons of this mixture = 1 (1-ounce) packet of taco seasoning. Thanks to my cousin's wife, Sarah, for this recipe!

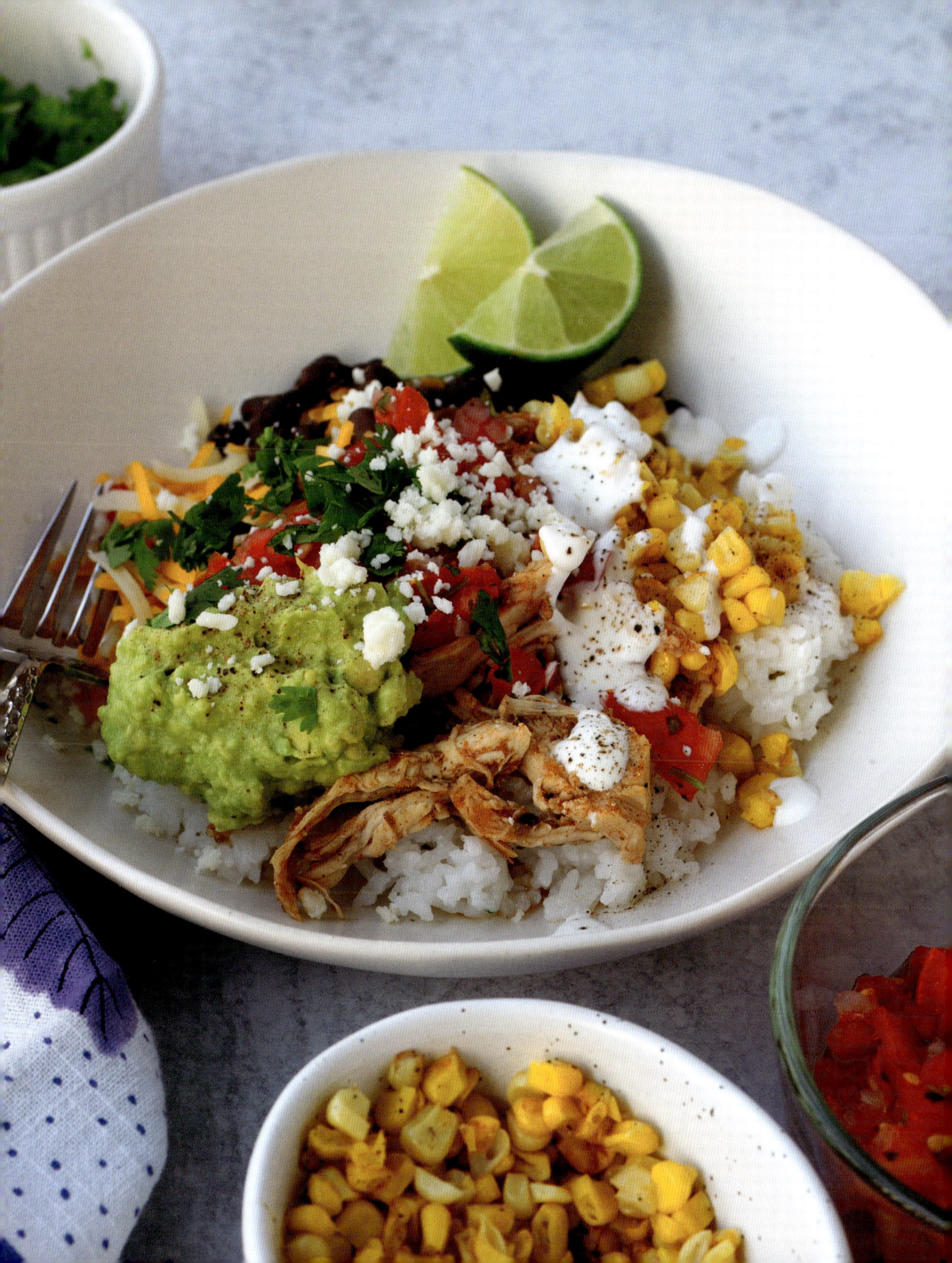

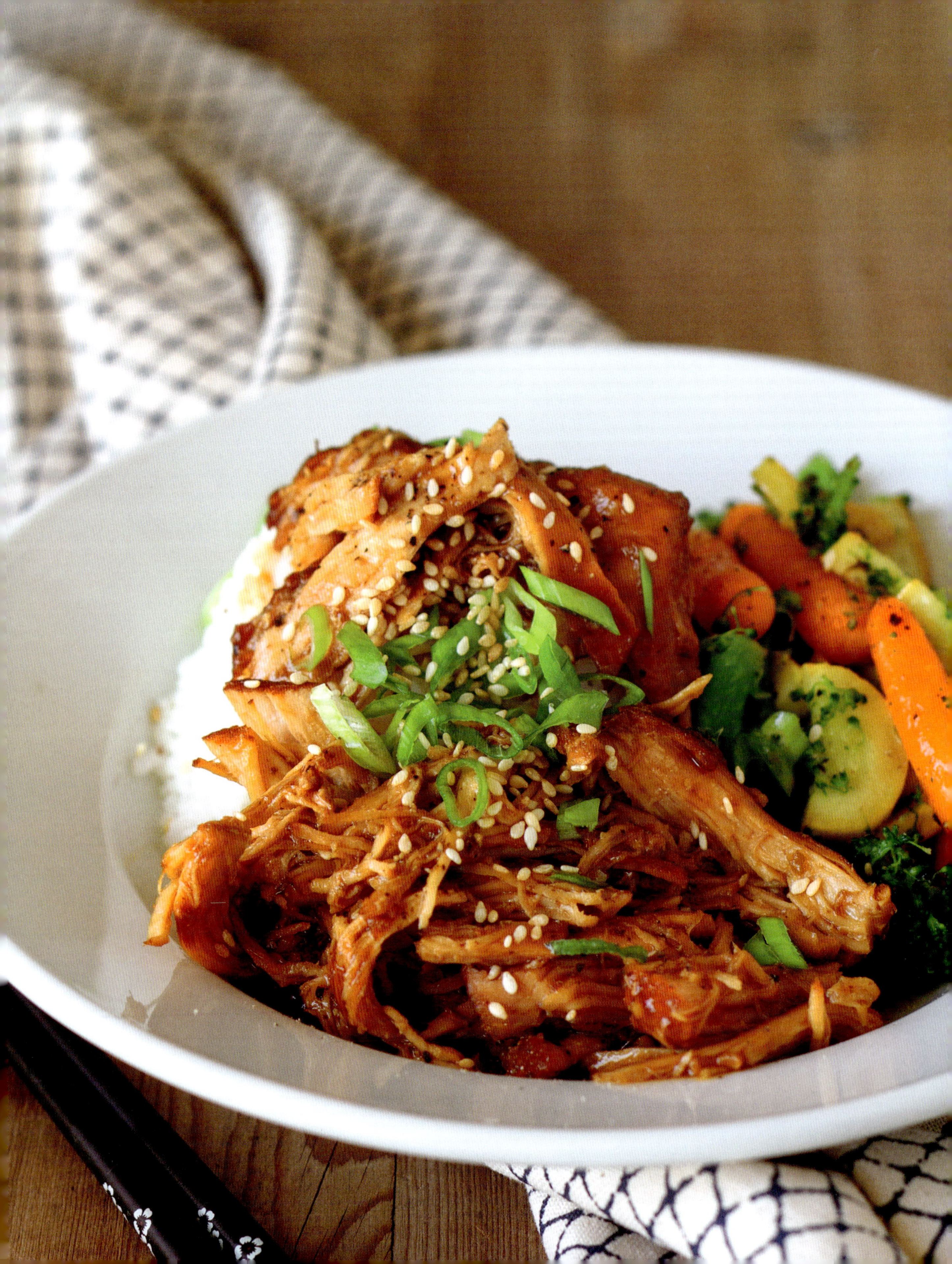

Teriyaki Chicken

One of our children loves teriyaki chicken and rice more than almost anything in the world, so this recipe has been a popular one in our family for years and years. Like all good slow cooker recipes, the amount of prep work you have to do is minimal—just mix the sauce and chop the green onions. You can mince or grate fresh ginger and garlic, or you can use the little frozen cubes of ginger and garlic from the grocery store, which are high on my list of favorite kitchen shortcuts. Cook a batch of white rice and make some steamed or stir-fried veggies while the chicken finishes cooking, and you'll have a very happy household come dinner time.

Prep: 10 minutes | Cook: 4 hours | Total: 4 hours 10 minutes | Serves 8

2½ to 3 pounds boneless, skinless chicken thighs or breasts, not frozen

¾ cup low-sodium soy sauce

¾ cup granulated sugar

4 tablespoons apple cider vinegar

1 tablespoon grated fresh ginger

2 teaspoons toasted sesame oil

1½ teaspoons minced garlic, or 1 to 2 garlic cloves, minced

Freshly ground black pepper

1 bunch green onions thinly sliced, white/light green parts separated from darker green parts

¼ cup cold water

2 tablespoons cornstarch

4 cups cooked white rice, for serving

Sesame seeds, for garnishing

1. Place the chicken in the bottom of a slow cooker.

2. In a medium bowl, combine the soy sauce, sugar, vinegar, ginger, sesame oil, and minced garlic. Whisk to combine, then pour over the chicken.

3. Season with freshly ground black pepper and top with the white and light green parts of the green onions.

4. Put the lid on the slow cooker and cook for 4 hours on low.

5. When the slow cooker has about 30 minutes left on the timer, make a cornstarch slurry to thicken the sauce. In a small bowl, whisk the cold water and cornstarch until smooth. Pour the slurry into the slow cooker, stir gently, and replace the lid. Continue cooking until the time is up.

6. Shred the chicken in the slow cooker with two forks. Serve over white rice, topped with the reserved darker green parts of the green onions and sesame seeds.

SHORTCUTS & NOTES

- Pre-minced ginger and garlic (frozen cubes, or a jar or squeeze tube)

Mom's Garlic Butter Chicken

My mom invented this recipe when I was growing up. It became an instant family favorite and remains a family favorite still. My kids love it, my siblings and their kids love it—everyone loves it! It's creamy, rich, and full of flavor. Throw some rice in the rice cooker, grab a green salad and some rolls from the grocery store, and you've got an easy, crowd-pleasing, comfort food hit on your hands.

Prep: 10 minutes | Cook: 4 hours | Total: 4 hours 10 minutes | Serves 8

½ cup (1 stick) butter

3 tablespoons minced garlic, or 9 garlic cloves, minced

1 (10.5-ounce) can cream of chicken soup

3 pounds boneless skinless chicken breasts, not frozen

Salt

Freshly ground black pepper

¼ cup minced fresh parsley

Cooked white rice, for serving

1. In a small saucepan over low heat, melt the butter. Add the garlic and cream of chicken soup and whisk until smooth.

2. Place the chicken breasts in the bottom of a slow cooker. Season with salt and pepper. Pour the garlic butter sauce over the chicken, cover, and cook on low for 4 hours, until the chicken is cooked through and very tender.

3. Shred the chicken with two forks or roughly chop it up with a wooden spoon. Sprinkle the parsley over the top. Serve over cooked white rice.

SHORTCUTS & NOTES

- Pre-minced garlic (frozen cubes, or a jar or squeeze tube)

Bonus Recipe! One of our favorite ways to cook green beans is in the oven with lots of garlic. Snap the ends off fresh green beans, toss with extra-virgin olive oil and 1 or 2 cloves of minced fresh garlic, and season with kosher salt, garlic salt, and freshly ground black pepper. Toss with your hands or a pair of tongs until evenly coated. Roast on a rimmed baking sheet in a 425°F oven until tender, about 15 minutes. My brother and sister-in-law make these green beans all the time and we all love them. The people and the green beans!

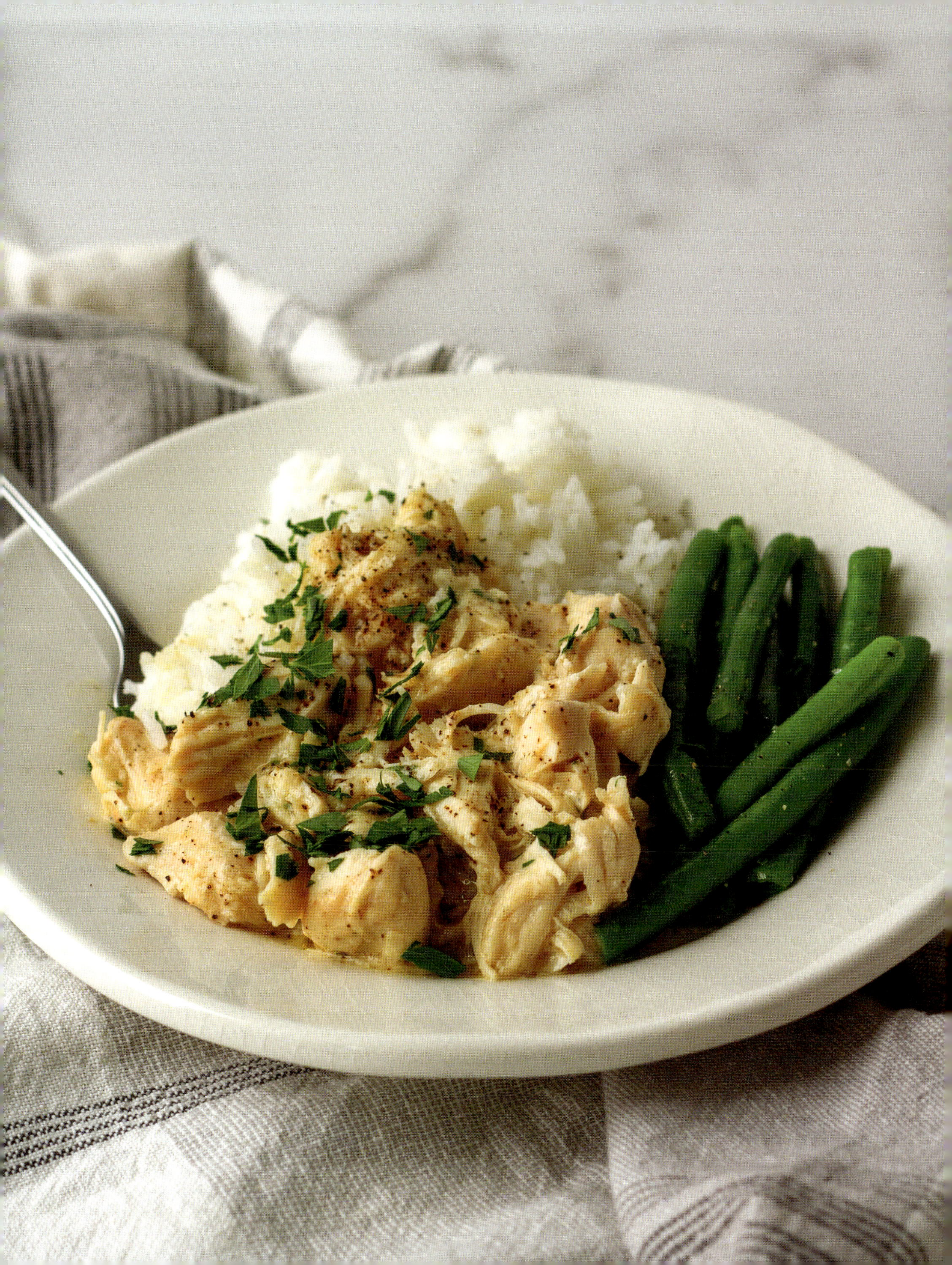

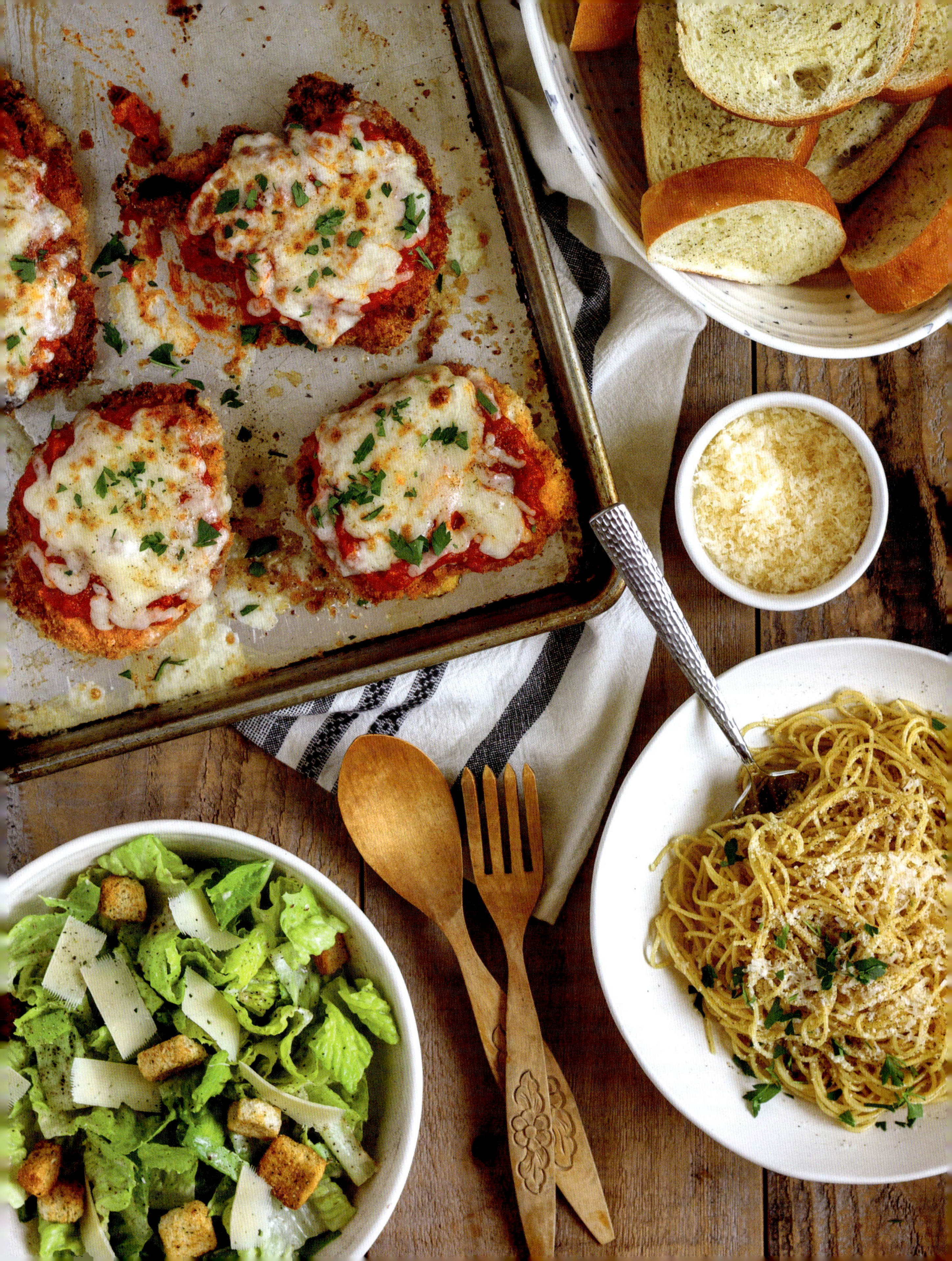

SKILLETS, SHEET PANS & BAKES

AFTER GETTING THROUGH all the other recipe categories for this book (Breakfast for Dinner, Soups, Salads, Sandwiches, Pastas, and Slow Cooker Entrées), these delicious entrées remained, so they're all lumped together in a sort of grab-bag category. We've got some stovetop skillet dinners, some oven bakes, and some recipes that use both the stove and the oven. They have a few important things in common that are absolute requirements for all weeknight dinners: They taste great, and they're ready quickly.

These dinners are a little more varied than some of the previous chapters, so I've created a couple of subgroups for serving suggestions.

Round these dinners out by serving them with:

A GREEN SALAD (PAGES 61–83)

FRENCH BREAD FROM THE GROCERY STORE BAKERY, CORNBREAD, MUFFINS, DINNER ROLLS, HAWAIIAN ROLLS, OR GARLIC BREAD

SAUTÉED, STEAMED, OR ROASTED VEGGIES (OUR FAVE GREEN BEANS ARE ON PAGE 144)

MASHED POTATOES, PASTA, OR STEAMED WHITE RICE

or

MEXICAN RESTAURANT-STYLE RICE OR LIME-CILANTRO RICE

BLACK BEANS (PAGE 154)

A GREEN SALAD (PAGES 61–83)

FRESH FRUIT

CHIPS AND GUACAMOLE (PAGE 154)

Bean & Cheese Tostadas

I took summer school PE one year in high school so that I could have more space in my schedule for electives. A girl who lived in my neighborhood had signed up for the class, too, so we carpooled. At least once a week, on a day when her mom was in charge of picking us up, she'd take us through the Taco Bell drive through for tostadas. Always tostadas, never anything else. And man, oh man, did I love those tostadas! As good as they were, these super simple homemade tostadas are a million times better. They are flavorful, filling, and easy to customize, and they make a fantastic meatless dinner.

Prep: 10 minutes | Cook: 20 minutes | Total: 30 minutes | Makes 16 tostadas, which feeds 6 to 8 people

2 (16-ounce) cans vegetarian or regular refried beans

¼ cup smooth salsa

½ cup shredded cheddar cheese

Oil, for frying

16 corn tortillas

Kosher salt

Shredded lettuce, minced fresh cilantro, your favorite shredded or crumbled cheese, diced tomatoes, taco sauce or hot sauce, guacamole (page 154) or diced avocado, sour cream, cilantro-lime crema (see bonus recipe on page 149), for topping

1. In a medium saucepan, combine the beans, salsa, and cheddar over medium heat. Cook until heated through, about 10 minutes, then cover and set aside.

2. Line a rimmed baking sheet with paper towels.

3. Pour an inch of oil in a small skillet over medium-low heat. When the oil is hot, fry the tortillas one at a time for 30 to 45 seconds on each side, until golden and crispy. (I test the temperature of the oil by dipping one edge of a tortilla in. If it bubbles right away, it's hot enough to start. If you don't see any tiny bubbles, let the oil get a little hotter first.) You might have to flip the tortillas a few times and cook them for a few minutes overall depending on how hot your oil is. Put the fried tortillas on the paper-towel-lined baking sheet to drain and cool, and sprinkle each with a pinch of kosher salt.

4. Top the fried tortillas with the bean mixture and any other toppings you like.

SHORTCUTS & NOTES

- Pre-shredded cheese

- We love these for Meatless Monday, but for a heartier meal, you can certainly add meat to the list of toppings. Seasoned ground beef, Taco Chicken (page 140), Carnitas (page 135), and Sweet Shredded Pork (page 139) are all great additions.

Bonus Recipe! Cilantro-lime crema is delicious, and once you make it, you'll want to put it on everything! Combine the following in a food processor or blender, and blend until smooth: ½ cup sour cream, 2 tablespoons mayonnaise, 2 tablespoons buttermilk, ¼ cup coarsely chopped cilantro, ¼ teaspoon minced garlic, 2 tablespoons crumbled cotija, the zest and juice of 1 small lime, and salt and pepper to taste.

SKILLETS, SHEET PANS & BAKES

Cornbread-Topped Tex-Mex Bake

A couple of years after my husband and I got married, I decided to put together a cookbook of my husband's family's favorite recipes. I had everyone submit recipes, and then I typed them up and had them spiral bound. It is still, nearly 20 years later, one of the most used cookbooks in my extensive cookbook collection, and I hear the same thing from one of my in-laws at least once a year. This hearty Tex-Mex casserole is based on a recipe my mother in-law submitted. We love how delicious and cozy it is.

Prep: 5 minutes | Cook: 50 minutes | Total: 55 minutes | Serves 8

FOR THE FILLING

1 pound ground beef

1 cup chopped onion

2 teaspoons minced garlic, or 2 garlic cloves, minced

1 teaspoon dried oregano

1 teaspoon ground cumin

1 (15.25-ounce) can corn, drained

1 (4-ounce) can chopped green chiles

1 (6.5-ounce) can sliced black olives, drained

1 (14.5-ounce) can diced tomatoes, drained

1 (15-ounce) can black or pinto beans, drained and rinsed

2 cups shredded cheddar cheese, divided

Garlic salt

Freshly ground black pepper

FOR THE CORNBREAD TOPPING

1 (8.5-ounce) box Jiffy corn muffin mix

1 (14.75-ounce) can creamed corn

½ cup sour cream

1 egg

FOR SERVING

Shredded lettuce, sour cream, minced green onions, minced fresh cilantro, pico de gallo, sliced avocado, or guacamole (page 154)

1. Preheat the oven to 375°F.

2. To make the filling, in a large, deep oven-safe skillet or Dutch oven, brown and crumble the ground beef and the chopped onion over medium heat, about 10 minutes. Drain off any excess grease. Add the garlic and cook for 2 minutes. Add the oregano, cumin, corn, green chiles, olives, tomatoes, beans, and 1 cup of the shredded cheese. Add the garlic salt and black pepper to taste.

3. Sprinkle the remaining 1 cup of shredded cheese evenly over the top.

4. To make the cornbread topping, in a medium bowl, combine the corn muffin mix, creamed corn, sour cream, and egg until well combined. Spread the cornbread mixture evenly over the cheese layer of the casserole, spreading it all the way to the edges of the pan.

5. Bake for 40 minutes, until the filling is bubbling on the sides and the cornbread is very golden on top.

6. Serve with toppings of choice.

SHORTCUTS & NOTES

- Pre-chopped onions

- Pre-minced garlic (frozen cubes, or a jar or squeeze tube)

- Pre-shredded cheddar cheese

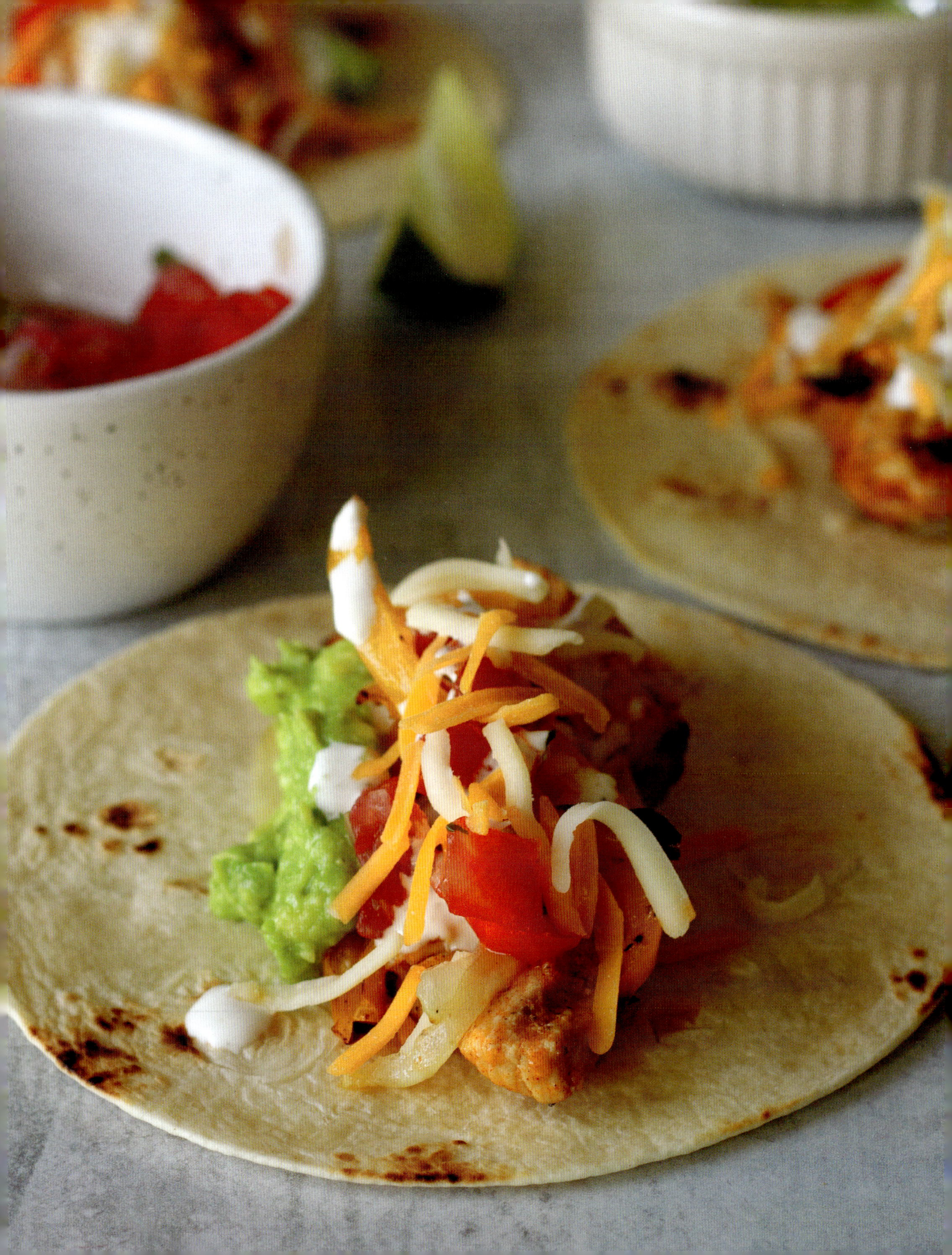

Sheet Pan Honey-Lime Chicken Fajitas

I love this recipe so much! Fajitas are such a treat to get at a restaurant, but I've found that most at-home recipes bear little if any resemblance to the sizzling restaurant favorites. A lot of times a slow cooker is involved, and while I'm a big fan of slow cookers, that's just not how I want my fajitas made! Using a baking sheet to roast the flavorful, marinated chicken in the oven and squeezing some fresh lime juice on at the end really makes these fajitas shine.

Prep: 15 minutes | Cook: 30 minutes | Total: 45 minutes | Serves 4

Zest and juice of 1 lime, plus lime wedges for serving

2 tablespoons extra-virgin olive oil or your favorite neutral cooking oil, plus more for drizzling

1 tablespoon honey

1 teaspoon minced garlic, or 1 garlic clove, minced

1 teaspoon kosher salt, plus more for seasoning

Freshly ground black pepper

½ teaspoon chili powder

½ teaspoon ground cumin

½ teaspoon dried oregano

½ teaspoon ground coriander

½ teaspoon smoked paprika

1¼ pounds boneless skinless chicken breasts, cut into strips

2 bell peppers, whatever color you like, seeded and thinly sliced

1 large onion, thinly sliced

Flour tortillas

Shredded cheese, guacamole (see page 154), pico de gallo, sour cream, etc., for topping

1. Preheat the oven to 450°F and line a rimmed baking sheet with foil for easy cleanup (you can skip this part if you just want to wash the pan).

2. In a medium bowl, whisk together the lime zest and juice, olive oil, honey, garlic, kosher salt, black pepper, chili powder, cumin, oregano, coriander, and smoked paprika. Add the chicken to the bowl, tossing gently to coat it with marinade. Set the chicken aside while you prepare the veggies.

3. Spread the peppers and onions out in a single layer on the prepared baking sheet. Drizzle lightly with olive oil and season with a pinch of kosher salt and black pepper. Roast the veggies in the oven for 10 minutes while the chicken marinates.

continued

4. After the veggies have been roasting for 10 minutes, add the chicken to the pan, season with a pinch of kosher salt and black pepper, and continue roasting for 15 to 17 more minutes, until the chicken is cooked through.

5. Squeeze a wedge or two of lime over the pan, toss, and serve immediately in warm flour tortillas with desired toppings.

SHORTCUTS & NOTES

- Pre-minced garlic (frozen cubes, or a jar or squeeze tube)

- Pre-sliced peppers and onions

- Buy chicken breasts that are already cut into strips. It's usually labeled as stir-fry chicken or something similar.

- Pre-shredded cheese (for topping)

- Store-bought guacamole (or make the following bonus recipe)

- Store-bought pico de gallo

- You can easily double this recipe. Move your oven racks so that one is just above center and one is just below. Put all of the veggies on one baking sheet on the top rack. Put all of the chicken on a second foil-covered baking sheet. When it's time for the chicken to go into the oven, put it on the bottom oven rack for 5 minutes, then switch the chicken to the top rack and the veggies to the bottom rack, and continue cooking until the chicken is cooked through and the veggies are tender, 10 to 12 more minutes.

Bonus Recipe! Our very favorite busy-night guacamole is simple and delicious. It only takes about 5 minutes to make. Mash avocados with a fork or one of those squiggly potato mashers. Add garlic salt, pepper, and lime juice to taste. So easy and so good!

Bonus Recipe! This is my favorite way to prepare black beans, and we have them at least once a month. Combine the following ingredients in a medium saucepan over medium heat, then simmer 10 minutes until heated through: 2 (15-ounce) cans black beans, drained and rinsed; 2/3 cup chicken or vegetable broth; 1/2 teaspoon garlic powder; 1/2 teaspoon onion powder; 1/2 teaspoon salt; 1/4 teaspoon ground cumin; 1/4 teaspoon ground coriander; 1/4 teaspoon dried oregano; and freshly ground black pepper. Before serving, squeeze the juice from half a lime on top and stir it in. So delicious!

Tropical Fried Rice

This recipe is a mix of family favorites. My husband grew up eating homemade fried rice and has made it for us for years. We took his go-to recipe and tweaked it to match the tropical fried rice a local Caribbean restaurant serves. The finished dish is loaded with veggies and bits of tart pineapple, and is a delicious mix of savory and sweet. To round out this yummy dinner, serve it with Hawaiian rolls and an Asian salad kit from the grocery store. If you need it to be even heartier, add your favorite frozen dumplings or potstickers to the menu.

Prep: 5 minutes | Cook: 25 minutes | Total: 30 minutes | Serves 6

2 cups rice

3 eggs, lightly beaten

Kosher salt

Freshly ground black pepper

1 tablespoon toasted sesame oil

¼ large red onion, thinly sliced

½ cup packed shredded carrots

½ cup frozen sweet peas

½ cup frozen corn kernels

1 cup diced fresh pineapple

½ bunch green onions, cut on the diagonal, divided into white/light green parts and dark green parts

1 tablespoon minced or grated fresh ginger

1 tablespoon minced garlic, or 3 garlic cloves, minced

¼ cup low-sodium soy sauce

¼ cup teriyaki sauce

1. Cook the rice according to the package directions. You should have about 6 cups of cooked rice.

2. While the rice cooks, make the scrambled eggs. Lightly grease a large skillet with nonstick cooking spray. Over medium heat, cook the eggs. Season with salt and pepper. When the eggs are cooked through, put them on a small plate and set them aside. Wash or scrape out the skillet if necessary.

3. Drizzle the toasted sesame oil in the bottom of the skillet. Add the red onion and carrots. Sauté over medium heat until beginning to get tender, 5 minutes.

continued

SKILLETS, SHEET PANS & BAKES

4. Add the peas, corn, pineapple, white/light green parts of the green onions, ginger, and garlic. Sauté until tender, 5 minutes.

5. Add the cooked rice, soy sauce, and teriyaki sauce, stirring to combine. Cook until heated through, 5 minutes more. Stir in the scrambled eggs. Add salt and pepper to taste (or soy sauce if it won't make the rice too wet), top with the dark green parts of the green onions, and serve.

SHORTCUTS & NOTES

- Pre-sliced red onions

- Pre-shredded carrots

- Pre-chopped pineapple from the produce section (just dice it a little smaller)

- Pre-minced ginger and garlic (frozen cubes, or a jar or squeeze tube)

- My husband grew up having crispy bacon pieces in his fried rice, and it tastes delicious in this, too. Chop up 6 slices of bacon and fry them until crispy before you cook the eggs. Scoop the cooked bacon out of the skillet, set it on a paper-towel-lined plate, and proceed with step 2. Add the bacon back in when you add the rice, soy sauce, and teriyaki sauce.

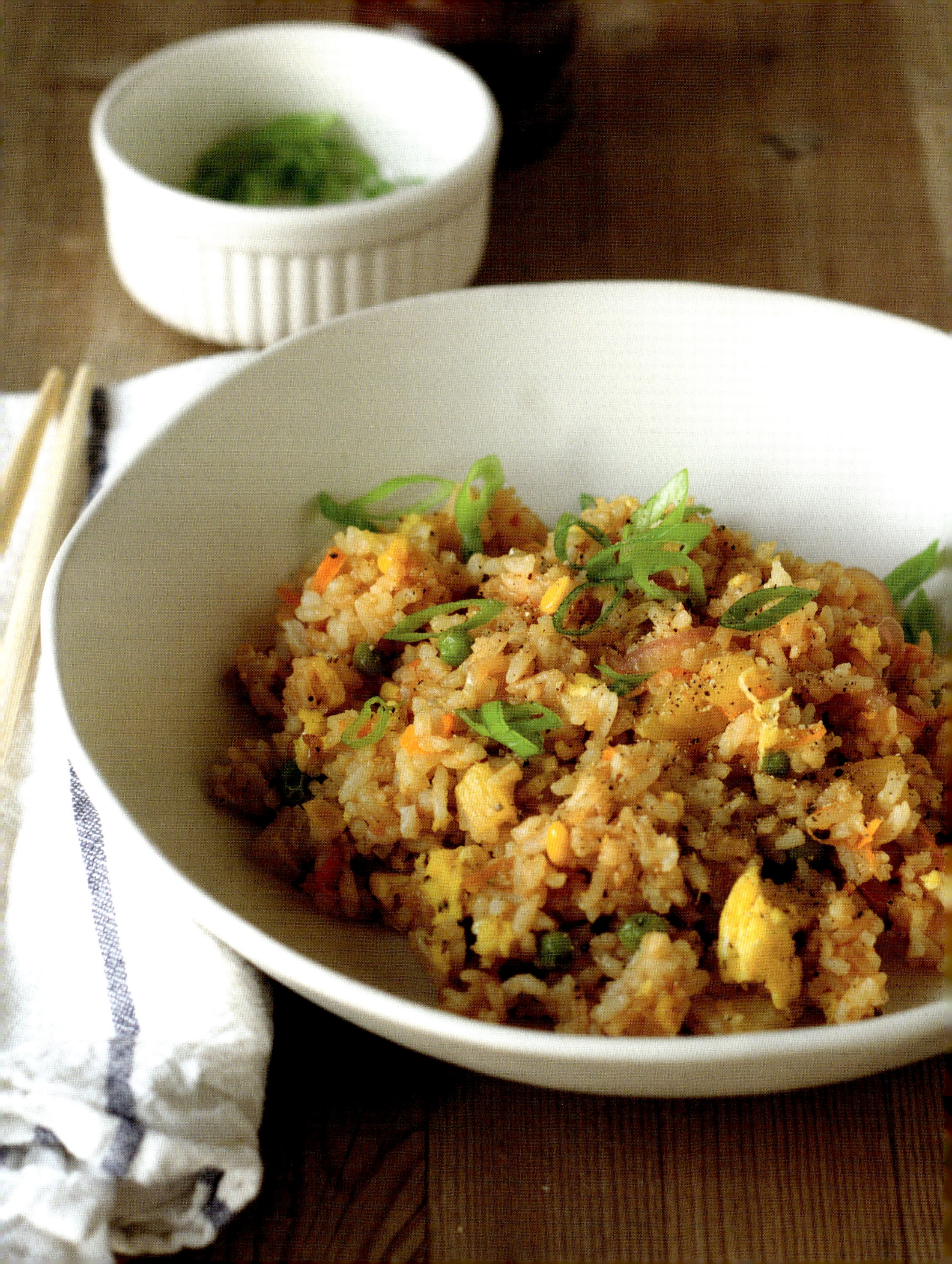

Emily's Cheesy Chicken & Stuffing Bake

When we were visiting my sister and her family a few years ago, we stopped for lunch at a darling shop in a darling town, as one often does in the New England countryside in early autumn. My sister ordered the stuffing casserole, a creamy, cheesy, saucy chicken dish covered in herby, savory stuffing. And we both fell in love with it immediately. My sister went straight home and came up with her own version, and this is my version of her version. Thank you to Simon's Market in Chester, Connecticut, for the original inspiration!

Prep: 10 minutes | Cook: 35 minutes | Total: 45 minutes | Serves 6

1 box stovetop stuffing (I like the savory herb variety)

¼ cup butter, divided

½ cup small diced onion

2 teaspoons minced garlic, or 2 garlic cloves, minced

2 tablespoons flour

1 cup whole milk

½ teaspoon salt

⅛ teaspoon freshly ground black pepper

⅛ teaspoon mustard powder

⅛ teaspoon paprika

1 cup shredded sharp white cheddar cheese

1 pound chopped cooked chicken breasts

1. Preheat the oven to 350°F.

2. In a medium saucepan on the stove, or in a medium microwave-safe bowl, prepare the stuffing according to the package directions using whatever amount of water the stuffing calls for and 2 tablespoons of butter. Set aside.

3. In an oven-safe skillet over medium heat, melt the remaining 2 tablespoons of butter. Add the onion and garlic and sauté until tender, about 8 minutes.

4. Whisk in the flour and cook for 1 minute. Add the milk, salt, pepper, mustard powder, and paprika, whisking constantly. Add the cheese, again whisking constantly. When the sauce has thickened and the cheese has melted, add the chicken and stir to combine. Remove from the heat.

5. Distribute the stuffing evenly over the top of the chicken mixture, then bake for 20 minutes, until the stuffing is golden and the sauce is bubbling.

SHORTCUTS & NOTES

- Pre-chopped onions

- Pre-minced garlic (frozen cubes, or a jar or squeeze tube)

- Pre-shredded sharp white cheddar cheese

- Rotisserie chicken

- If you don't have a large, oven-safe skillet or some other casserole pan that can handle both the stove and the oven, you can still make this! Use a skillet or saucepan to make the chicken mixture, then pour it into an 8-inch square baking dish. Top with the stuffing and bake as previously directed.

- I've gone back and forth a hundred times about the serving size on this recipe. It's a tricky one. I think that this recipe can serve exactly 6 people, especially if you serve it with some dinner rolls, cooked veggies, and maybe a green salad. But you won't have any leftovers, and if you have more than 6 people, you should probably double it.

SKILLETS, SHEET PANS & BAKES

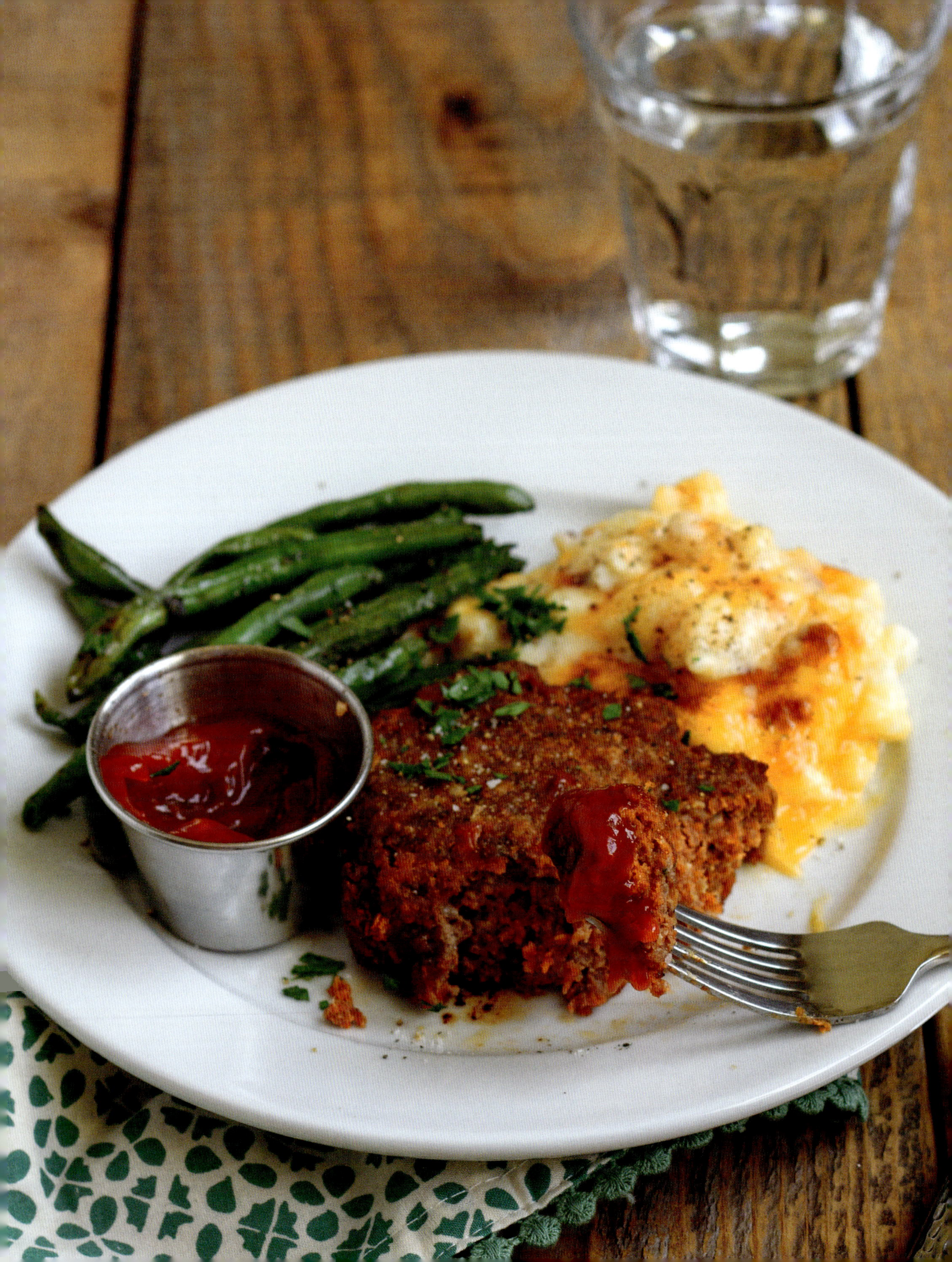

Mini Meatloaves

I've been making this recipe for individual meatloaves for almost two decades, and after tinkering with it for so long, I think I can confidently say that it is perfect. Beefy and full of savory flavor and, thanks to the small size, ready in a heartbeat.

Prep: 20 minutes | Cook: 20 minutes | Total: 40 minutes | Serves 8

---

2 pounds ground beef

2 eggs

1 cup Italian-style breadcrumbs

⅓ cup grated Parmesan cheese (nothing fancy, just the one in the plastic shaker jar)

½ cup grated onion (grate on the large holes of a box grater)

2 tablespoons minced garlic, or 6 garlic cloves, minced

¼ cup tomato paste

1½ teaspoons kosher salt

Freshly ground black pepper

Extra-virgin olive oil or your favorite neutral cooking oil

Ketchup, for serving

1. Preheat the oven to 425°F. Spray a rimmed baking sheet with nonstick cooking spray.

2. In a large bowl, combine the ground beef, eggs, breadcrumbs, Parmesan, onion, garlic, tomato paste, salt, and pepper. Mix with your hands until all of the ingredients are evenly distributed.

3. Divide the meat mixture into 8 equal portions. Pat each portion into a patty about 1 inch thick. Place the patties on the prepared baking sheet and drizzle lightly with olive oil.

4. Roast for 20 minutes, until the meatloaves are browned and sizzling. Serve with ketchup.

SHORTCUTS & NOTES

- Pre-minced garlic (frozen cubes, or a jar or squeeze tube)

Crispy Chicken Parmesan

Crispy, breaded chicken cutlets covered in marinara sauce and melty cheese have always been a favorite of mine, and I worked really hard to get an easy version of chicken parm for this cookbook. I tried oven-baking on a baking sheet because that is such an easy method, and I tried panfrying because the results taste so good. I ended up with a hybrid method to get the best of both worlds: juicy chicken inside, perfectly crispy crust outside.

Prep: 20 minutes | Cook: 20 minutes | Total: 40 minutes | Serves 4

4 chicken cutlets or thin-sliced chicken breast fillets

½ cup all-purpose flour

2 teaspoons salt, divided

1 teaspoon onion powder

1 teaspoon garlic powder

1 teaspoon paprika

Freshly ground black pepper

2 large eggs

1 tablespoon water

1 cup panko breadcrumbs

2 tablespoons grated Parmesan cheese (nothing fancy, just the one in the plastic shaker jar)

Zest of 1 lemon

Neutral oil, for frying

1 cup marinara sauce

1½ cups shredded mozzarella cheese

Minced fresh parsley, for garnishing

1. Preheat the oven to 350°F.

2. If your chicken cutlets aren't uniform in size and thickness, fix that first. You can pound any spots that are too thick with a meat mallet, and feel free to trim any fillets that are bigger than the rest.

3. In a large, resealable bag, combine the flour, 1½ teaspoons of salt, onion powder, garlic powder, paprika, and black pepper. Toss gently to combine.

4. In a shallow dish or pie plate, whisk the eggs with the water until combined.

5. In another shallow dish or pie plate, combine the breadcrumbs, Parmesan cheese, lemon zest, and remaining ½ teaspoon of salt, and pepper to taste. Toss with a fork or your fingers to combine.

6. Put the chicken in the bag, close it tightly, and shake gently until the chicken fillets are all uniformly coated in flour.

7. Lay one of the chicken fillets in the egg mixture on one side, then flip it over to make sure both sides are coated. Do the same thing with the chicken fillet and

continued

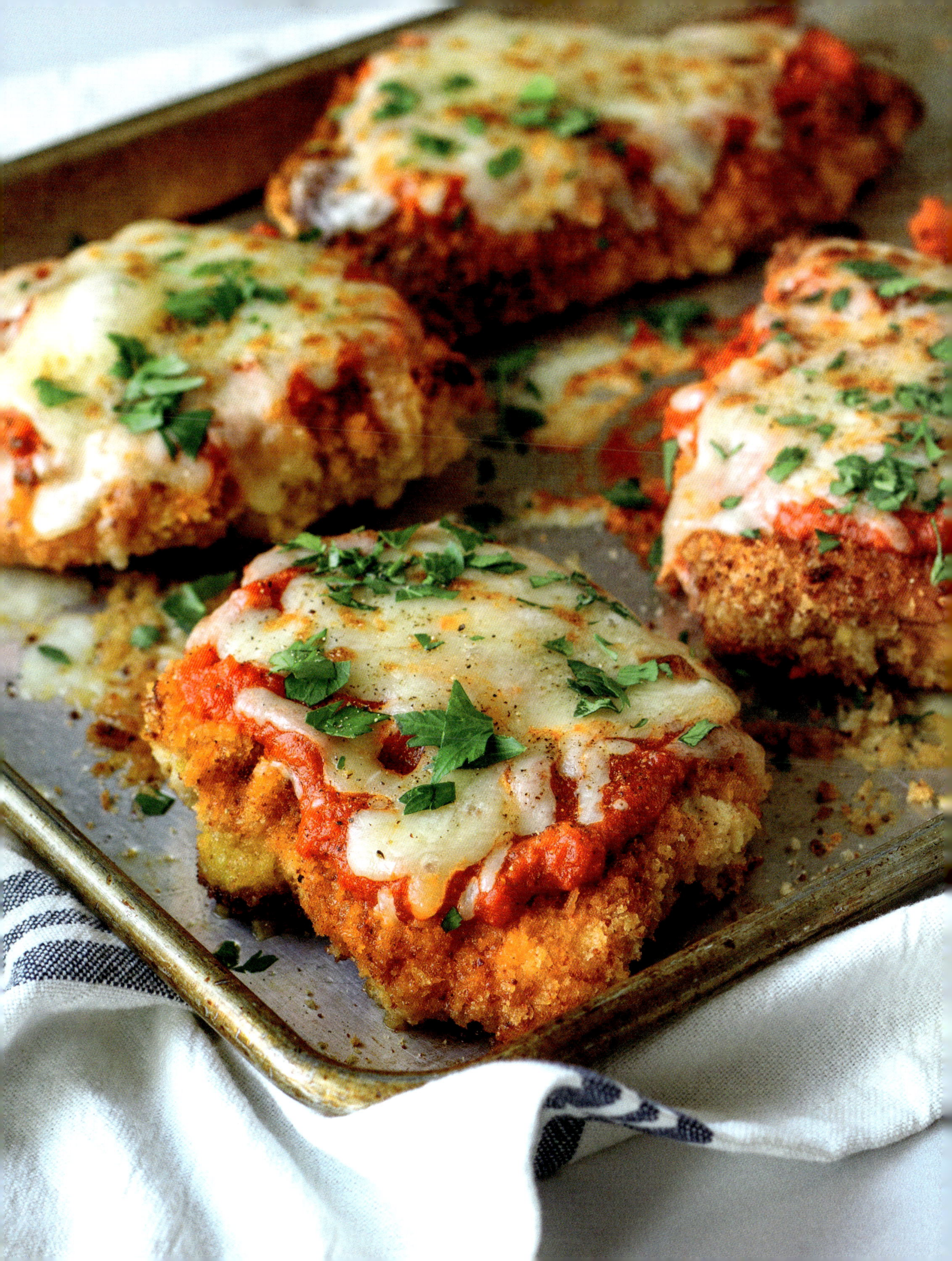

the breadcrumb mixture, using your hands to gently pat breadcrumbs onto both sides of the chicken. Place the chicken fillet on a rimmed baking sheet and repeat the process with the remaining chicken fillets.

8. Cover the bottom of a large skillet with a thin layer of your favorite cooking oil and put it over medium heat. You'll know the oil is hot enough to start frying when you get your fingers wet with water, flick the water into the oil, and hear the oil sizzle. Use a pair of tongs to gently place the chicken fillets in the hot oil. Sauté for 3 minutes, until golden on the bottom, then use the tongs and a thin metal spatula to flip the chicken over. Sauté for another 3 minutes, until both sides are golden.

9. Use the spatula to place the chicken back on the baking sheet, and bake for 10 minutes until the internal temperature of the chicken is 165°F.

10. Remove the baking sheet from the oven and turn the oven to broil. Spoon the marinara sauce evenly over the chicken breasts, then top with the mozzarella. Put the baking sheet back in the oven and broil just until the cheese is melted, bubbly, and beginning to brown. This will happen within 2 or 3 minutes, so watch carefully. Remove from the oven and serve immediately with a sprinkle of parsley.

SHORTCUTS & NOTES

- Pre-shredded mozzarella cheese

- Our favorite store-bought marinara is Rao's.

- These chicken cutlets are great in all kinds of sandwiches and chopped up for crispy chicken salads.

- Try topping the chicken with a slice of deli ham and some Swiss cheese to make a chicken cordon bleu-inspired version.

- Use prosciutto, fontina, and a pinch of dried sage for an easy take on chicken saltimbocca.

Easy Flatbread Pizzas

Every Friday night is pizza night at our house. There are lots of different options for pizza, from store-bought to takeout to homemade. These flatbread pizzas are one of the fastest and most delicious of the homemade options. Naan is our favorite flatbread pizza crust because it is soft and fluffy to begin with, so it doesn't get too hard or crusty after baking for this long in the oven. Feel free to use your favorite kind of flatbread if naan isn't your thing.

Prep: 10 minutes | Cook: 15 minutes | Total: 25 minutes | Makes 4 personal-size pizzas

4 pieces of naan

½ to ¾ cup pizza sauce of choice

2 cups shredded mozzarella cheese

Toppings: see page 166 for our favorite ideas

1. Preheat the oven to 400°F.

2. Place the naan in a single layer on two rimmed baking sheets. Spread 2 to 3 tablespoons of sauce on each piece of naan, then top with shredded cheese and your choice of toppings.

3. Put one baking sheet on the top rack of the oven and the other on the bottom rack. Bake for 12 to 15 minutes, until the cheese is melted and the pizzas are heated through, switching the rack placement of the baking sheets after the first 6 or 7 minutes.

continued

SKILLETS, SHEET PANS & BAKES

SHORTCUTS & NOTES

- Our favorite red pizza sauce to use is Rao's Marinara. It's such a great all-purpose red sauce. And our favorite pesto is Kirkland Signature Basil Pesto from Costco.

- Now for the variations...

- Loaded Hawaiian: red sauce; mozzarella; diced deli ham; cooked, crumbled bacon; chopped roasted red peppers; chopped pineapple (canned or fresh)

- Pesto Bacon: pesto; fresh mozzarella slices; cooked, crumbled bacon

- Chicken Bacon Ranch: ranch dressing; mozzarella and cheddar; chopped, cooked chicken; cooked, crumbled bacon

- Supreme: red sauce; mozzarella; pepperoni; cooked, crumbled Italian sausage; diced peppers; diced onion; sliced black olives

- BBQ Chicken: BBQ sauce; mozzarella; chopped cooked chicken; thinly sliced red onion; fresh cilantro sprinkled on after cooking

- Potato Pesto: pesto; mozzarella; thinly sliced, pre-cooked baby potatoes; kosher salt

- Meat Lovers: red sauce; mozzarella; pepperoni; cooked, crumbled Italian sausage; cooked, crumbled bacon; diced deli ham

- Margherita: red sauce; fresh mozzarella slices; kosher salt; thinly sliced fresh basil sprinkled on after cooking

- Tostada: a drizzle of extra-virgin olive oil; mozzarella; cooked chicken; black or pinto beans (drained and rinsed); fresh salsa; shredded lettuce; shredded cheddar; thinly sliced green onions; and a drizzle of ranch dressing after cooking

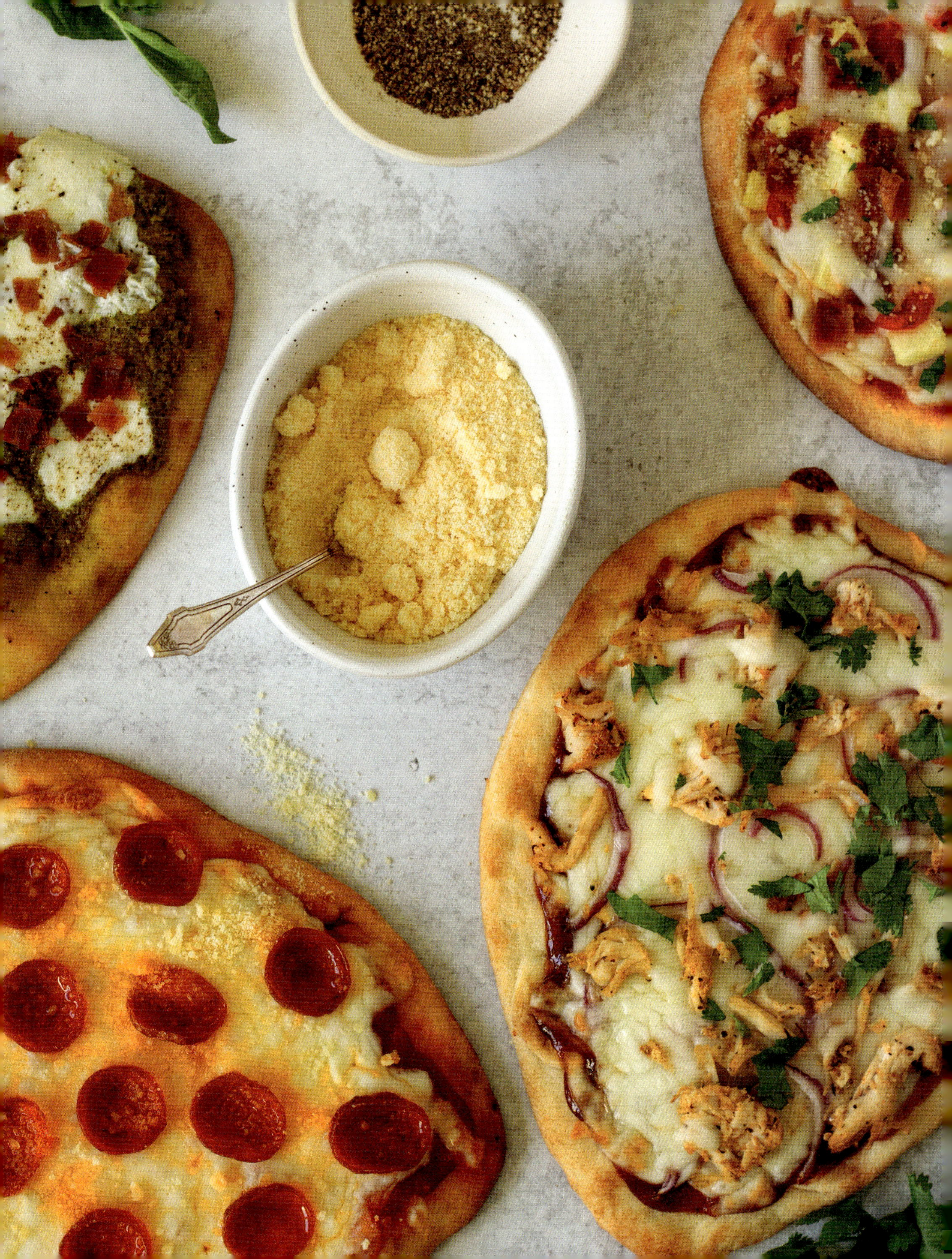

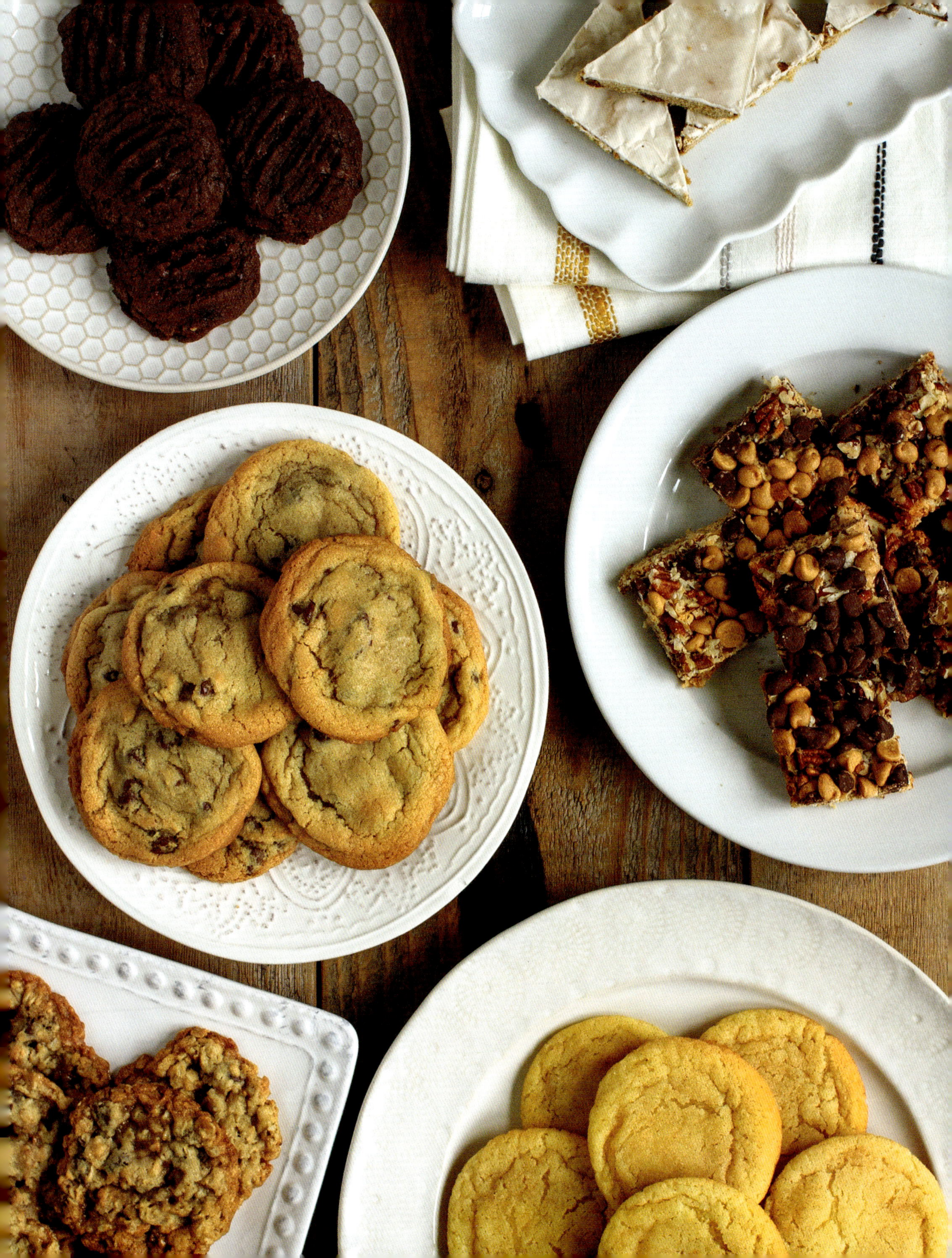

AFTER-DINNER TREATS

WHAT WOULD A weeknight cookbook be without some easy, sweet treats to cap things off?! The recipes in this chapter are some of our favorite desserts that don't take long to make and that we all love. Most can be made at the last minute and eaten right away. A few work a little better if you make them at least a couple of hours before you want to dig in. But they're all pretty effortless and make the end of your day a little sweeter.

Oatmeal Toffee Cookies

My family always defaults to Chocolate Chip Cookies (page 177), but if pressed, they'll admit that these chewy sweets, loaded with oatmeal, toffee chunks, and, yes, chocolate chips, are truly a delight. So buttery and sweet, with the perfect texture. They are not a second fiddle cookie; they deserve a little time in the spotlight!

Prep: 20 minutes | Cook: 11 minutes per batch | Total: 31 minutes for the first batch | Makes about 40 cookies

1 cup (2 sticks) butter, softened

1 cup granulated sugar

1 cup dark brown sugar

2 eggs

1 teaspoon vanilla extract

3 cups old-fashioned rolled oats

2 cups all-purpose flour

1 teaspoon salt

1 teaspoon baking soda

1 teaspoon baking powder

1 cup semisweet chocolate chips

1 (8-ounce) package English toffee bits (about 1⅓ cups)

1. Preheat the oven to 350°F. Line at least one baking sheet with parchment paper or a silicone baking mat.

2. In a large bowl or in the bowl of a stand mixer, beat the butter, granulated sugar, and brown sugar on medium speed until smooth, about 1 minute. Add the eggs and vanilla, and beat to combine.

3. In a separate bowl, mix the oats, flour, salt, baking soda, and baking powder. Add the dry ingredients to the butter mixture and beat just until combined. Stir in the chocolate chips and toffee bits and mix until evenly distributed.

4. Scoop the dough into 2-inch balls. Place 12 dough balls on the prepared baking sheet, evenly spaced out, and bake for 11 minutes. Repeat with the remaining dough balls or freeze the extras. The cookies can be baked from frozen at the same temperature, just increase the baking time to 12 to 13 minutes.

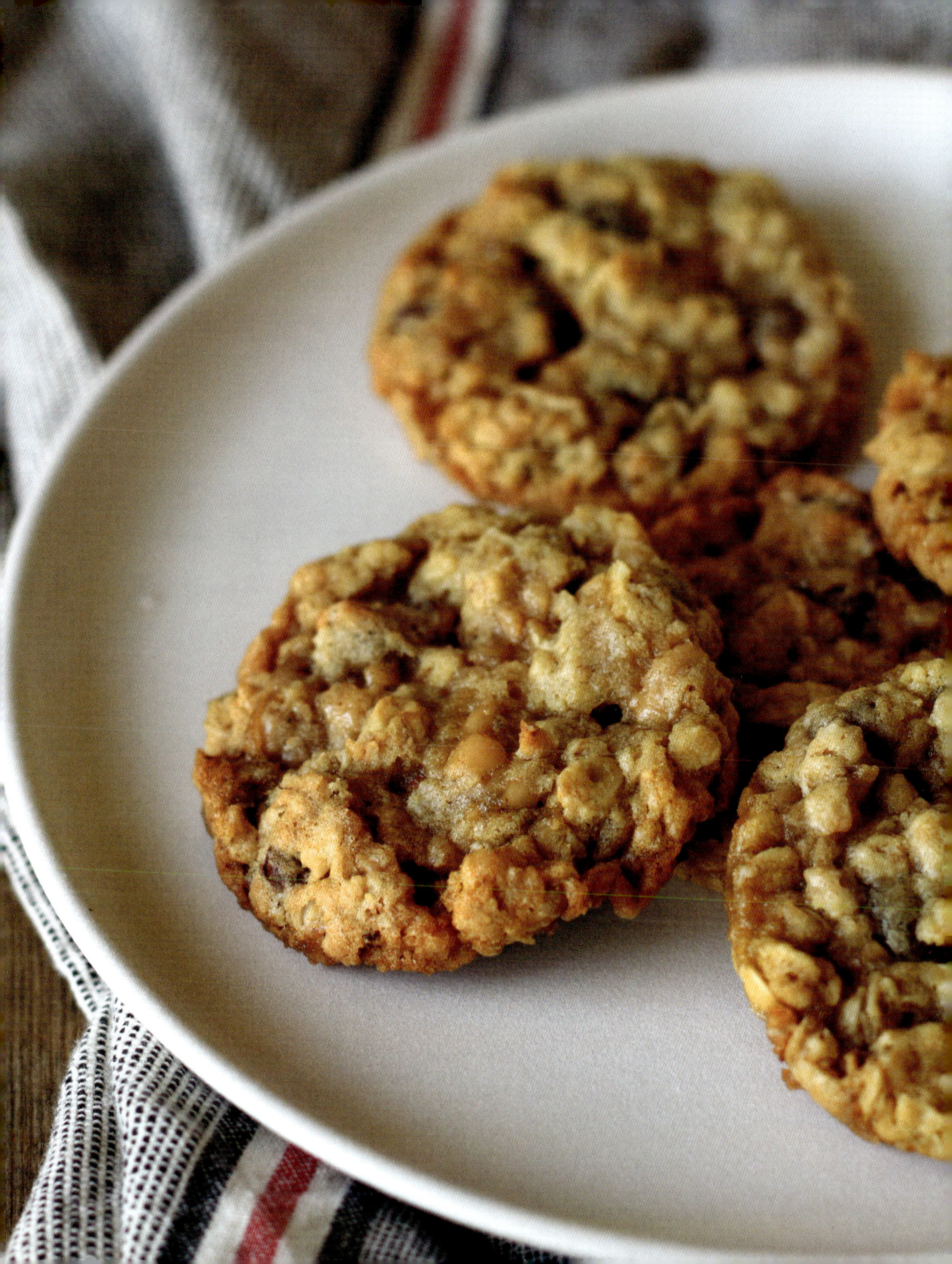

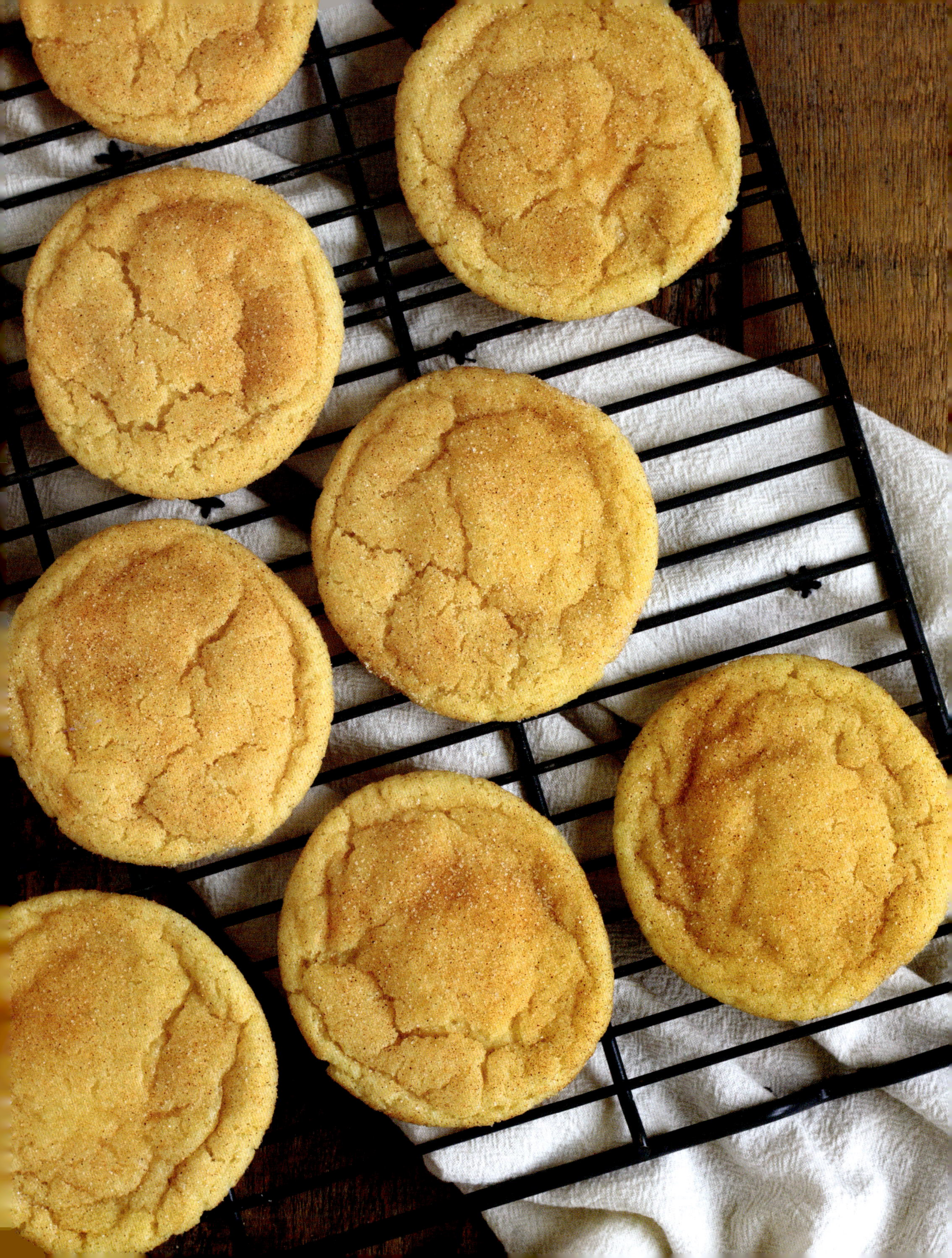

Snickerdoodles

This snickerdoodle recipe is a winner. Some snickerdoodles just taste like plain cookies that have nothing in them but are rolled in cinnamon sugar, but these are special. They turn out super chewy and buttery, with exactly the right amount of cinnamon and sugar coating the outside, and that pleasant tanginess that is the hallmark of a spectacular snickerdoodle. They'll easily earn their place on your holiday cookie or bake sale short list.

Prep: 25 minutes | Cook: 9 minutes per batch | Total: 34 minutes for the first batch | Makes about 30 cookies

1 cup (2 sticks) butter, softened

1½ cups plus 4 tablespoons granulated sugar, divided

2 eggs

2¾ cups all-purpose flour

2 teaspoons cream of tartar

1 teaspoon baking soda

¼ teaspoon salt

2 teaspoons ground cinnamon

1. Preheat the oven to 350°F. Line at least one rimmed baking sheet with parchment paper or a silicone baking mat.

2. Beat the butter and 1½ cups sugar on medium speed until light and fluffy, about 1 minute. Add the eggs and beat until combined.

3. In a medium bowl, combine the flour, cream of tartar, baking soda, and salt. Add the dry ingredients to the wet ingredients and mix until just combined.

4. In a small bowl, combine the remaining 4 tablespoons of sugar and cinnamon for the cinnamon-sugar topping. Scoop the cookie dough into 1½-inch balls. Roll each ball thoroughly in cinnamon sugar.

5. Place 12 dough balls 2 inches apart on the prepared baking sheet, and bake for 8 to 10 minutes, until the cookies look set. These snickerdoodles will puff up as they bake, and then flatten as they cool. Allow the cookies to cool on the baking sheets for 3 to 5 minutes before transferring them to a cooling rack. Cool completely before eating.

Speedy's Chocolate No-Bake Cookies

These cookies were a staple in my husband's family growing up, and my kids request them often, especially if they're craving a last-minute, unplanned dessert. They're basically oats and coconut held together with rich, chocolatey fudge! Lots of no-bake cookie recipes call for peanut butter, but we always make these with mini marshmallows instead, and even though those two things aren't even remotely the same, this version always turns out the perfect texture and is our very favorite.

Prep: 15 minutes | Cook: 15 minutes | Total: 30 minutes | Makes about 24 cookies

3 cups old-fashioned rolled oats

1 cup sweetened coconut flakes

1 cup mini marshmallows

2 cups granulated sugar

½ cup milk

½ cup (1 stick) butter

3 tablespoons natural, unsweetened cocoa powder (such as Hershey's)

1 teaspoon salt

1 teaspoon vanilla extract

1. In a large bowl, combine the oats, coconut flakes, and marshmallows. Set aside.

2. Lay a large piece of parchment paper on the counter.

3. In a medium saucepan, combine the sugar, milk, butter, cocoa powder, and salt. Bring the mixture to a boil over medium-high heat. Boil, stirring constantly, for about 4 minutes, until the mixture reaches the soft ball stage. My husband aims for 237°F on a candy-making thermometer (see below for how to do this without a thermometer). Remove from the heat and whisk in the vanilla extract.

4. Pour the chocolate mixture over the oat mixture and stir until evenly combined. Scoop Ping Pong ball–size spoonfuls of the batter onto the parchment paper. Use the back of the spoon to gently spread and flatten each spoonful slightly so that they look like cookies. Allow to cool completely. Or don't! We start eating them as soon as they're cool enough to touch and solid enough not to fall apart.

SHORTCUTS & NOTES

- The names for the various candy-making stages come from the behavior of the mixture when dropped into cold water. After boiling for 4 minutes, if you drop a little spoonful of the chocolate mixture into a small amount of cold water, it should form a soft, sticky ball. If it falls apart or smooshes, boil it a minute longer and try again. If it forms a firm ball, you've boiled it a little too much, but your cookies will still taste great. They'll just be more crumbly and less creamy.

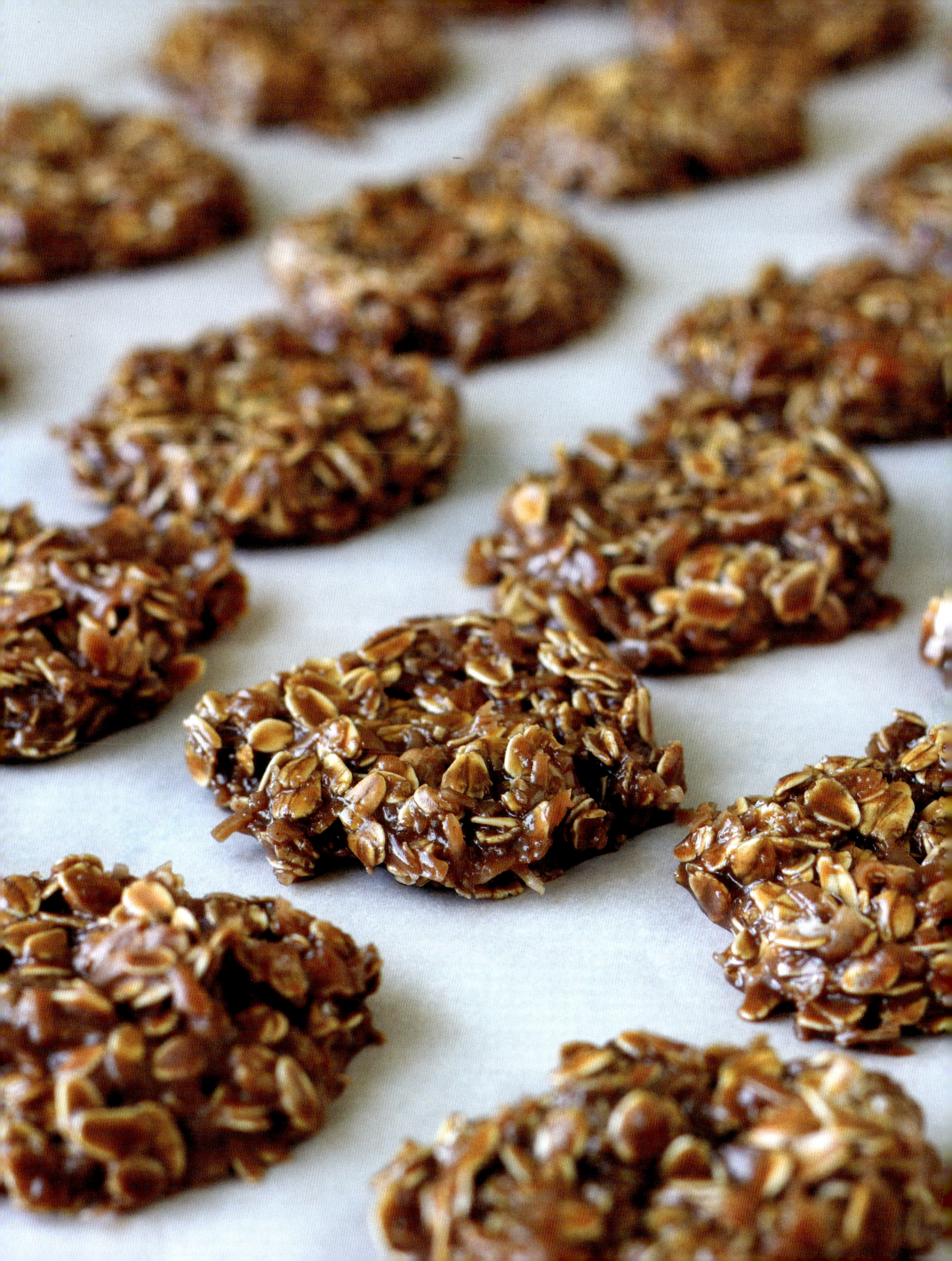

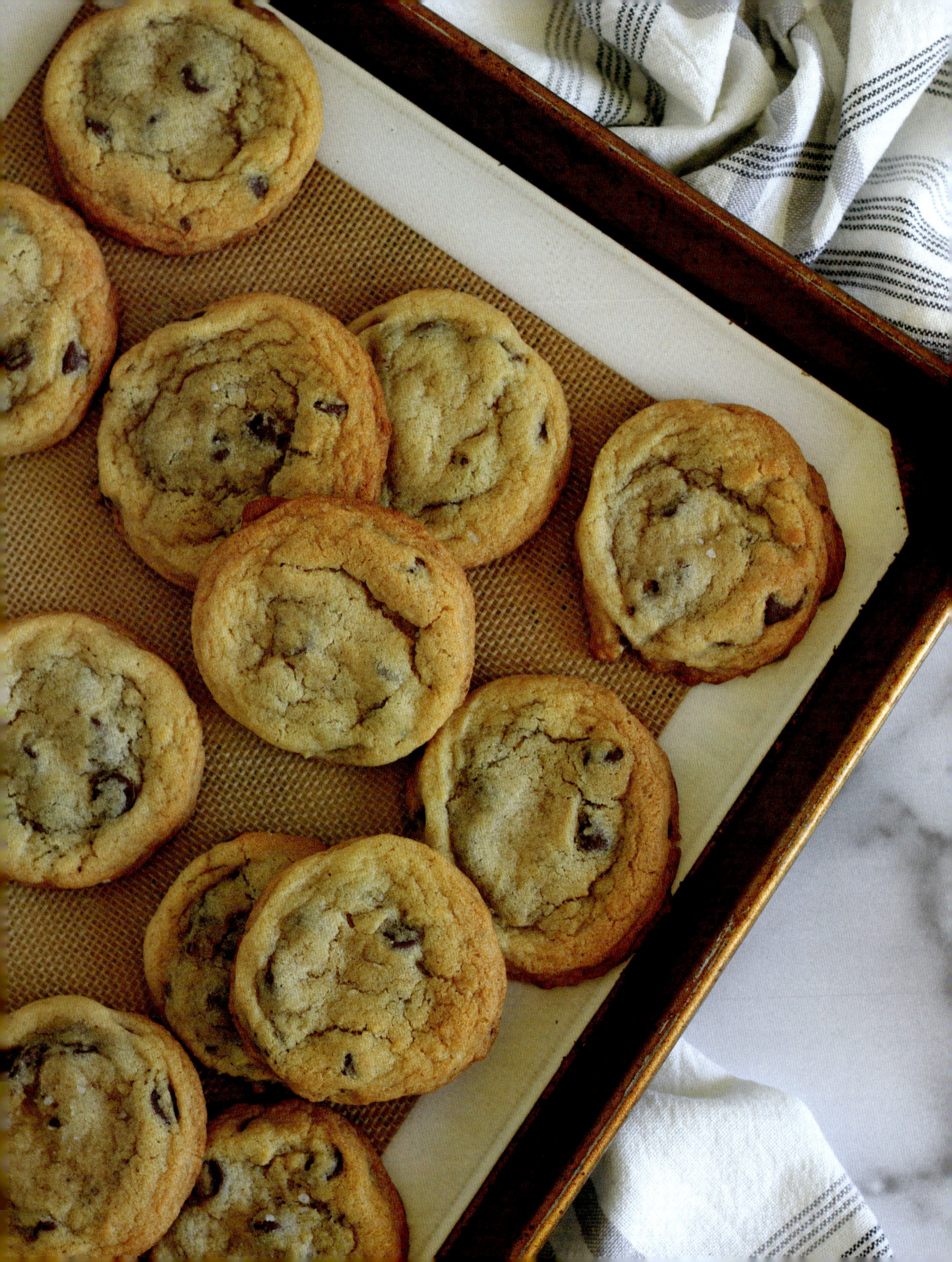

Chocolate Chip Cookies

Everybody has their idea of what makes a perfect chocolate chip cookie. Some people like a fluffy, cakey cookie, while others prefer a cookie that is crispy and thin. This recipe is my family's all-time favorite. It's a stripped-down version of a famous *New York Times* chocolate chip cookie recipe that makes really good cookies but is a little high maintenance and, in my opinion, takes too long to make. This version has all of the good things about that recipe (lots of butter and brown sugar) and can be made in less than an hour with ingredients you probably already have in your pantry. We started making them several years ago and haven't made any other recipe since. The cookies turn out buttery and chewy, with soft centers and crispy edges, which is my idea of the perfect chocolate chip cookie.

Prep: 18 minutes | Cook: 11 minutes per batch | Total: 29 minutes for the first batch | Makes about 40 cookies

3½ cups plus 2 teaspoons all-purpose flour

1½ teaspoons baking powder

1¼ teaspoons baking soda

1½ teaspoons kosher salt

1¼ cups (2½ sticks) butter, softened

1¼ cups brown sugar

1 cup plus 2 tablespoons granulated sugar

2 eggs

2 teaspoons vanilla extract

2 cups chocolate chips

1. Reheat the oven to 350°F and line at least one rimmed baking sheet with parchment paper or a silicone baking mat.

2. In a medium bowl, combine the flour, baking powder, baking soda, and salt.

3. In a large bowl or in the bowl of a stand mixer, beat the butter, brown sugar, and granulated sugar until smooth. Add the eggs and vanilla and beat again until just combined. Add the dry ingredients and mix on low speed until just combined. Mix in the chocolate chips until they are evenly distributed.

4. Scoop dough into 2-inch balls. Place 12 dough balls on the prepared baking sheet, evenly spaced out, and bake for 11 minutes. Repeat with the remaining dough balls or freeze the extras. The cookies can be baked from frozen at the same temperature, just increase the baking time to 13 minutes.

Triple Chocolate Cookies

These cookies are for the chocolate lovers! They have three different types of chocolate in them already, but if you want to up the chocolate factor, you can use as many different kinds of chocolate chips as you want. Something I love about this cookie recipe is that unlike a lot of other chocolate cookie recipes I've made over the years, this one doesn't require any chill time for the dough, and the dough is a regular cookie dough texture, not gooey or sticky. It makes this recipe a great one for satisfying weeknight chocolate cravings.

Prep: 20 minutes | Cook: 9 minutes per batch | Total: 29 minutes for the first batch | Makes about 36 cookies

1 cup (2 sticks) butter, softened

¾ cup lightly packed brown sugar

⅓ cup granulated sugar

1 (3.9-ounce) box instant chocolate pudding

2 large eggs

2 teaspoons vanilla extract

2⅓ cups all-purpose flour

⅓ cup natural, unsweetened cocoa powder (such as Hershey's)

1 teaspoon baking soda

½ teaspoon salt

2 cups semisweet chocolate chips

1. Preheat the oven to 350°F and line at least one rimmed baking sheet with parchment paper on a nonstick silicone baking mat.

2. Cream the butter, both sugars, and pudding on medium speed until well mixed, about 1 minute. Add the eggs and vanilla, and mix 1 more minute on medium speed, scraping down the sides of the bowl with a rubber spatula as needed.

3. Add the flour, cocoa powder, baking soda, and salt and mix on low speed just until combined, about 30 seconds. Add the chocolate chips and mix until they are evenly distributed and the dry ingredients are fully mixed in.

4. Scoop the dough into 2-inch balls. Place 12 dough balls evenly spaced out on the prepared baking sheet. Use the tines of a fork to gently flatten the cookie dough balls to a thickness of about ½ inch. Bake for 9 minutes. Repeat with the remaining dough balls or freeze the extras. Allow the cookies to cool for a few minutes before eating.

SHORTCUTS & NOTES

- You can use any kind or combination of chocolate chips (or even other flavors) that you like in these cookies. "Triple chocolate" is much easier to say than "quadruple chocolate" or "quintuple chocolate," so I stuck to just semisweet in this recipe. But you can do half semisweet, half milk chocolate, or add some white chocolate chips in there. You can even try butterscotch or peanut butter chips! Just keep the total amount of chips to 2 cups.

- The cookies can be baked from frozen at the same temperature, just increase the baking time to 11 to 12 minutes, and flatten them with a fork to a thickness of ½ inch after they've baked for about 8 minutes.

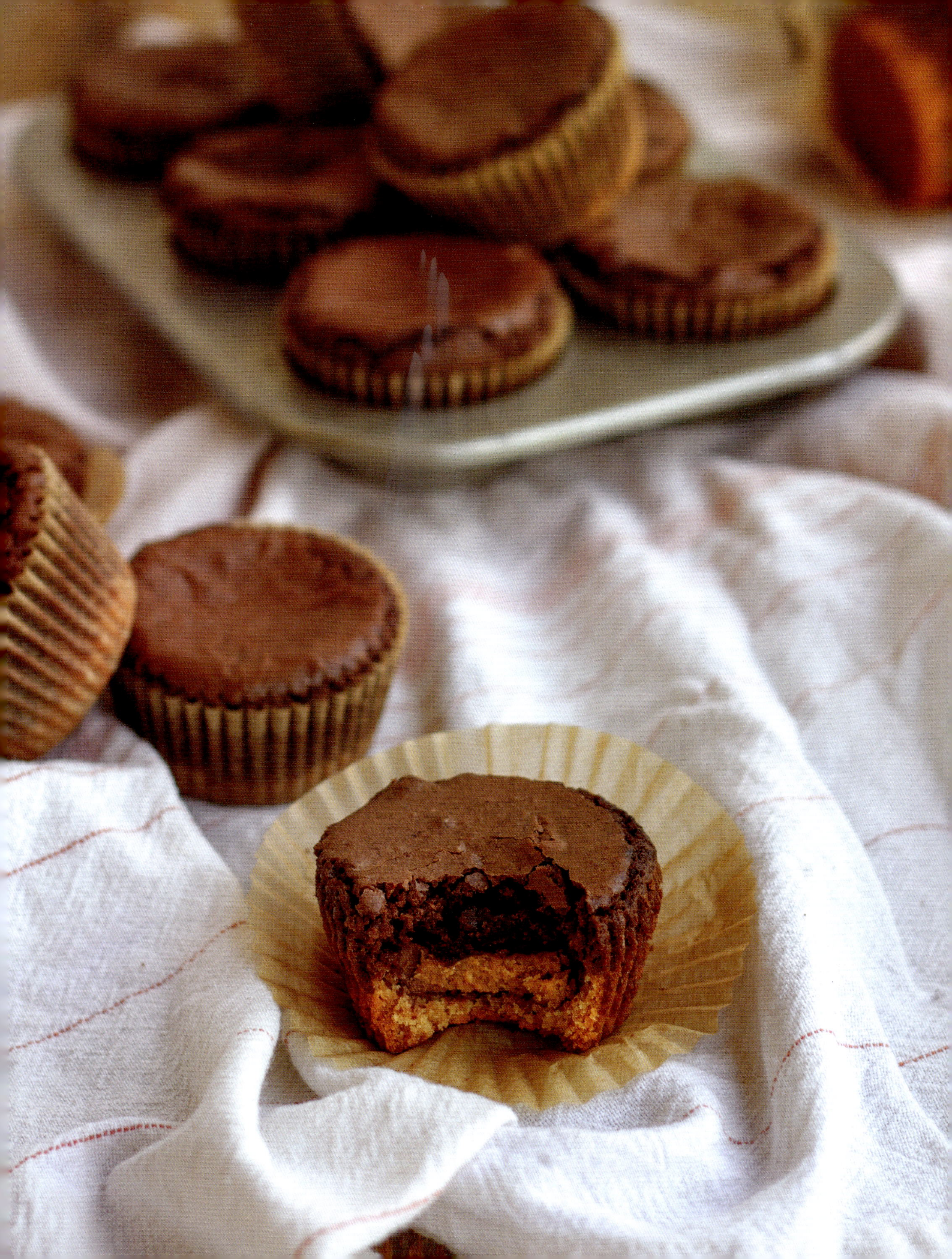

Easy Peanut Butter Cup Brownies

School fundraiser auctions are really popular around here. Almost every school we've had a child at has hosted one at some point. And almost every auction has included something called the Dessert Dash, where local businesses or school families donate desserts and the auction attendees bid for first pick at the dessert table. These unassuming brownies were left over after the dash one year, so the committee auctioned them off to the highest bidder as an afterthought, and not wanting whoever donated them to feel bad, we bid on them. The joke was on everyone who passed them up that night because once we unwrapped them, we could see that they weren't plain old brownies. They had a layer of peanut butter cookie at the bottom and were stuffed with decadent peanut butter cups. They've been a family favorite ever since! Their individual "packaging" makes them great for potlucks and bake sales, but they're also just perfect as a midweek dessert.

Prep: 15 minutes | Cook: 25 minutes | Total: 40 minutes | Makes 18 brownies

1 (16-ounce) package peanut butter cookie dough

18 Reese's peanut butter cups (the full-size ones, not the minis)

1 (16- to 18-ounce) box brownie mix, plus the ingredients to make it (usually vegetable oil, water, and 1 egg)

1. Preheat the oven to 350°F and line 18 muffin cups with paper liners. Lightly spray the top of the muffin pan with nonstick baking spray.

2. Divide the peanut butter cookie dough evenly among the muffin cups. Press the dough down into the bottom of the paper liners.

3. Place an unwrapped peanut butter cup into each muffin cup on top of the cookie dough.

4. In a medium bowl, prepare the brownie mix according to the package directions. Divide the brownie batter evenly among the muffin cups, pouring it over the peanut butter cups and cookie dough. If you have empty muffin cups in your pans, pour 1 to 2 tablespoons of water in each empty cup so that the brownies bake evenly.

5. Bake the brownies for 22 to 25 minutes. Allow the brownies to cool before eating.

SHORTCUTS & NOTES

- The packaged peanut butter cookie dough I buy comes pre-scooped into 24 little balls of dough. Just put 18 of them in their own cup, then divide each of the remaining 6 into 3 smaller dough balls, and add 1 to each of the 18 cups.

- Not all of the grocery stores I shop at stock ready-to-bake peanut butter cookie dough, but all of them carry peanut butter cookie mix on the baking aisle near boxed cake and muffin mixes. A 17.5-ounce package of peanut butter cookie mix will work for this recipe in a pinch. Just make the dough according to the instructions on the package. It will probably require oil, eggs, and water.

Aunt Myrl's German Cookies

My mom's Aunt Myrl gave her the recipe for these yummy and unique bar cookies at her bridal shower. They've been a family favorite for many generations now and are easy and delicious. We love the mix of spices, the chocolate chips, and the thin, shiny layer of sugary glaze. They frequently pop up on our holiday baking list, or just whenever someone has a hankering for these old-fashioned sweets.

Prep: 15 minutes | Cook: 15 minutes | Total: 30 minutes | Makes 48 cookies

FOR THE COOKIE BARS

4 eggs

2¼ cups brown sugar

2½ cups all-purpose flour

1 teaspoon ground cinnamon

¼ teaspoon salt

½ teaspoon ground cloves

1 cup semisweet chocolate chips

FOR THE ICING

1½ cups powdered sugar

1 teaspoon butter, softened

2½ tablespoons milk

⅛ teaspoon vanilla or maple extract

A pinch of salt

1. Preheat the oven to 350°F. Grease a 12 x 17-inch rimmed baking sheet (this is a regular, half-sheet, cookie baking size) with nonstick baking spray.

2. To make the cookie bars, in a large bowl or in the bowl of a stand mixer, beat the eggs and brown sugar until smooth.

3. In a medium bowl, combine the flour, cinnamon, salt, and cloves and mix well. Add to the egg and brown sugar mixture. Mix until just combined. The batter will be very thick. Gently stir in the chocolate chips.

4. Spread the batter evenly in the rimmed baking sheet and bake for 15 minutes. The bars should look set and should be golden on the edges. Remove from the oven and set aside while you make the icing.

5. While the cookies are cooling, make the icing. Combine the powdered sugar, softened butter, milk, vanilla, and salt in a medium bowl and beat until smooth. You can use an electric mixer or just a whisk if you don't mind an arm workout. Pour the icing evenly over the warm cookie bars and spread it all the way to the edges. Allow the icing to set before cutting and serving the bars. I like to cut it into a 4 x 6-inch grid, then cut each rectangle in half diagonally to make 48 triangles. I just think they look fancy that way.

SHORTCUTS & NOTES

- The original recipe from Aunt Myrl says you can also add 1 cup chopped nuts, chopped dates, or raisins.

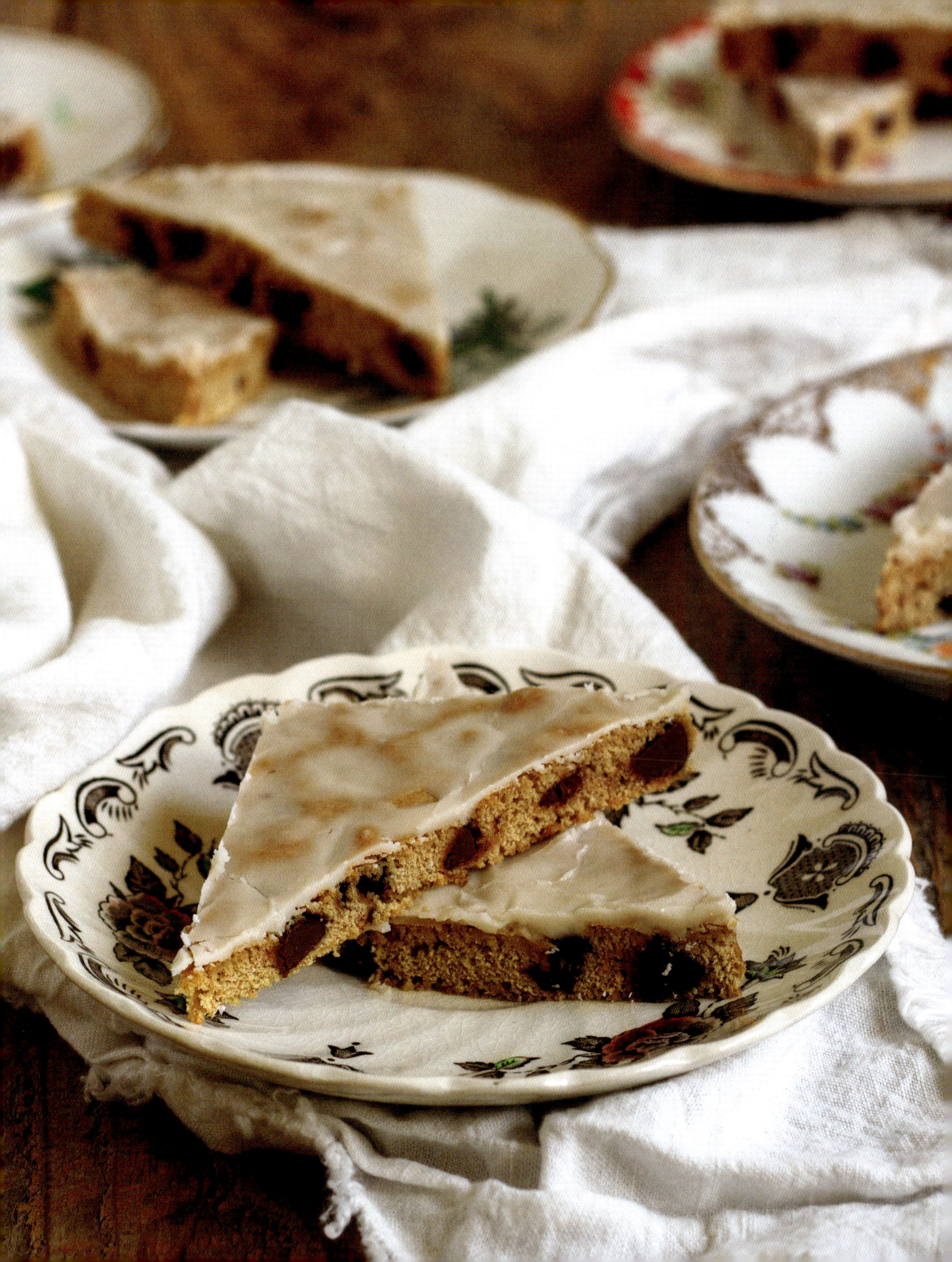

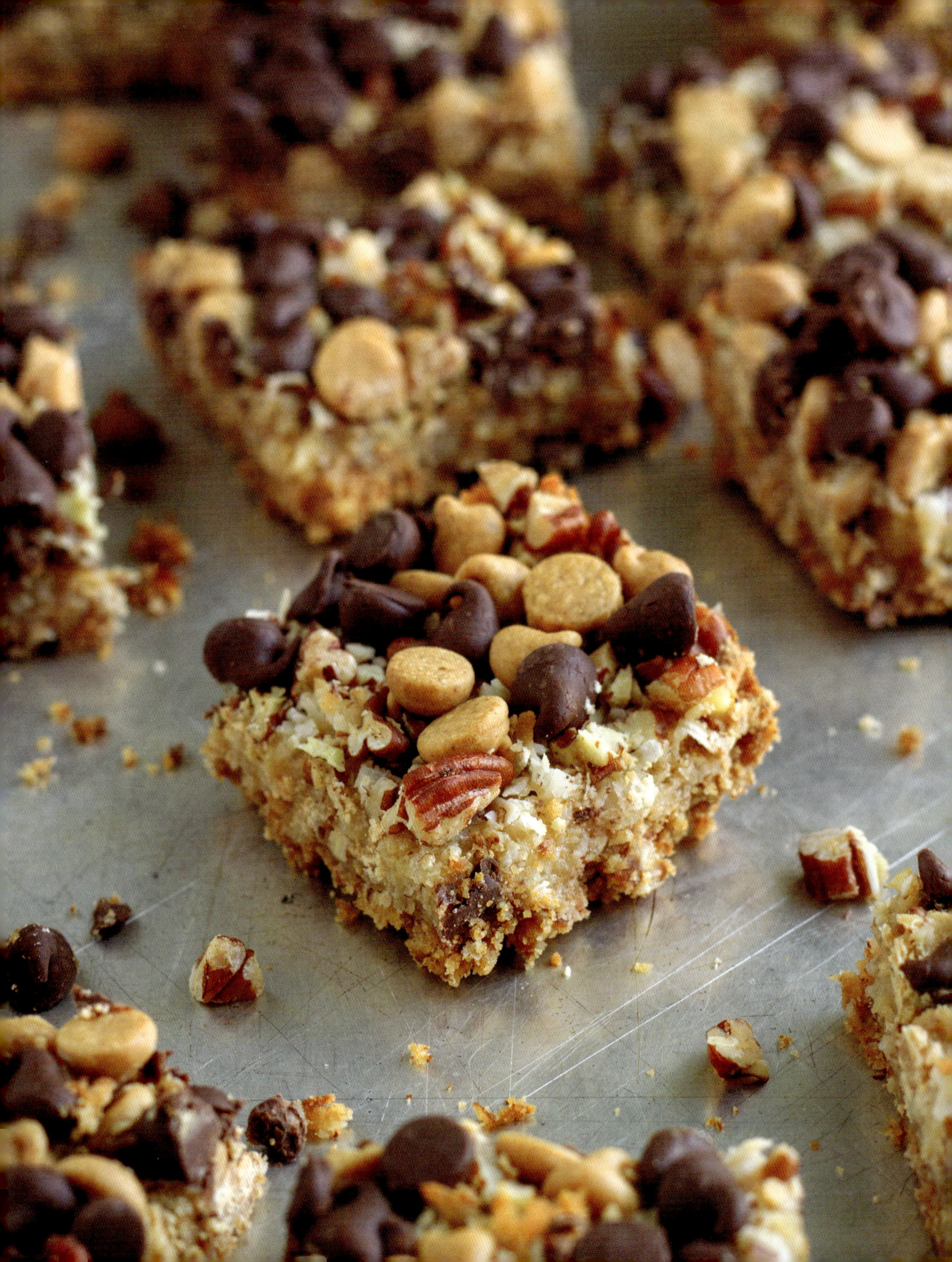

Peanut Butter Pretzel Magic Cookie Bars

Magic cookie bars are an easy, weeknight dessert staple. We usually have all of the ingredients floating around in the pantry (or in the refrigerator), and they bake up pretty quickly. If you want them to cut cleanly, you'll have to let them cool, but I'll admit I'm not always that patient or conscientious! We've thrown a lot of different kinds of baking chips on these over the years, and our current favorite combo is a classic: chocolate and peanut butter, with a yummy pretzel crust.

Prep: 10 minutes | Cook: 25 minutes | Total: 35 minutes | Makes 24 bars

- ¾ cups graham cracker crumbs (from 7 sheets of graham crackers)
- ¾ cups pretzel crumbs (about 3 ounces mini pretzels)
- ½ cup (1 stick) butter, melted
- 1 tablespoon granulated sugar
- 1 (14-ounce) can sweetened condensed milk
- 1 cup sweetened flaked coconut
- 1 cup chopped pecans
- 1 cup chocolate chips
- 1 cup peanut butter chips

1. Preheat the oven to 350°F. Spray a 9 x 13-inch baking pan with nonstick spray.

2. Combine the graham cracker crumbs, pretzel crumbs, melted butter, and granulated sugar. Press the mixture into the bottom of the pan. Pour the sweetened condensed milk evenly over the top, using a rubber spatula to spread it gently all the way to the edges of the pan. Sprinkle the coconut and pecans evenly over the top of the sweetened condensed milk, followed by the chocolate and peanut butter chips. Press everything down firmly with your hands or the back of a spatula.

3. Bake for 25 minutes, until golden brown on top.

4. Remove from the oven and allow to cool before cutting and serving.

SHORTCUTS & NOTES

- Pre-chopped pecans

- Substitute your favorite kind of chips for all or some of the chocolate and peanut butter chips. We've tried white chocolate, butterscotch, and milk chocolate, and they're all delicious.

- If you just want a graham cracker crust, use 1½ cups graham cracker crumbs and omit the pretzel crumbs and granulated sugar.

AFTER-DINNER TREATS

Peanut Butter Scotcheroos

It's hard to overstate just how much my family loves these delicious little peanut buttery treats. I can't remember where I got the recipe, but I've been making them for at least 20 years now, and they are a perennial favorite. Take a crispy cereal treat and swap out the normal marshmallow-butter sauce for a chewy, caramelly, stick-to-your-teeth peanut butter sauce, then top it with a layer of chocolate-butterscotch icing. Amazing, right? There must be something magical about them because they disappear almost as soon as they're made.

Prep: 5 minutes | Cook: 10 minutes | Total: 15 minutes | Makes 18 bars

6 cups crispy rice cereal

1 cup corn syrup

1 cup granulated sugar

1 cup peanut butter

1 cup semisweet chocolate chips

1 cup butterscotch chips

1. Pour the cereal into a large bowl and set aside.

2. In a medium saucepan, combine the corn syrup and sugar. Cook over medium heat until the sugar is dissolved and the mixture has come to a boil, 6 to 7 minutes. Remove from the heat immediately and stir in the peanut butter. Pour the mixture over the rice cereal and stir gently with a large spoon until well combined. Make sure you dig all the way to the bottom to get all of the cereal evenly coated.

3. Spray a 9 x 13-inch pan with nonstick cooking spray and press the mixture gently into the pan. Don't worry about getting the bars completely even on top; the chocolate layer will help even everything out. Also, pushing too hard on the bars will make them very dense and hard to chew.

4. Pour the semisweet and butterscotch chips into a medium microwave-safe bowl. Microwave for 30 seconds, then stir. Repeat until the chips are melted and smooth. This will take several 30-second cycles of microwaving and stirring. Pour the chocolate mixture over the cereal bars and spread evenly with an offset spatula. Allow to cool completely before serving.

SHORTCUTS & NOTES

- We usually get impatient and stick these in the refrigerator for 20 minutes or so to cool faster. You don't want them cold, but this will help them cool and be ready to eat a lot sooner. Do not store them in the refrigerator!

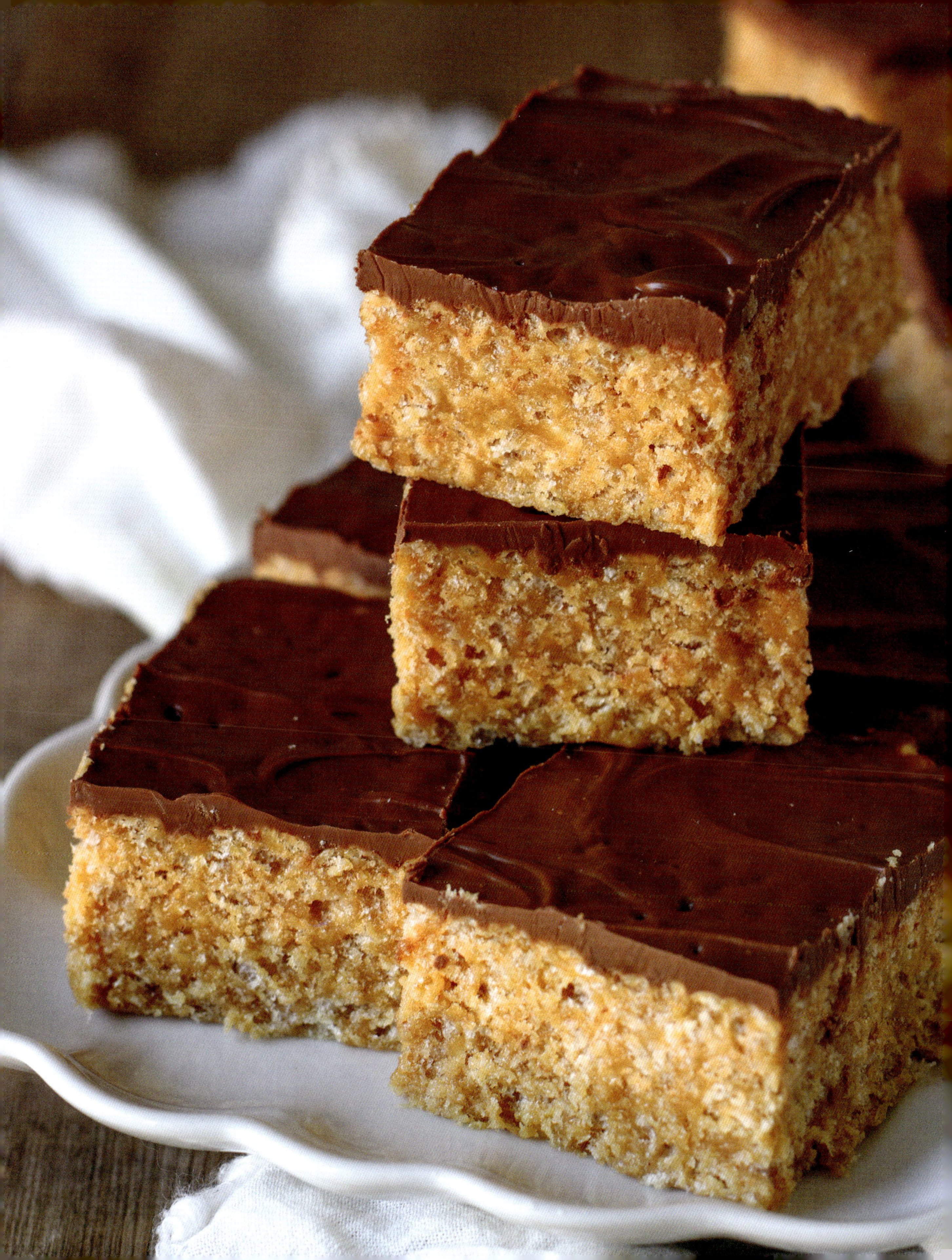

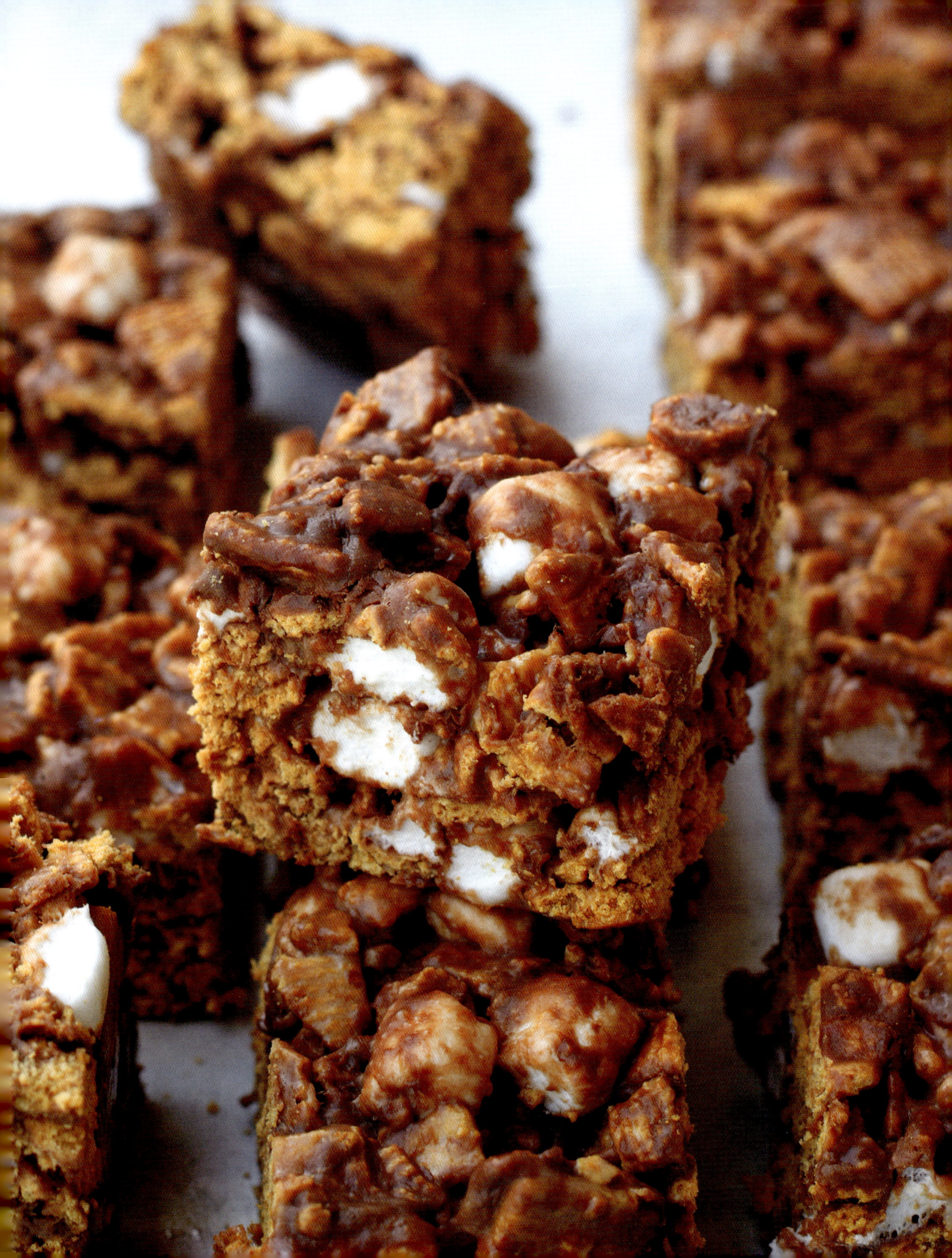

S'mores Bars

I started making these when my kids were little, and over the years, we've gone through many eras where we make them once a week for months. It took me a couple of tries to get the recipe just right (which absolutely nobody minded), and it is safe to say that they are just about perfect. They capture all the best things about summer s'mores in every gooey bite: crispy, sweet graham crackers, melty milk chocolate, and fluffy bits of sugary marshmallow.

Prep: 5 minutes | Cook: 15 minutes | Total: 20 minutes | Makes 24 bars

10 cups graham cereal (almost a whole 18.9-ounce "Family Size" box)

1 (12-ounce) bag milk chocolate chips

2 (10-ounce) bags mini marshmallows

10 tablespoons butter

1 teaspoon vanilla extract

A big pinch of kosher salt

1. Spray a 9 x 13-inch pan with nonstick cooking spray and set aside.

2. Put the graham cereal in a very large bowl. Crush it gently with your hands or with the bottom of a cup (hands work better). You don't need to crush it all to dust, just make the pieces smaller. Add the milk chocolate chips and stir gently to combine.

3. Measure out 2 cups of mini marshmallows and set them aside.

4. Melt the butter in a medium saucepan over medium-low heat, 2 to 3 minutes.

5. Add the rest of the marshmallows to the butter. Continue cooking over medium-low heat until the marshmallows are melted and the mixture is smooth, about 5 more minutes. Remove from the heat and stir in the vanilla and salt.

6. Pour the marshmallow mixture over the cereal and chocolate chips and stir until evenly coated. Add the reserved 2 cups of mini marshmallows and stir until they are evenly distributed.

7. Pour the gooey cereal mixture into the prepared pan, scraping as much as possible out of the bowl with a spatula.

8. Spray your hands with nonstick cooking spray. Make sure you get in between your fingers, too! Use your hands to press the cereal mixture firmly into the pan. Allow to cool before cutting into bars.

Brown Butter Crispy Cereal Treats

We're taking the classic crispy rice cereal and marshmallow treat and turning up the flavor to make them even better! The bake sale fave is already so good, but thanks to a quick browning of the butter, a little vanilla, and a generous pinch of kosher salt, these tasty treats will be yummier than ever.

Prep: 5 minutes | Cook: 15 minutes | Total: 20 minutes | Makes 24 big squares

12 cups crispy rice cereal

¾ cup (1½ sticks) butter

2 (10-ounce) bags mini marshmallows

A splash of vanilla extract

A big pinch of kosher salt

1. Spray a 9 x 13-inch baking pan with nonstick cooking spray.

2. Measure out the cereal into a large bowl.

3. In a large pot over medium heat, melt the butter and cook it until it starts to bubble and turn golden brown, about 8 minutes. Turn the heat down to low, add the mini marshmallows, and stir continuously until the marshmallows are completely melted and the mixture is smooth, about 5 minutes. Turn off the heat and stir in the vanilla and salt.

4. Pour the cereal into the marshmallow mixture and stir until the cereal is well distributed.

5. Transfer the gooey cereal mixture to the prepared pan, scraping as much as possible out of the pot with a rubber spatula.

6. Spray your hands with nonstick cooking spray. Make sure you get in between your fingers, too! Use your hands to press the cereal mixture firmly into the pan. Allow to cool before cutting into bars.

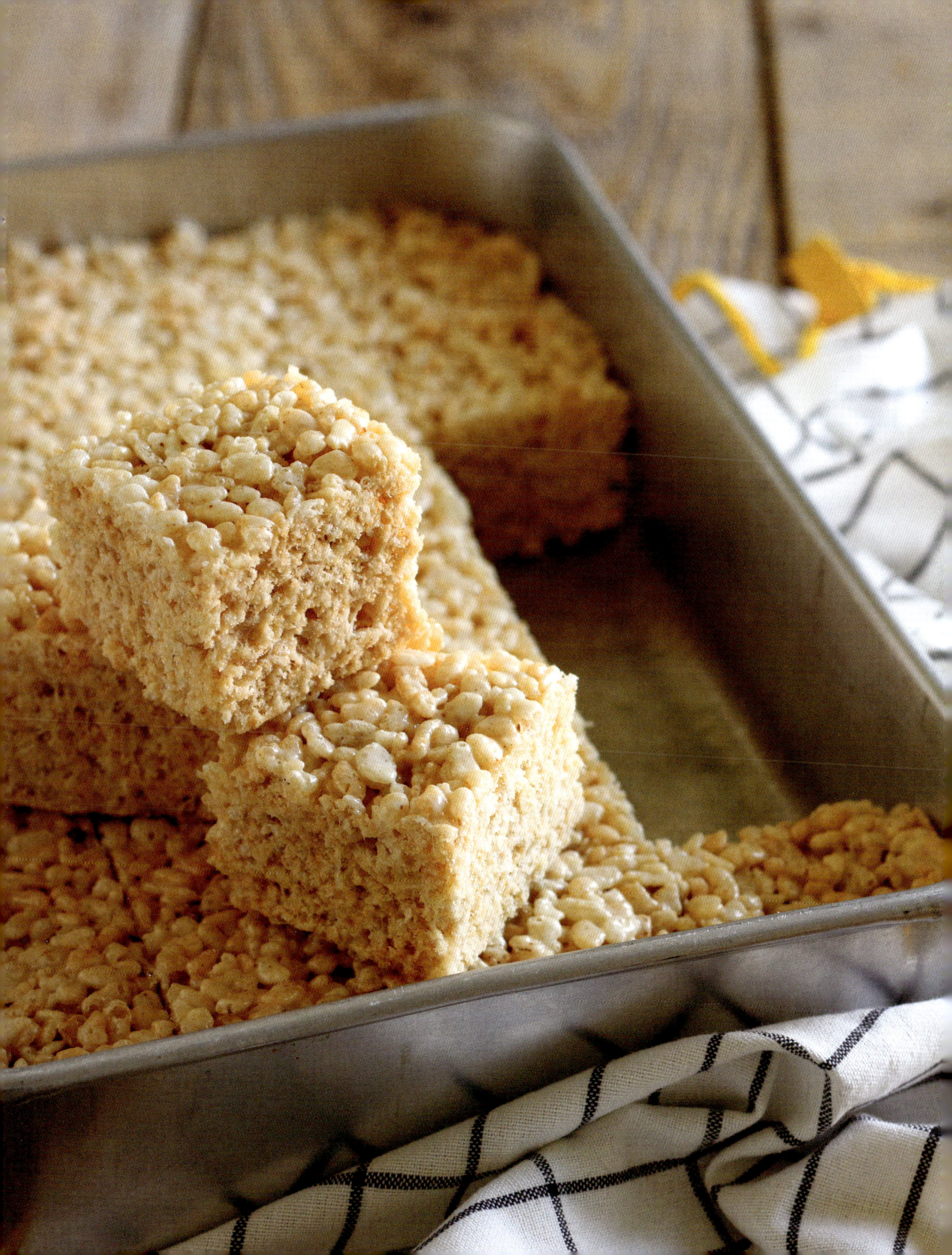

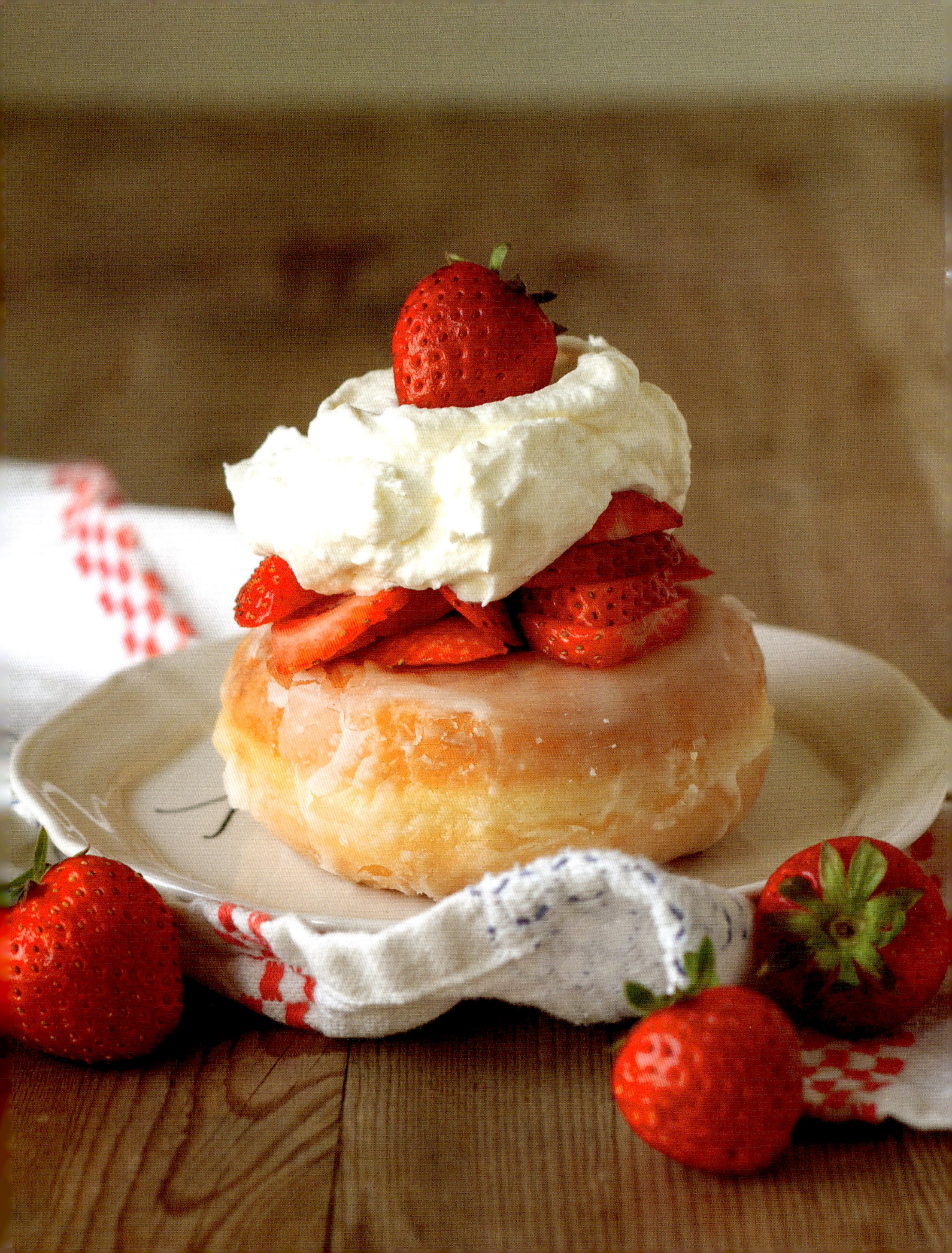

Donut Shortcake

There's a really amazing food truck here called Locals Donuts. They make donuts and giant soft pretzels, and they are delicious enough that we drive 30 minutes and wait in long lines to get them. They have a special every week, yummy things like cheesy pretzel dogs and donuts filled with homemade lemon curd and covered in powdered sugar. Swoon! At the beginning of summer, their weekly special was a glazed donut topped with a mound of sweetened whipped cream and freshly picked local strawberries. Never in my life had it occurred to me to use a glazed donut as the base for strawberry shortcake, but let me tell you, it was pure heaven. Do you need a detailed recipe to make it? Not really. But do you need to know that donut shortcake is a thing? A thousand times yes.

Prep: 10 minutes | Cook: 0 minutes | Total: 10 minutes | Serves 4

4 glazed raised donuts

Sweetened whipped cream

1 pound fresh strawberries, topped and sliced

¼ cup Nutella, optional

1. Place the donuts on individual plates.

2. Top with the whipped cream and sliced strawberries.

3. If using, put the Nutella in a small, microwave safe bowl, and microwave until runny, about 30 seconds. Use a spoon to drop dollops of Nutella over the strawberries, and serve immediately.

Double Chocolate Cake

This cake is a very old family favorite. My mom got the recipe from a friend when I was in elementary school, and we've all made it regularly in the intervening decades. It's basically a really tasty, from-scratch chocolate cake with chocolate chips in it. Simple and delicious, and ready in a flash.

Prep: 10 minutes | Cook: 30 to 35 minutes | Total: 40 to 45 minutes | Serves 12 to 16

1½ cups water

⅔ cup neutral oil such as vegetable or canola oil

2 eggs

1 teaspoon vanilla extract

2⅓ cups all-purpose flour

2 cups granulated sugar

3 heaping tablespoons natural, unsweetened cocoa powder (such as Hershey's)

1 teaspoon baking soda

1 teaspoon salt

1 cup semisweet chocolate chips

1. Preheat the oven to 350°F and grease a 9 x 13-inch baking pan with nonstick cooking spray.

2. In a large bowl, whisk together the water, oil, eggs, and vanilla until well blended. Add the flour, sugar, cocoa powder, baking soda, and salt and whisk until smooth.

3. Pour the batter into the prepared pan and sprinkle the chocolate chips evenly over the top.

4. Bake for 30 to 35 minutes, until a toothpick inserted in the center comes out clean. Serve warm or at room temperature.

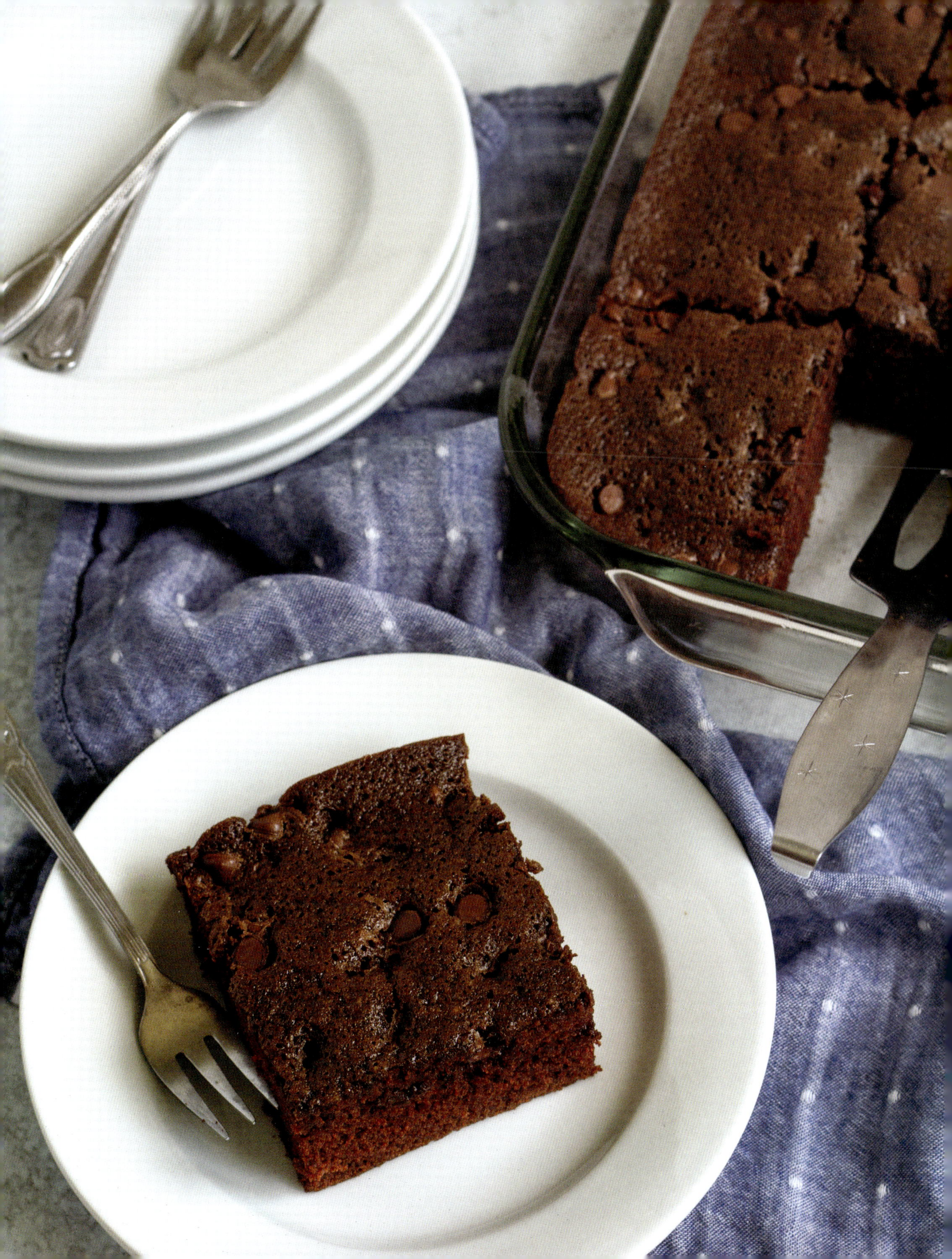

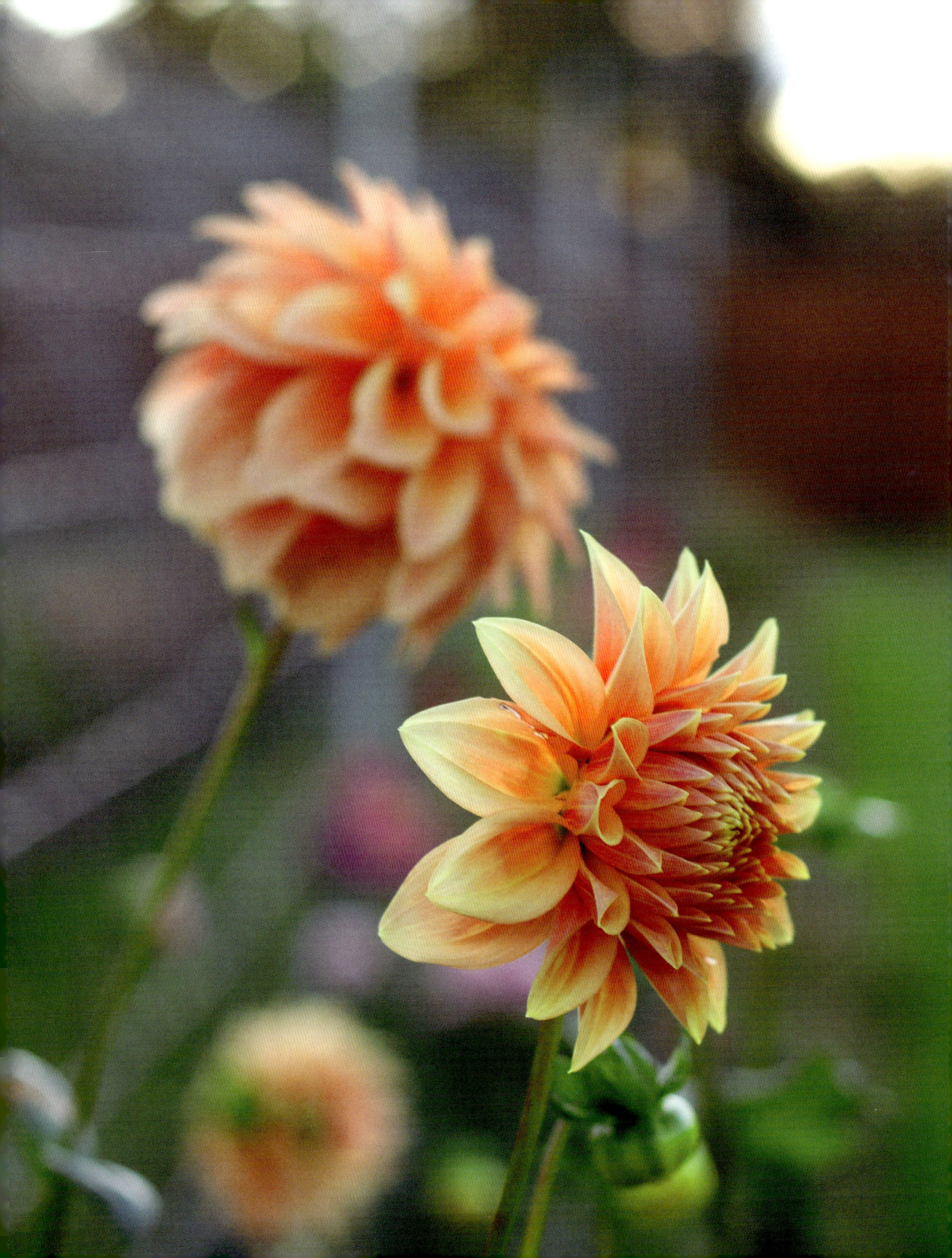

ACKNOWLEDGMENTS

WRITING A BOOK is always a marathon, never a sprint. But sometimes it feels like sprinting a marathon! There are so many people who helped me get this book over the finish line.

Thank you to everyone at Gibbs Smith who worked on *Farmhouse Weeknights*. To my wonderful editor, Michelle Branson: You are always beyond a pleasure to work with. To Ryan Thomann, Sheryl Dickert, Renee Bond, and everyone else at Gibbs Smith: thank you!

Thank you to my amazing agent, Lilly Ghahremani at Full Circle Literary. Lilly, thank you for answering every insane text and rambling email. Thank you for being my teammate and cheerleader.

Endless thanks to everyone who generously shared a recipe with me and let me include it in this book: my mom, Marci; my sister, Emily; my brother, Chaz, and my sister-in-law, Jasmine; my Nana; my aunt Kari; my mother-in-law, Toni; and my friends Anne, Annie, and Brooke. And thank you to those I have no way to thank, but whose recipes we love just as much: Dr. B., Aunt Myrl, and Chef Gaspar.

Thank you to all of the people who tested recipes for me to make sure I hadn't skipped a step or forgotten an ingredient.

And last but not least, in fact most of all, thank you to my family, who I love more than anything: Speedy, Addie, Ellie, James, and George. Writing this book, developing all of the recipes, and then taking all of the pictures over the span of a single summer break was a lot. I think we're all pretty tired of dinner at this point! Thank you for your support, your encouragement, your (mostly kind!) feedback, and all of your help. Thank you for running props and garnishes up and down the stairs for me. Thank you for doing extra dishes when I had four photo shoots in a single day. And thank you for eating all of those dinners! XO

VEGETARIAN RECIPES

Anne's Lentil Soup, 32

Annie & Brooke's Kale Salad, 62

Aunt Myrl's German Cookies, 182

Bean & Cheese Tostadas, 148

Black Bean Soup, 36

Blue Valley Spinach Salad with Feta & Avocado, 65

Caprese Grilled Cheese Sandwiches, 93

Cheese Tortellini with Pesto & Veggies, 110

Cheesy Egg & Hashbrown Breakfast Bake (variation in notes), 23

Cheesy Eggs-in-a-Basket, 19

Chocolate Chip Cookies, 177

Creamy Tomato Cheese Soup, 44

Donut Shortcake, 193

Double Chocolate Cake, 194

Easy Flatbread Pizzas, 165

Easy Peanut Butter Cup Brownies, 181

French Toast Waffles, 28

Garden Minestrone, 41

Green Goddess Veggie Sandwiches, 86

Lemon Garlic Spaghetti, 113

Lulu the Baker's Famous Cheesy Chowder, 48

Mac & Cheese with Toasted, Buttered Breadcrumbs, 124

Mediterranean Quinoa Salad, 81

Oatmeal Toffee Cookies, 170

Peanut Butter Pretzel Magic Cookie Bars, 185

Peanut Butter Scotcheroos, 186

Roasted Cauliflower & White Cheddar Soup, 47

Snickerdoodles, 173

Stella Blues' Pasta, 127

Triple Chocolate Cookies, 178

Tropical Fried Rice, 155

30-MINUTE (OR LESS!) RECIPES

Annie & Brooke's Kale Salad, 62

Aunt Myrl's German Cookies, 182

Bean & Cheese Tostadas, 148

Blue Valley Spinach Salad with Feta & Avocado, 65

Breakfast Sandwiches, 16

Brown Butter Crispy Cereal Treats, 190

Cajun Alfredo Pasta with Kielbasa, 123

Caprese Grilled Cheese Sandwiches, 93

Cheese Tortellini with Pesto & Veggies, 110

Cheesy Eggs-in-a-Basket, 19

Chicken Pesto Paninis, 94

Chicken Salad Sandwiches, 97

Chocolate Chip Cookies, 177

Classic Cobb Salad with Lemon-Shallot Vinaigrette, 69

Donut Shortcake, 193

Easy Flatbread Pizzas, 165

Emily's South Lane Chopped Salad with Cilantro-Lime Vinaigrette, 71

French Toast Waffles, 28

Green Goddess Veggie Sandwiches, 86

Harvest Salad with Creamy Herb-Dijon Vinaigrette, 74

Lemon Garlic Spaghetti, 113

Loaded, Lemony Caesar Salad with Homemade Dressing, 66

Meatball Subs, 102

Mediterranean Quinoa Salad, 81

Nana's Quick & Hearty Soup, 57

Peanut Butter Scotcheroos, 186

Philly Cheesesteaks, 105

San Antonio Breakfast Tacos, 27

Sausage & Pesto Pasta, 119

S'mores Bars, 189

Speedy's Chocolate No-Bake Cookies, 174

Stella Blues' Pasta, 127

Taco Salad, 82

Taco Soup, 54

Toasted Ramen Noodle Salad, 78

Triple Chocolate Cookies, 178

Tropical Fried Rice, 155

Turkey & Cranberry Plymouth Rock Sandwiches, 101

Turkey-Bacon-Avocado Clubs, 98

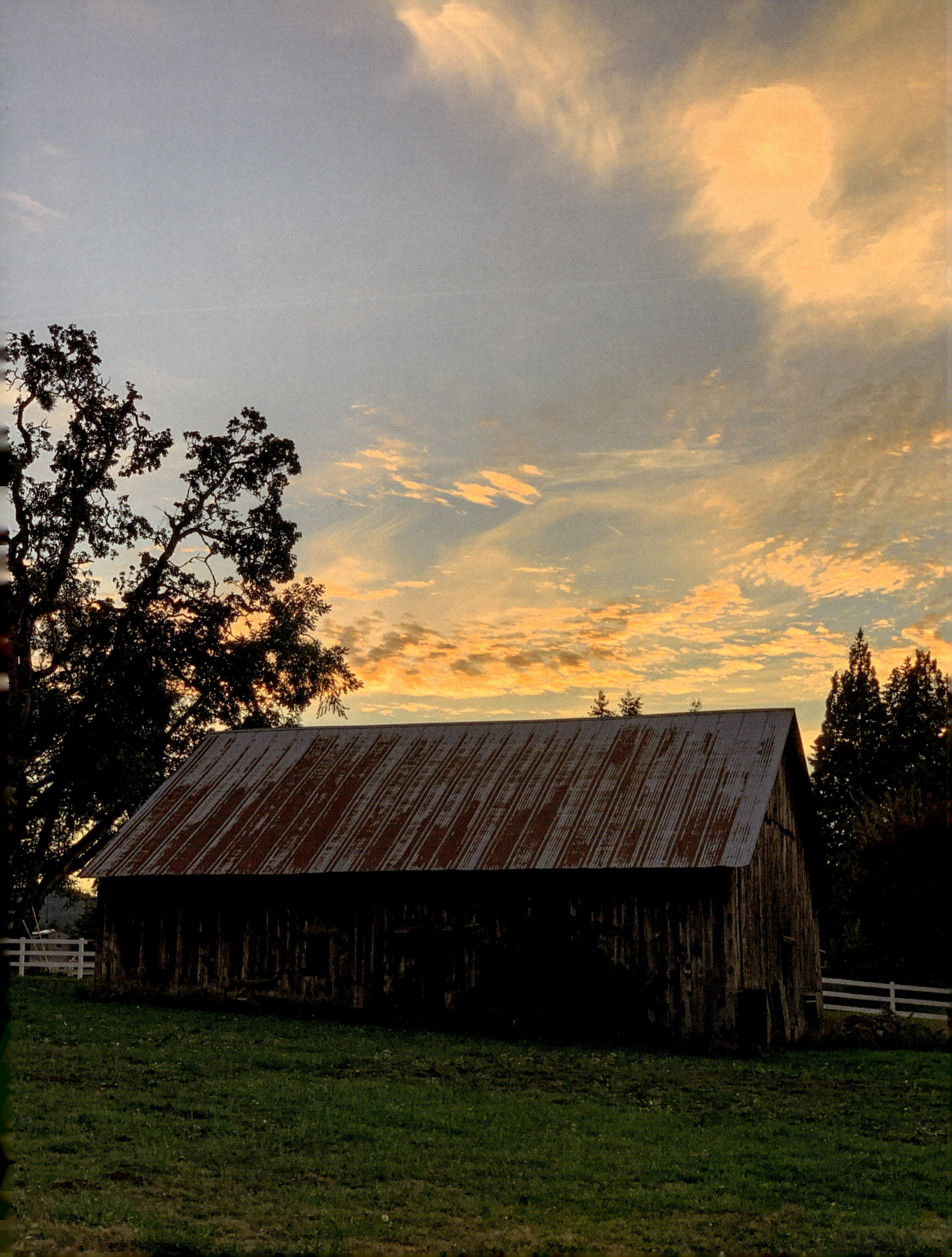

INDEX

A

almonds
    Blue Valley Spinach Salad with Feta & Avocado, 65
    Loaded, Lemony Caesar Salad with Homemade Dressing, 66
    Mediterranean Quinoa Salad, 81
    Toasted Ramen Noodle Salad, 78
Anne's Lentil Soup, 32
Annie & Brooke's Kale Salad, 62
artichoke hearts
    Italian Pasta Salad, 77
arugula
    Chicken Pesto Paninis, 94
Aunt Myrl's German Cookies, 182
avocados
    Blue Valley Spinach Salad with Feta & Avocado, 65
    Classic Cobb Salad with Lemon-Shallot Vinaigrette, 69–70
    Emily's South Lane Chopped Salad with Cilantro-Lime Vinaigrette, 71–73
    Green Goddess Veggie Sandwiches, 86–88
    Guacamole, 154
    Loaded, Lemony Caesar Salad with Homemade Dressing, 66
    Turkey-Bacon-Avocado Clubs, 98

B

bacon
    Classic Cobb Salad with Lemon-Shallot Vinaigrette, 69–70
    Coffee Shop Bacon & Cheese Egg Bites, 24
    Croissant-wich, 16–18
    Double Cheese Bagel-wich, 16–18
    English Muffin-wich, 16–18
    Loaded, Lemony Caesar Salad with Homemade Dressing, 66
    San Antonio Breakfast Tacos, 27
    Turkey-Bacon-Avocado Clubs, 98
Bagel-wich, Double Cheese, 16–18
Barbecue Chicken Sandwiches, Slow Cooker, 89–90
bars
    Aunt Myrl's German Cookies, 182
    Brown Butter Crispy Cereal Treats, 190
    Peanut Butter Pretzel Magic Cookie Bars, 185
    Peanut Butter Scotcheroos, 186
    S'mores Bars, 189
basil
    Lemon Garlic Spaghetti, 113
    Stella Blues' Pasta, 127
beans
    Bean & Cheese Tostadas, 148–149
    Black Bean Soup, 36
    Cornbread-Topped Tex-Mex Bake, 150–151
    Dr. B.'s Southwest Three-Bean Soup, 39–40
    Garden Minestrone, 41–43
    Taco Salad, 82
    Taco Soup, 54
    White Bean & Ham Soup, 35
    See also green beans
beef
    Cornbread-Topped Tex-Mex Bake, 150–151
    Easy Pot Roast, 132
    Mini Meatloaves, 161
    Nana's Quick & Hearty Soup, 57
    One-Pan Weeknight Lasagna, 116–117
    Pasta Fagioli, 58
    Philly Cheesesteak, 105
    Taco Salad, 82
    Taco Soup, 54
    Weeknight Beef Stroganoff, 128
bell peppers
    Black Bean Soup, 36
    Dr. B.'s Southwest Three-Bean Soup, 39–40
    Philly Cheesesteak, 105
    Sausage & Pesto Pasta (variation), 119
    Sheet Pan Honey-Lime Chicken Fajitas, 153–154
    Slow Cooker Sausage & Pepper Sandwiches, 106
black beans
    Black Bean Soup, 36
    Dr. B.'s Southwest Three-Bean Soup, 39–40
    preparation recipe, 154
Blue Valley Spinach Salad with Feta & Avocado, 65
Bobbie Sandwich, 101
breadcrumbs
    Crispy Chicken Parmesan, 162–163
    Mac & Cheese with Toasted, Buttered Breadcrumbs, 124
breads, kitchen shortcuts, 12
Breakfast Sandwiches, 16–18
broccoli
    Lulu the Baker's Famous Cheesy Chowder, 48
broccoli slaw
    Annie & Brooke's Kale Salad, 62
    Brown Butter Crispy Cereal Treats, 190
Brownies, Easy Peanut Butter Cup, 181
butterscotch chips
    Peanut Butter Scotcheroos, 186

C

cabbage
    Coleslaw, 90
Cajun Alfredo Pasta with Kielbasa, 123
Cake, Double Chocolate, 194

Canadian bacon
　Dr. B.'s Southwest Three-
　　Bean Soup, 39–40
　See also ham
Caprese Grilled Cheese
　Sandwiches, 93
Carnitas, 135
carrots
　Anne's Lentil Soup, 32
　Easy Pot Roast, 132
　Garden Minestrone, 41–43
　Homestyle Chicken Noodle Soup, 51
　Italian Pasta Salad, 77
　Lulu the Baker's Famous
　　Cheesy Chowder, 48
　Nana's Quick & Hearty Soup, 57
　Pasta Fagioli, 58
　Tropical Fried Rice, 155–156
　White Bean & Ham Soup, 35
Cauliflower, Roasted, & White
　Cheddar Soup, 47
cheddar cheese
　Bean & Cheese Tostadas, 148–149
　Cheesy Egg & Hashbrown
　　Breakfast Bake, 23
　Cheesy Eggs-in-a-Basket, 19–20
　Cornbread-Topped Tex-
　　Mex Bake, 150–151
　Creamy Tomato Cheese Soup, 44
　Croissant-wich, 16–18
　Double Cheese Bagel-wich, 16–18
　Emily's Cheesy Chicken &
　　Stuffing Bake, 158–159
　English Muffin-wich, 16–18
　Harvest Salad with Creamy
　　Herb-Dijon Vinaigrette, 74
　Lulu the Baker's Famous
　　Cheesy Chowder, 48
　Mac & Cheese with Toasted,
　　Buttered Breadcrumbs, 124
　One-Pan Weeknight Lasagna, 116–117
　Roasted Cauliflower & White
　　Cheddar Soup, 47
　San Antonio Breakfast Tacos, 27
cheese
　Annie & Brooke's Kale Salad, 62
Bean & Cheese Tostadas, 148–149
Blue Valley Spinach Salad
　with Feta & Avocado, 65
Cajun Alfredo Pasta with
　Kielbasa, 123
Caprese Grilled Cheese
　Sandwiches, 93
Cheese Tortellini with
　Pesto & Veggies, 110
Cheesy Egg & Hashbrown
　Breakfast Bake, 23
Cheesy Eggs-in-a-Basket, 19–20
Chicken Pesto Paninis, 94
Chicken Tetrazzini, 114
Classic Cobb Salad with Lemon-
　Shallot Vinaigrette, 69–70
Coffee Shop Bacon &
　Cheese Egg Bites, 24
Cornbread-Topped Tex-
　Mex Bake, 150–151
Creamy Tomato Cheese Soup, 44
Crispy Chicken Parmesan, 162–163
Croissant-wich, 16–18
Double Cheese Bagel-wich, 16–18
Easy Flatbread Pizzas, 165–166
Emily's Cheesy Chicken &
　Stuffing Bake, 158–159
English Muffin-wich, 16–18
Harvest Salad with Creamy
　Herb-Dijon Vinaigrette, 74
Italian Pasta Salad, 77
Loaded, Lemony Caesar Salad
　with Homemade Dressing, 66
Lulu the Baker's Famous
　Cheesy Chowder, 48
Mac & Cheese with Toasted,
　Buttered Breadcrumbs, 124
Meatball Subs, 102
Mediterranean Quinoa Salad, 81
Mini Meatloaves, 161
One-Pan Weeknight Lasagna, 116–117
Philly Cheesesteak, 105
Roasted Cauliflower & White
　Cheddar Soup, 47
San Antonio Breakfast Tacos, 27
Sausage & Pesto Pasta, 119
Taco Salad, 82
Turkey & Cranberry Plymouth
　Rock Sandwiches, 101
Turkey-Bacon-Avocado Clubs, 98
See also cottage cheese;
　cream cheese
chicken
　Chicken Pesto Paninis, 94
　Chicken Salad Sandwiches, 97
　Chicken Tetrazzini, 114
　Classic Cobb Salad with Lemon-
　　Shallot Vinaigrette, 69–70
　Crispy Chicken Parmesan, 162–163
　Emily's Cheesy Chicken &
　　Stuffing Bake, 158–159
　Emily's South Lane Chopped
　　Salad with Cilantro-Lime
　　Vinaigrette, 71–73
　Harvest Salad with Creamy
　　Herb-Dijon Vinaigrette, 74
　Homestyle Chicken Noodle Soup, 51
　Loaded, Lemony Caesar Salad
　　with Homemade Dressing, 66
　Mom's Chicken Tortilla Soup, 52–53
　Mom's Garlic Butter Chicken, 144
　Sheet Pan Honey-Lime
　　Chicken Fajitas, 153–154
　Slow Cooker Barbecue Chicken
　　Sandwiches, 89–90
　Taco Chicken, 140
　Teriyaki Chicken, 143
chiles, green
　Cornbread-Topped Tex-
　　Mex Bake, 150–151
　Mom's Chicken Tortilla Soup, 52–53
　Sweet Shredded Pork, 139
chocolate
　Aunt Myrl's German Cookies, 182
　Chocolate Chip Cookies, 177
　Double Chocolate Cake, 194
　Easy Peanut Butter Cup Brownies, 181
　Oatmeal Toffee Cookies, 170
　Peanut Butter Pretzel Magic
　　Cookie Bars, 185
　Peanut Butter Scotcheroos, 186
　S'mores Bars, 189

Speedy's Chocolate No-Bake Cookies, 174
Triple Chocolate Cookies, 178–179

cilantro
Cilantro-Lime Crema, 149
Emily's South Lane Chopped Salad with Cilantro-Lime Vinaigrette, 71–73
Salsa Verde Ranch Dressing, 139

Classic Cobb Salad with Lemon-Shallot Vinaigrette, 69–70

coconut
Peanut Butter Pretzel Magic Cookie Bars, 185
Speedy's Chocolate No-Bake Cookies, 174

Coffee Shop Bacon & Cheese Egg Bites, 24
Coleslaw, 90

cookies
Aunt Myrl's German Cookies, 182
Chocolate Chip Cookies, 177
Oatmeal Toffee Cookies, 170
Peanut Butter Pretzel Magic Cookie Bars, 185
Snickerdoodles, 173
Speedy's Chocolate No-Bake Cookies, 174
Triple Chocolate Cookies, 178–179
See also bars

corn
Cheese Tortellini with Pesto & Veggies, 110
Cornbread-Topped Tex-Mex Bake, 150–151
Emily's South Lane Chopped Salad with Cilantro-Lime Vinaigrette, 71–73
Taco Salad, 82
Taco Soup, 54
Tropical Fried Rice, 155–156

Cornbread-Topped Tex-Mex Bake, 150–151

cottage cheese
Coffee Shop Bacon & Cheese Egg Bites, 24

One-Pan Weeknight Lasagna, 116–117

cranberries, dried
Annie & Brooke's Kale Salad, 62
Blue Valley Spinach Salad with Feta & Avocado, 65

cranberry sauce
Bobbie Sandwich, 101
Turkey & Cranberry Plymouth Rock Sandwiches, 101

cream cheese
Double Cheese Bagel-wich, 16–18
Green Goddess Veggie Sandwiches, 86–88

Creamy Tomato Cheese Soup, 44
Crispy Chicken Parmesan, 162–163
Croissant-wich, 16–18

cucumbers
Classic Cobb Salad with Lemon-Shallot Vinaigrette, 69–70
Green Goddess Veggie Sandwiches, 86–88
Mediterranean Quinoa Salad, 81

D

desserts
Aunt Myrl's German Cookies, 182
Brown Butter Crispy Cereal Treats, 190
Chocolate Chip Cookies, 177
Donut Shortcake, 193
Double Chocolate Cake, 194
Easy Peanut Butter Cup Brownies, 181
Oatmeal Toffee Cookies, 170
Peanut Butter Pretzel Magic Cookie Bars, 185
Peanut Butter Scotcheroos, 186
S'mores Bars, 189
Snickerdoodles, 173
Speedy's Chocolate No-Bake Cookies, 174
Triple Chocolate Cookies, 178–179

Dijon mustard
Harvest Salad with Creamy Herb-Dijon Vinaigrette, 74

Honey-Dijon-Ranch Marinade, 70
Donut Shortcake, 193
Double Cheese Bagel-wich, 16–18
Double Chocolate Cake, 194
Dr. B.'s Southwest Three-Bean Soup, 39–40

dressings, salad
Cilantro-Lime Vinaigrette, Emily's South Lane Chopped Salad with, 71–73
Creamy Herb-Dijon Vinaigrette, Harvest Salad with, 74
Greek Dressing, in Mediterranean Quinoa Salad, 81
Homemade Dressing, Loaded, Lemony Caesar Salad with, 66
Lemon-Shallot Vinaigrette, Classic Cobb Salad with, 69–70
Salsa Verde Ranch Dressing, 139

E

Easy Flatbread Pizzas, 165–166
Easy Peanut Butter Cup Brownies, 181
Easy Pot Roast, 132

eggs
Cheesy Egg & Hashbrown Breakfast Bake, 23
Cheesy Eggs-in-a-Basket, 19–20
Classic Cobb Salad with Lemon-Shallot Vinaigrette, 69–70
Coffee Shop Bacon & Cheese Egg Bites, 24
Croissant-wich, 16–18
Double Cheese Bagel-wich, 16–18
English Muffin-wich, 16–18
Harvest Salad with Creamy Herb-Dijon Vinaigrette, 74
San Antonio Breakfast Tacos, 27
Tropical Fried Rice, 155–156

Emily's Cheesy Chicken & Stuffing Bake, 158–159
Emily's South Lane Chopped Salad with Cilantro-Lime Vinaigrette, 71–73
English Muffin-wich, 16–18

INDEX 203

F

Fajitas, Sheet Pan Honey-Lime Chicken, 153–154
feta cheese
    Blue Valley Spinach Salad with Feta & Avocado, 65
    Mediterranean Quinoa Salad, 81
Flatbread Pizzas, Easy, 165–166
French Toast Waffles, 28
fruits, kitchen shortcuts, 12

G

Garden Minestrone, 41–43
garlic
    Lemon Garlic Spaghetti, 113
    Mom's Garlic Butter Chicken, 144
    Stella Blues' Pasta, 127
graham cereal
    S'mores Bars, 189
graham crackers
    Peanut Butter Pretzel Magic Cookie Bars, 185
green beans
    Harvest Salad with Creamy Herb-Dijon Vinaigrette, 74
    Nana's Quick & Hearty Soup, 57
Green Goddess Veggie Sandwiches, 86–88
green onions
    Chicken Salad Sandwiches, 97
    Classic Cobb Salad with Lemon-Shallot Vinaigrette, 69–70
    Green Goddess Veggie Sandwiches, 86–88
    Soy & Citrus Marinade, 70
    Teriyaki Chicken, 143
    Toasted Ramen Noodle Salad, 78
    Tropical Fried Rice, 155–156
greens
    Emily's South Lane Chopped Salad with Cilantro-Lime Vinaigrette, 71–73
    Harvest Salad with Creamy Herb-Dijon Vinaigrette, 74
    See also arugula; kale; lettuce; spinach
Guacamole, 154

H

ham
    Cheesy Egg & Hashbrown Breakfast Bake, 23
    Croissant-wich, 16–18
    English Muffin-wich, 16–18
    White Bean & Ham Soup, 35
    See also Canadian bacon
Harvest Salad with Creamy Herb-Dijon Vinaigrette, 74
hashbrowns
    Cheesy Egg & Hashbrown Breakfast Bake, 23
    San Antonio Breakfast Tacos, 27
Homestyle Chicken Noodle Soup, 51
Honey-Dijon-Ranch Marinade, 70

I

Italian Pasta Salad, 77

K

kale
    Annie & Brooke's Kale Salad, 62
    Mediterranean Quinoa Salad, 81
kidney beans
    Dr. B.'s Southwest Three-Bean Soup, 39–40
    Garden Minestrone, 41–43
    Taco Soup, 54

L

leeks
    Garden Minestrone, 41–43
lemons
    Classic Cobb Salad with Lemon-Shallot Vinaigrette, 69–70
    Lemon Garlic Spaghetti, 113
    Loaded, Lemony Caesar Salad with Homemade Dressing, 66
Lentil Soup, Anne's, 32

lettuce
    Classic Cobb Salad with Lemon-Shallot Vinaigrette, 69–70
    Green Goddess Veggie Sandwiches, 86–88
    Loaded, Lemony Caesar Salad with Homemade Dressing, 66
    Mediterranean Quinoa Salad, 81
    Taco Salad, 82
    Turkey & Cranberry Plymouth Rock Sandwiches, 101
    Turkey-Bacon-Avocado Clubs, 98
limes
    Carnitas (*see* sausage)
    Cilantro-Lime Crema, 149
    Emily's South Lane Chopped Salad with Cilantro-Lime Vinaigrette, 71–73
    Sheet Pan Honey-Lime Chicken Fajitas, 153–154
Loaded, Lemony Caesar Salad with Homemade Dressing, 66
Lulu the Baker's Famous Cheesy Chowder, 48

M

Mac & Cheese with Toasted, Buttered Breadcrumbs, 124
marinades
    Honey-Dijon-Ranch Marinade, 70
    Soy & Citrus Marinade, 70
marinara sauce
    Crispy Chicken Parmesan, 162–163
    Meatball Subs, 102
    One-Pan Weeknight Lasagna, 116–117
marshmallows
    Brown Butter Crispy Cereal Treats, 190
    S'mores Bars, 189
    Speedy's Chocolate No-Bake Cookies, 174
Meatball Subs, 102
meats, kitchen shortcuts, 12
Mediterranean Quinoa Salad, 81

Mini Meatloaves, 161
Mom's Chicken Tortilla Soup, 52–53
Mom's Garlic Butter Chicken, 144
Monterey jack cheese
    Coffee Shop Bacon & Cheese Egg Bites, 24
    Emily's South Lane Chopped Salad with Cilantro-Lime Vinaigrette, 71–73
    Taco Salad, 82
mozzarella cheese
    Caprese Grilled Cheese Sandwiches, 93
    Chicken Pesto Paninis, 94
    Crispy Chicken Parmesan, 162–163
    Easy Flatbread Pizzas, 165–166
    Italian Pasta Salad, 77
    One-Pan Weeknight Lasagna, 116–117

N

Nana's Quick & Hearty Soup, 57
noodles
    Homestyle Chicken Noodle Soup, 51
    One-Pan Weeknight Lasagna, 116–117
    Toasted Ramen Noodle Salad, 78
    Weeknight Beef Stroganoff, 128

O

oats
    Oatmeal Toffee Cookies, 170
    Speedy's Chocolate No-Bake Cookies, 174
olives
    Cornbread-Topped Tex-Mex Bake, 150–151
    Mediterranean Quinoa Salad, 81
    Taco Salad, 82
One-Pan Weeknight Lasagna, 116–117
onions
    Chicken Pesto Paninis, 94
    Green Goddess Veggie Sandwiches, 86–88
    Philly Cheesesteak, 105
    Pickled Red Onions, 65
    Sheet Pan Honey-Lime Chicken Fajitas, 153–154
    Slow Cooker Barbecue Chicken Sandwiches, 89–90
    Slow Cooker Sausage & Pepper Sandwiches, 106
    Smothered Pork Chops, 136
    Tropical Fried Rice, 155–156
    Turkey-Bacon-Avocado Clubs, 98
    See also green onions

P

Parmesan cheese
    Cajun Alfredo Pasta with Kielbasa, 123
    Chicken Tetrazzini, 114
    Crispy Chicken Parmesan, 162–163
    Italian Pasta Salad, 77
    Loaded, Lemony Caesar Salad with Homemade Dressing, 66
    Mini Meatloaves, 161
    One-Pan Weeknight Lasagna, 116–117
    Sausage & Pesto Pasta, 119
pasta
    Cajun Alfredo Pasta with Kielbasa, 123
    Cheese Tortellini with Pesto & Veggies, 110
    Chicken Tetrazzini, 114
    Garden Minestrone, 41–43
    Italian Pasta Salad, 77
    Lemon Garlic Spaghetti, 113
    Mac & Cheese with Toasted, Buttered Breadcrumbs, 124
    One-Pan Weeknight Lasagna, 116–117
    Pasta Fagioli, 58
    Sausage & Pesto Pasta, 119
    Shrimp Scampi, 119
    Stella Blues' Pasta, 127
peanut butter
    Easy Peanut Butter Cup Brownies, 181
    Peanut Butter Pretzel Magic Cookie Bars, 185
    Peanut Butter Scotcheroos, 186
peas
    Cajun Alfredo Pasta with Kielbasa, 123
    Tropical Fried Rice, 155–156
pecans
    Annie & Brooke's Kale Salad, 62
    Peanut Butter Pretzel Magic Cookie Bars, 185
pesto
    Caprese Grilled Cheese Sandwiches, 93
    Cheese Tortellini with Pesto & Veggies, 110
    Chicken Pesto Paninis, 94
    Sausage & Pesto Pasta, 119
Philly Cheesesteak, 105
Pickled Red Onions, 65
pine nuts
    Cheese Tortellini with Pesto & Veggies, 110
    Lemon Garlic Spaghetti, 113
pineapple
    Shrimp Scampi, 119
    Tropical Fried Rice, 155–156
pinto beans
    Dr. B.'s Southwest Three-Bean Soup, 39–40
    Taco Soup, 54
Pizzas, Easy Flatbread, 165–166
pork
    Carnitas, 135
    Smothered Pork Chops, 136
    Sweet Shredded Pork, 139
    See also bacon; ham; sausage
Pot Roast, Easy, 132
potatoes
    Cheesy Egg & Hashbrown Breakfast Bake, 23
    Easy Pot Roast, 132
    Lulu the Baker's Famous Cheesy Chowder, 48
    San Antonio Breakfast Tacos, 27

Pretzel Magic Cookie Bars, Peanut Butter, 185
provolone cheese
    Chicken Pesto Paninis, 94
    Meatball Subs, 102

Q

Quinoa Salad, Mediterranean, 81

R

radishes
    Toasted Ramen Noodle Salad, 78
refried beans
    Bean & Cheese Tostadas, 148–149
Rice, Tropical Fried, 155–156
rice cereal, crispy
    Brown Butter Crispy Cereal Treats, 190
    Peanut Butter Scotcheroos, 186
Roasted Cauliflower & White Cheddar Soup, 47

S

salads
    Annie & Brooke's Kale Salad, 62
    Blue Valley Spinach Salad with Feta & Avocado, 65
    Classic Cobb Salad with Lemon-Shallot Vinaigrette, 69–70
    Coleslaw, 90
    Harvest Salad with Creamy Herb-Dijon Vinaigrette, 74
    Italian Pasta Salad, 77
    Loaded, Lemony Caesar Salad with Homemade Dressing, 66
    Mediterranean Quinoa Salad, 81
    Taco Salad, 82
    Toasted Ramen Noodle Salad, 78
salami
    Italian Pasta Salad, 77
salsa
    Bean & Cheese Tostadas, 148–149
    Dr. B.'s Southwest Three-Bean Soup, 39–40
    Taco Chicken, 140
    Taco Salad, 82
Salsa Verde Ranch Dressing, 139
San Antonio Breakfast Tacos, 27
sandwiches
    Bobbie Sandwich, 101
    Breakfast Sandwiches, 16–18
    Caprese Grilled Cheese Sandwiches, 93
    Chicken Pesto Paninis, 94
    Chicken Salad Sandwiches, 97
    Croissant-wich, 16–18
    Double Cheese Bagel-wich, 16–18
    English Muffin-wich, 16–18
    Green Goddess Veggie Sandwiches, 86–88
    Meatball Subs, 102
    Philly Cheesesteak, 105
    Slow Cooker Barbecue Chicken Sandwiches, 89–90
    Slow Cooker Sausage & Pepper Sandwiches, 106
    Turkey & Cranberry Plymouth Rock Sandwiches, 101
    Turkey-Bacon-Avocado Clubs, 98
sausage
    Cajun Alfredo Pasta with Kielbasa, 123
    Sausage & Pesto Pasta, 119
    Slow Cooker Sausage & Pepper Sandwiches, 106
Shallot Vinaigrette, Lemon-, Classic Cobb Salad with, 69–70
Sheet Pan Honey-Lime Chicken Fajitas, 153–154
Shortcake, Donut, 193
shortcuts, 12
Shrimp Scampi, 119
Slow Cooker Barbecue Chicken Sandwiches, 89–90
Slow Cooker Sausage & Pepper Sandwiches, 106
S'mores Bars, 189
Smothered Pork Chops, 136
Snickerdoodles, 173
soups
    Anne's Lentil Soup, 32
    Black Bean Soup, 36
    Creamy Tomato Cheese Soup, 44
    Dr. B.'s Southwest Three-Bean Soup, 39–40
    Homestyle Chicken Noodle Soup, 51
    Lulu the Baker's Famous Cheesy Chowder, 48
    Mom's Chicken Tortilla Soup, 52–53
    Roasted Cauliflower & White Cheddar Soup, 47
    Taco Soup, 54
    White Bean & Ham Soup, 35
sour cream
    Cilantro-Lime Crema, 149
    Weeknight Beef Stroganoff, 128
Soy & Citrus Marinade, 70
Speedy's Chocolate No-Bake Cookies, 174
spinach
    Blue Valley Spinach Salad with Feta & Avocado, 65
    Green Goddess Veggie Sandwiches, 86–88
Stella Blues' Pasta, 127
strawberries
    Donut Shortcake, 193
stuffing (boxed)
    Bobbie Sandwich, 101
    Emily's Cheesy Chicken & Stuffing Bake, 158–159
sunflower seeds
    Toasted Ramen Noodle Salad, 78
Sweet Shredded Pork, 139

T

Taco Chicken, 140
Taco Salad, 82
Taco Seasoning, 140
Taco Soup, 54
Tacos, San Antonio Breakfast, 27
Teriyaki Chicken, 143
30-minute (or less!) recipes, 199
Toasted Ramen Noodle Salad, 78
Toffee Cookies, Oatmeal, 170

tomatoes
    Anne's Lentil Soup, 32
    Cajun Alfredo Pasta with Kielbasa, 123
    Caprese Grilled Cheese Sandwiches, 93
    Cheese Tortellini with Pesto & Veggies, 110
    Chicken Pesto Paninis, 94
    Classic Cobb Salad with Lemon-Shallot Vinaigrette, 69–70
    Cornbread-Topped Tex-Mex Bake, 150–151
    Creamy Tomato Cheese Soup, 44
    Emily's South Lane Chopped Salad with Cilantro-Lime Vinaigrette, 71–73
    Garden Minestrone, 41–43
    Green Goddess Veggie Sandwiches, 86–88
    Harvest Salad with Creamy Herb-Dijon Vinaigrette, 74
    Loaded, Lemony Caesar Salad with Homemade Dressing, 66
    Mom's Chicken Tortilla Soup, 52–53
    Pasta Fagioli, 58
    Shrimp Scampi, 119
    Slow Cooker Sausage & Pepper Sandwiches, 106
    Stella Blues' Pasta, 127
    Taco Salad, 82
    Taco Soup, 54
    Turkey-Bacon-Avocado Clubs, 98
tomatoes, sun-dried
    Mediterranean Quinoa Salad, 81
tortilla chips
    Mom's Chicken Tortilla Soup, 52–53
    Taco Salad, 82
tortillas, corn
    Bean & Cheese Tostadas, 148–149
tortillas, flour
    San Antonio Breakfast Tacos, 27
    Sheet Pan Honey-Lime Chicken Fajitas, 153–154
Tostadas, Bean & Cheese, 148–149
Triple Chocolate Cookies, 178–179
Tropical Fried Rice, 155–156
turkey
    Bobbie Sandwich, 101
    Pasta Fagioli, 58
    Turkey & Cranberry Plymouth Rock Sandwiches, 101
    Turkey-Bacon-Avocado Clubs, 98

V

vegetables
    Cheese Tortellini with Pesto & Veggies, 110
    kitchen shortcuts, 12
    See also specific vegetables
vegetarian recipes, 198
vinaigrettes
    Cilantro-Lime Vinaigrette, Emily's South Lane Chopped Salad with, 71–73
    Creamy Herb-Dijon Vinaigrette, Harvest Salad with, 74
    Lemon-Shallot Vinaigrette, Classic Cobb Salad with, 69–70

W

Waffles, French Toast, 28
Weeknight Beef Stroganoff, 128
whipped cream
    Donut Shortcake, 193
white beans
    Garden Minestrone, 41–43
    White Bean & Ham Soup, 35

Y

yellow squash
    Garden Minestrone, 41–43

Z

zucchini
    Cheese Tortellini with Pesto & Veggies, 110
    Garden Minestrone, 41–43
    Italian Pasta Salad, 77

Metric Conversion Chart

VOLUME MEASUREMENTS	
U.S.	Metric
1 teaspoon	5 ml
1 tablespoon	15 ml
¼ cup	60 ml
⅓ cup	75 ml
½ cup	125 ml
⅔ cup	150 ml
¾ cup	175 ml
1 cup	250 ml

WEIGHT MEASUREMENTS	
U.S.	Metric
½ ounce	15 g
1 ounce	30 g
3 ounces	90 g
4 ounces	115 g
8 ounces	225 g
12 ounces	350 g
1 pound	450 g
2¼ pounds	1 kg

TEMPERATURE CONVERSION	
Fahrenheit	Celsius
250	120
300	150
325	160
350	180
375	190
400	200
425	220
450	230

ABOUT THE AUTHOR

MELISSA BAHEN is the creator of *Lulu the Baker*, a blog about simple food and modern country life. She's the author of two previous cookbooks. Her first book, *Scandinavian Gatherings*, includes recipes and projects inspired by her beloved Nordic heritage. Her second book, *Farmhouse Weekends*, is full of recipes for relaxing meals inspired by the slow pace of life in the country. Melissa lives on a small hobby farm in Western Oregon with her husband and kids. They collect eggs from their little flock of chickens, pick apples and pears from their orchard, and grow a few dozen varieties of dahlias, all in their own backyard. And while writing this book, she went back to school and got her MBA at the University of Oregon. Go Ducks!

Photo by Nicki Bergeson